National Responses
to the Holocaust

National Responses to the Holocaust

National Identity and Public Memory

Edited by
Jennifer Taylor

UNIVERSITY OF DELAWARE PRESS
Newark

Published by University of Delaware Press
Co-published with The Rowman & Littlefield Publishing Group, Inc.
4501 Forbes Boulevard, Suite 200, Lanham, Maryland 20706
www.rowman.com

10 Thornbury Road, Plymouth PL6 7PP, United Kingdom

British Library Cataloguing in Publication Information Available

Library of Congress Cataloging-in-Publication Data
National response to the Holocaust : nation, identity and public memory / [compiled by] Jennifer Taylor.
    pages cm
  Includes bibliographical references and index.
  ISBN 978-1-61149-056-5 (cloth : alk. paper)
  ISBN 978-1-61149-598-0 (pbk : alk. paper) 1. Holocaust, Jewish (1939–1945)—Historiography. 2. Holocaust, Jewish (1939–1945)—Influence. 3. Holocaust, Jewish (1939–1945), in art. 4. Holocaust, Jewish (1939–1945), in literature. I. Taylor, Jennifer, 1961– editor of compilation. II. Taylor, Jennifer, 1961– Reading Holocaust Fiction at the End of the Twentieth Century : Jakob the Liar and Life is Beautiful.
  D804.348.N38 2014
  940.53'1814—dc23   2012051220

Printed in the United States of America

This book is dedicated to the memory of Robert Southard.

Contents

PART II: THE UNITED STATES AND ISRAEL: LIVING WITH THE PAST IN NEW LANDS

Acknowledgments

Excerpts from five poems included in *New and Collected Poems: 1931–2001* by Czeslaw Milosz. "In Milan," "City Without a Name," "Earth," "Legend," and "Song on Porcelain" from New and Collected Poems: 1931–2001 by Czeslaw Milosz. Copyright © 1988, 1991, 1995, 2001 By Czeslaw Milosz Royalties, Inc. Reprinted by permission of HarperCollins Publishers.

Also forty-one lines from *A Treatise on Poetry* by Czeslaw Milosz, translation copyright © 2001 by Robert Hass. Reprinted by permission of Harper-Collins Publishers.

While I have made every effort to communicate with copyright holders of material used in this volume, I would be grateful to hear from any I have been unable to contact.

I would like to thank the College of William and Mary for the research opportunities that helped me edit this volume. I would also like to acknowledge my gratitude to Michael Schuldiner for getting this book project started and for his subsequent help and advice. Phyllis Lassner provided helpful direction, support, and suggestions throughout the process. And I want to thank Tim Schulte for all of his suggestions and careful reading of early drafts.

Introduction

Jennifer Taylor

Two distinct and yet intimately connected issues inform the essays in this collection. First, the essays examine *how* and *whether* the Holocaust, an enormously complex event, can be adequately represented in artistic works and memorials from Eastern and Western Europe as well as from the United States and Israel. In other words, can this story be told in its totality? The question of validity or authenticity of representation has been debated and discussed vigorously in many excellent books, including Saul Friedlander's *Probing the Limits of Representation: Nazism and the "Final Solution,"* Michael Rothberg's *Traumatic Realism: The Demands of Holocaust Representation*, and Berel Lang's *Writing and the Holocaust*, to name but a few of the volumes that open up questions about the complexity of describing this trauma. Who, for instance, should tell the story? Does the more authentic narrative belong to the first generation of victims of the Nazis—such as Elie Wiesel, whose memoir, *Night*, is seen by many as the quintessential Holocaust text? What authority belongs to the second generation—the children of Holocaust survivors, such as Art Spiegelman, whose *Maus I* and *II* depict how his parents' trauma hangs over his family? And how are we to read works by people with no direct connection to the Holocaust—such as American writer Philip Roth, whose *The Counterlife* asks us to examine how complex the notion of Jewish identity has become in a post-Holocaust world. Given the variations in approaches to and histories of the Holocaust, it is challenging to decide, to paraphrase Cynthia Ozick, who "owns" the Holocaust.[1]

The question of "ownership" is not limited to the kind of intergenerational struggles depicted so movingly in Art Spiegelman's *Maus*, however. Ownership or authority also comes into play when we begin to think about the national context of a Holocaust work. After all, although the Holocaust is, to some degree, understood to be an international event that affects all of us, the fact remains that the events that make up what we call the Holocaust are very specific, local, and unique. There are numerous works of both fiction and nonfiction that remind us that specificity matters when we talk and write about the Holocaust. Christopher Browning's *Ordinary Men: Reserve Police Battalion 101 and the Final Solution in Poland*, for example, depicts how German police units murdered Jewish villagers, shooting them one at a time in rural Poland, while Ruth Klüger's *Weiter leben: eine Jugend* (*Living On: A Childhood*) paints a vivid portrait of her and her mother's brutal experiences in Vienna and later in Theresienstadt, Auschwitz-Birkenau, and in Christianstadt/Groß-Rosen. And in the documentary film *Shoah*, Claude Lanzmann underlines again and again the importance of remembering the specifics of a traumatic event, directing the viewer's attention to language, to place, and to local space. To put it very simply, we cannot ignore questions of what we will refer to as national identity when we read Holocaust texts. People do not create texts without contexts; we always have a relationship to a place, a language, to a cultural or political identity.

The second issue informing this volume is then the complex and often ambiguous relationship between national identity and the legacy of the Holocaust. What, though, do we mean when we talk about national identity? The concept of the nation, let alone of national identity, is very complicated, and before we go on to discuss the works in this volume more concretely, it would be useful to establish some common understanding of the concept "national." This book is not meant to be a history of or a philosophical treatise on the meaning of nationality or nationalism (centuries of heated philosophical debate can be found on library shelves), but for the purposes of this volume, concerned as it is with postwar national depictions of the Holocaust, Ernest Gellner's 1997 book *Nationalism*, offers a deeply compelling and useful (if sexist) model of the nation, although, as I will discuss later, his model is problematic when we consider the identity of post-Holocaust Jews in Europe. A philosopher interested in the relationship between the emergence of the nation-state and modernity, Gellner urges us to imagine the beginnings of a nation as a marriage. He asks us to think of the bride as a common cultural understanding among a people that includes language among other shared systems. The groom, in his theory, can be thought of as the political structure that figuratively shields the nation under a canopy or protective dome.[2] Furthermore, Gellner's theory attempts to explain why some nations have been in place longer than others, especially in the case of Europe. He paints a map of Europe divided into zones, with the strongest, earliest "marriages" on the west coast, where culture and politics came together in Spain, France, and England because the "couple was living together in a kind of customary marriage for ages, long before the Age of Nationalism."[3] Germany and Italy, in the second zone, saw marriages only after they were politically made possible through unification in the mid-1800s (despite a cohesive cultural readiness, there were no grooms to be found!). Finally, in zones three and four, Eastern Europe, such marriages were not yet possible due to fractured cultures and a weaker political structure.

Marriages are, of course, complicated, messy, and always changing. Stories about marriages are equally difficult to read. There is, for instance, the story the couple presents to the public, what I will call the official narrative, and then there are the private stories that are known only to immediate family members, if that. We can think of those private or unofficial stories as counter-narratives. Nations whose populations witnessed, ignored, planned, or took part in murder, who were bystanders, perpetrators, or rescuers, all have narratives about the event we now call the Holocaust. Those narratives, whether dominant and official or unofficial and perhaps subversive, are found in films, monuments, paintings, poems, and histories, to name but a few forms. The essays in this book attempt to uncover, expose, and interpret the roles both official and competing or counter-narratives play in a nation dominated by the official discourse(s).

The national stories questioned in the volume are, by definition, incomplete or flawed; they each reflect a point of view in time, a political ideology, a series of omissions or sometimes elaborations or exaggerations. How can we as readers deal productively with the competing narratives about this deeply traumatic historical event without falling into the very unproductive trap of trying to determine whose narratives are most factual or most complete? While we can certainly label some narratives as absurd (that the Holocaust did not occur at all, for instance), we cannot and must not ignore them altogether. We should, rather, search for what is missing, what is exaggerated, and why these distortions occur, in order to open up new questions, and perhaps find new answers. Dominick LaCapra suggests a productive way of reading that answers some of the questions posed above.[4] We will only begin to work through the trauma of the Holocaust, he suggests, when we read Holocaust texts and imagine ourselves to be psychologists, listening to the stories; we, as psychologist-readers believe that the Holocaust is real and traumatic, and yet our role is to look for what the stories reveal about the people telling them rather than whether the stories reveal some ultimate truth (or lie) about the Holocaust.

Angel Loureiro, in his book *The Ethics of Autobiography: Replacing the Subject in Modern Spain*, offers an equally compelling way of reading Holocaust literature that, like LaCapra's, attempts to get beyond linguistic debates about the limits of language. While Loureiro is concerned primarily with autobiographical Holocaust texts, his ideas are useful for our texts as well. Specifically, he proposes we label texts as ethically engaged if they are conscious of their own incompleteness and engaged in a discussion with the self, with the other, and with those who are reading.[5] Ethical texts engage in a back-and-forth with the reader, asking her to engage with the past, to explore painful topics. The texts we explore in this collection all attempt to function ethically; that is, we are opening up texts that raise ethical questions about national Holocaust narratives.

LaCapra's picture of the reader as psychologist provides useful ways of reading about the Holocaust; many of the works we explore here, especially the European texts, picture the Holocaust as a traumatic departure from an earlier harmony, as a rupture in identity, and even, we might imagine, as a divorce between the bride and groom. Holocaust texts, like other works about trauma, depict families, marriages, and their vulnerabilities, from Haneke's deeply disturbed Austrian family in *The Seventh Continent* to the broken families in *Gebürtig*. Gellner's image of the weakening marriage zones as we move east, moreover, provides a context for understanding the enormous national changes (and the accompanying changes in national stories about the Holocaust) that have occurred across Europe since the end of World War II, from the collapse of the Soviet Union to the fall of the Berlin Wall in 1989.

The Eastern European narratives explored in this volume are thus especially interesting because the dominant stories have undergone the most change since the end of Communism. More than the Western Europeans or the Americans, Eastern Europeans have been faced with the contradictions that arise when they read the Holocaust outside of the context of Communism. The Southards' essay takes up the question of how three important Lithuanian museums balance acknowledging the contentious past with expressing national pride. Donna Coffey describes the Catholic, Lithuanian-born Polish Nobel Prize-winning poet, Czeslaw Milosz, a writer who calls into question both the official Holocaust stories of the Communist regime in Poland, as well as those of the nationalist right wing. By asking questions about Polish complicity with the Nazis during the Holocaust, Milosz creates counter-narratives to two ideologically opposed and yet similar dominant narratives. Dr. Lesinska's essay, too, investigates the contradictions in Polish cultural memory in an analysis of *Medallions*, the 1946 memoir of poet Zofia Nałkowska.

Western Europe, though it has not gone through the ruptures that Eastern Europe has experienced in the last twenty years, also presents us with deeply entrenched dominant narratives that need to be reexamined. As I discussed earlier, the image of the family in crisis is central. The first essay, for example, explores how the novel *Gebürtig* (1992) and its 2002 film version call into question Austrian notions of normalcy, especially across generations. At the heart of *Gebürtig* is a critique of the Austrian national myth, perpetuated in the 1980s under Austrian President and former SS-member Kurt Waldheim, of a homogenous and "normal" society unaffected by generational strife and by the ravages of World War II and the Holocaust. I read Austrian filmmaker Michael Haneke's film *The Seventh Continent* as a critique of the fragile myth of the postwar middle-class Austrian family seemingly unaffected by history. In the film, a family is shown to be deeply harmed, even destroyed, by the Nazi past it has refused to acknowledge. Finally, in Ferzina Banaji's essay, we are asked to reread groundbreaking French Holocaust documentaries, including Alain Resnais's *Nuit et Brouillard* (1955), Marcel Ophuls's *Le Chagrin et la pitié* (1971), and Claude Lanzmann's *Shoah* (1985), in order to understand their role in engaging questions of memory in France.

I suggested earlier that Gellner's picture of the nation as a marriage becomes problematic when we talk about post-Holocaust Jewish identity, specifically in Europe. This is in part because the Holocaust itself was a genocidal event that was meant to erase Jewish ethnic, religious, and cultural identity from the Earth, while simultaneously underlining the importance of national identity for the perpetrators. This presents a huge problem for post-Holocaust Jewish survivors and later generations; after surviving genocide, do Jewish Germans or Poles want to come back into Gellner's imagined marriage? In the 1980s, Dan Diner suggested the term "negative symbiosis" to describe the highly problematic relationship between post-Holocaust Germans and Jews, where they are each forced to identify themselves in terms of the other without the possibility of resolution. His term is a response to the widely held perception that there had been a positive symbiosis that had existed between Germans and Jews before the Holocaust, particularly in the Weimar Republic.[6] According to the symbiotic theory, the debates originating in the eighteenth century among such scholars as Moses Mendelssohn, Christian Wilhelm von Dohm and Gotthold Ephraim Lessing about the nature of Judaism, and whether it is an ethnicity, a religion, a culture or a nationality, had all been largely resolved to allow the possibility of a true Jewish German identity. It was possible, for example, for German or Italian Jews before the Holocaust to think of themselves as German or Italian first, and then as Jewish. This was simply not the case after this event. The bureaucracy, policies, ideology, apathy, and killing machinery of the Holocaust made Jewishness the primary marker of identity for Jews who had once primarily identified themselves as German, Italian, Norwegian, Austrian, Dutch or, to a lesser degree—because of the more overt anti-Semitism in certain lands—Polish, Lithuanian, or Romanian.

The Nazis attempted to erase, with a great deal of success, unfortunately, the European Jews' pre-Holocaust national identities and ties to their countries. The Holocaust, in a very real way, made both European national identity as well as a sense of Jewish identity very complex for Jews. Many works by Jewish Holocaust survivors return again and again to the rupture from their culture of birth, even those by survivors who, like Edgar Hilsenrath or Jurek Becker, returned to Germany (Becker was born in Poland but moved to East Germany after the war, and always insisted that German did not feel native to him despite his clear mastery of the language) and wrote in their native or, in the case of Becker, second language. Works by survivors in their home country are concerned in a central way with the survivor's fraught relationship to his or her European home.

Leaving Europe was certainly one answer for many Holocaust survivors, and the idea of America as a "melting pot," and as the "land of opportunity," was clearly appealing, even if survivor authors such as Ruth Klüger do express some disappointment with the realities of the New World.[7] In her discussion in her memoir *Weiter leben; eine Jugend* (*Living On: A Childhood*), about her life as a German professor in California, for instance, Klüger paints a highly ironic portrait of America, and specifically of California, as a place where everyone is trying, with varying degrees of success, to escape their past identities. Texts such as Klüger's *Weiter leben* as well as Spiegelman's *Maus* make painfully clear that, while many Holocaust survivors have sought a new life in the United States, it is difficult, if not impossible, to re-invent oneself after a trauma as horrific as the Holocaust. Nevertheless, American film companies, as well as other institutions including the United States Holocaust Memorial Museum, have been instrumental in creating an American national narrative in which the United States symbolizes a place for starting anew, for shedding old identities and for providing redemption. Three chapters in this book deal specifically with American narratives about the Holocaust. Dr. Hagelin's work explores Spielberg's portrayal of Oskar Schindler as specifically American, linking America with saving Holocaust victims. Schindler, whose easygoing optimism codes him as American, offers hope and safety for some of the Jews in his factories through his courage as well as through his dedication to commerce. In chapter 8, Phyllis Lassner takes a critical look at how Jewish women are sexualized in two American Holocaust texts—Sherri Szeman's 1994 novel *The Kommandant's Mistress*, and Steven Spielberg's *Schindler's List*. Szeman's novel specifically opens up a dialogue with texts such as *Schindler's List*, inviting the reader to rethink the American cultural myth of escape and new beginnings. And finally, my chapter explores the way that two late twentieth-century texts—the American-French film, *Jakob the Liar*, and Italian director Roberto Benigni's film *Life Is Beautiful*—have created narratives in which redemption and hope are understood to be the natural consequences of trauma, whereas earlier texts, such as East German

Jurek Becker's *Jacob the Liar*, stubbornly remind the reader time and again that mass murder does not inspire optimism and hope in the survivors. In Becker's novel, there is also no redemptive hope for the dead.

If the United States, with its cultural myth of the melting pot and new beginnings poses critical problems for Holocaust survivors and their children, how much more complex are the issues faced by survivors in the state of Israel. Fictional and non-fictional Holocaust representations (for example, the Yad Vashem Holocaust History Museum) in Israel have been and continue to be compelling and very complex. Questions about Jewish identity in the European Diaspora abound. Was it an actual diaspora? Was there an authentic European identity for Jews before the Holocaust and can it still exist? Why didn't more persecuted European Jews come to Palestine before the Holocaust? Furthermore, there are questions about Jewish identity in Israel that are hard to answer. Are the Jews who came to Palestine early on more authentic or privileged than the European immigrants who came later? Is Israel a site of new beginnings and redemption or does the trauma of the Holocaust follow survivor immigrants to the new, and yet old, homeland?

For many who do not live there, the story of the Israeli response to the Holocaust is very complicated. To return for a moment to Gellner's image of the nation as a marriage, Israel is a fraught case; this couple has reunited after an endless separation, after murderously violent experiences outside of the marriage. And so, while many European Holocaust texts focus on the moment of rupture, or divorce, many Israeli texts are caught up in the return to the old marriage, a narrative about going home and finding, or not finding, redemption. In this case, the bride and groom are, at least in the beginning, almost like strangers to each other. Israel, at first, is a nation of immigrants, made up of ethnically diverse people, most of whom escaped mass murder, who share a desire to live in the Jewish homeland, but who have culturally little in common. Chapter 10 of this book provides a very clear and succinct overview of the history of the Israeli fictional response to the Holocaust, from the early years in Palestine and Israel right after the war to the present. The chapter then goes on to explore how various seminal Israeli texts have engaged the Israeli national myth of coming home and of redemption through a critical re-reading of the happy domestic space, the home.

The contributors to this collection challenge us to engage critically and ethically with national stories about an international event. We are concerned with texts that question national stories about the destruction of European Jewry, investigating the very complex relationship between a country's dominant (and often official) national narrative(s) and potential counter-narratives. This collection is meant to open up questions about the boundaries between dominant and counter narratives both within and across national borders. Ultimately, asking the question of who "owns" the Holocaust is less illuminating than continuing an authentic and ongoing ethical engagement with how nations represent trauma.

NOTES

1. Cynthia Ozick, "Who Owns Anne Frank?" *The New Yorker*, October 6, 1997.
2. Ernest Gellner, *Nationalism* (New York: New York University Press, 1997), 20.
3. Ibid., 51.
4. Dominick LaCapra, "Representing the Holocaust: Reflections on the Historian's Debate," in *Probing the Limits of Representation: Nazism and the "Final Solution,"* ed. Saul Friedlander (Cambridge, MA: Harvard University Press, 1992), 108ff.
5. Angel Loureiro, *The Ethics of Autobiography: Replacing the Subject in Modern Spain* (Nashville: Vanderbilt University Press, 2000).
6. Dan Diner, "Negative Symbiosis. *Deutsche und Juden nach Auschwitz,*" *Babylon* 1 (1986).
7. Ruth Klüger, *Weiter leben: eine Jugend* (Göttingen: Wallstein, 1992).

BIBLIOGRAPHY

Becker, Jurek. *Jacob the Liar [Jakob der Luegner]*. 1st ed. New York: Harcourt Brace Jovanovich, 1975.
Becker, Jurek and Leila Vennewitz. *Jacob the Liar [Jakob der Luegner]*. 1st U.S. ed. New York: Little, Brown and Co., 1996.
Browning, Christopher. *Ordinary Men: Reserve Police Battalion 101 and the Final Solution in Poland*. New York: Harper Collins, 1993.
Diner, Dan. "*Negative Symbiosis. Deutsche und Juden nach Auschwitz.*" *Babylon* 1 (1986).
Friedlander, Saul. *Probing the Limits of Representation: Nazism and the "Final Solution."* Cambridge, MA: Harvard University Press, 1992.
Gebürtig. DVD. Directed by Robert Schindel and Lukas Stepanik. Vienna: Cult-Film Produktion, 2002.
Gellner, Ernest. *Nationalism*. New York: New York University Press, 1997.
Jakob the Liar. Directed by Peter Kassovitz. Culver City, CA: Columbia Tristar Home Video, 2000.
Jakob Der Luegner. Directed by Vlastimil Brodskây, Armin Mueller-Stahl, Erwin Geschonneck, et al. Northampton, MA: Icestorm International, 1999.
Klüger, Ruth. *Weiter leben: eine Jugend*. Göttingen: Wallstein, 1992.
Lang, Berel, ed. *Writing and the Holocaust*. New York: Holmes and Meier, 1989.
Le Chagrin et la pitié. Directed by Marcel Ophuls. NDR/Télévision Rencontre/TSR. Switzerland/France, 1971.

Life Is Beautiful. Directed by Roberto Benigni. Burbank, CA: Miramax Home Entertainment; Distributed by Buena Vista Home Entertainment, 1999.

Loureiro, Angel. *The Ethics of Autobiography: Replacing the Subject in Modern Spain.* Nashville: Vanderbilt University Press, 2000.

Nałkowska, Zofia. *Medallions.* Translated and introduction by Diana Kuprel. Evanston, IL: Northwestern University Press, 2000.

Nuit et Brouillard. Directed by Alain Resnais. Paris: Argos Films, 1955.

Ozick, Cynthia. "Who Owns Anne Frank?" *The New Yorker*, October 6, 1997, 76–97.

Roth, Philip. *The Counterlife.* New York: Vintage, 1996.

Rothberg, Michael. *Traumatic Realism: The Demands of Holocaust Representation.* Minneapolis: University of Minnesota Press, 2000.

Schindel, Robert. *Gebürtig.* Frankfurt am Main: Suhrkamp, 1992.

Schindler's List. DVD. Directed by Steven Spielberg. Hollywood, CA: Universal Pictures, 1993.

The Seventh Continent. Directed by Michael Haneke. Vienna: Wega Film, 1989.

Shoah. Directed by Claude Lanzmann. Paris: Les Films Aleph/Historia, 1985.

Spiegelman, Art. *Maus I, A Survivor's Tale: My Father Bleeds History.* New York: Pantheon, 1986.

———. *Maus II, A Survivor's Tale: And Here My Troubles Began.* New York: Pantheon, 1992.

Szeman, Sherri. *The Kommandant's Mistress.* New York: Harper Perennial, 1993.

Wiesel, Elie. *Night.* New York: Hill and Wang; Revised Edition, 2006.

Part I

EUROPE: LIVING IN THE SHADOW OF THE HOLOCAUST

Chapter One

Staging Austria's Past in Contemporary Vienna

Robert Schindel's 2002 Film Adaptation of Gebürtig

Christina Guenther

Robert Schindel's 1992 first novel, *Gebürtig*,[1] and its 2002 film adaptation[2] revolve around the way in which children of Holocaust perpetrators and Holocaust survivors process transgenerational trauma in Vienna in the mid-1980s. The sociopolitical context of the two works is key. The novel is set on the eve of the controversial Kurt Waldheim candidacy and presidential election in 1983 and goes through 1986, while the film seems to play during the first years of Waldheim's presidency. In the new millennium, the so-called Waldheim affair in 1986 is considered the *Wendejahr* (turning year) in Austria, and the novel *Gebürtig* and its film variant chronologically frame this significant turning point, a year during which—after forty years of nationally sanctioned amnesia—a public vigorous, thorough, and very painful debate about Austria's involvement in the Nazi war crimes took place.[3] In fact, the two texts are testaments to the way in which, in the late 1980s, a generation of Viennese began to come to terms with their experience of an unacknowledged mediated past. Marianne Hirsch has called this form of secondhand memory "postmemory," a term that "characterizes the experience of those who grow up dominated by narratives that preceded their birth, whose belated stories are evacuated by the stories of the previous generation shaped by traumatic events that can be neither understood nor recreated."[4] Indeed, the two texts explore and illustrate how especially the Viennese second generation, children of Holocaust survivors, confront what Eva Hoffman calls "transferred loss, more than transferred memory . . . loss that has no concrete shape or face." For Hoffman, this secondhand experience of memory "belongs to the realm of the psychological, the internal theater of body and mind, rather than to the stage of external events."[5] Taken together, the novel and film adaptation represent contrasting yet complementary imaginative contributions to the processing of postmemory in Austria at the turn of the twenty-first century.

The 1992 novel *Gebürtig* or *Born-Where*,[6] its title in English translation, followed the Waldheim era. By contrast, the film, directed by Robert
Schindel and Lukas Stepanik appeared on the heels of the formation of a
new right-wing coalition that included the Austrian People's Party as well as
the Freedom Party with its populist, xenophobic rhetoric. *Gebürtig*, the film,
enjoyed a modicum of success in Austria.[7] It opened the 2002 Austrian Film
Festival *Diagonale* in Graz and received Austria's nomination in the Best
Foreign Film category at the Oscars.

The novel called forth significant debate in the German-speaking media
upon its publication, reaping both euphoric praise as well as a few scathing
critiques. Literary scholars agree, however, that the central question of this
novel about contemporary Viennese society revolves around the tension
between genealogical origin (*Herkunft*), familial and cultural memory and
its impact on identity formation among Jewish Austrians of the second generation, and the complex relationship between Jews and non-Jews in Austria
today. In her 1987 film essay *Paper Bridge*,[8] which appeared five years before *Gebürtig*, fellow Viennese filmmaker and writer Ruth Beckermann had
already begun to explore the perception of identity among Viennese Jews of
the second generation who, growing up in a social environment of repressed
familial memories and public cultural erasure, struggled with the sense of
not belonging, of living in a "no-man's-land," in postwar Austria.[9] Schindel
ventures one step further in *Gebürtig* by proposing a new response to the
long-delayed process of *Vergangenheitsaufarbeitung*—coming to terms with
the past—in the Austrian context. With his novel, he reframes the question
of Jewish post-*Shoah* identity in Austria by problematizing the relationships
among Jewish and non-Jewish grandchildren of the Habsburgian doubled ea-
gle, between members of the second generation and the children of perpetrators and bystanders—i.e., gentile Austrians. His image of a "*gläserne Wand*,"
a glass wall that may be transparent and even invisible ("*stumm, unsichtbar,
hermetisch*" or mute, invisible, and hermetic),[10] but that clearly continues to
hinder open dialogue, captures the complexity of such relationships.

Most literary scholars read the novel as confirmation that normalcy in
the relations between these grandchildren—Viennese gentiles and Jews in
the 1980s—is still impossible.[11] In fact, Hildegard Nabbe observes that the
novel exemplifies continued and inevitable "negative symbiosis" between
the grandchildren of both groups, in which prejudices and incrimination
originating from different familial histories abound on both sides.[12] More
recently, in her thorough and thoughtful study of *Gebürtig*, the novel, Erin
McGlothlin, too, points to the duality of experience—rooted and uprooted
family histories and familial location—on the part of Schindel's Jewish and
non-Jewish Austrian main characters. For McGlothlin, the novel suggests

that, as a result of their different legacies, the divide between Austrian Jews and non-Jews cannot yet be bridged after only one generation.[13] By contrast, Dagmar Lorenz's reading of the novel is somewhat more hopeful. Although for Lorenz, too, most of Schindel's characters never really escape "a polarization" of perceptions between Jewish and gentile Austrians of the 1980s, she concludes that the "glass wall" between them in the novel is attributable to a "lack of communication, rather than the legacy of the past or ancestry"—an obstacle that at least for a few individuals can be scaled when the "characters are motivated by curiosity, sexual attraction, or ambition to interact with the 'other.'"[14] Schindel's own observation shortly after publication of the novel in March 1992 seems to support Lorenz's more optimistic interpretation. Born in 1944 to Jewish Communists—to a mother who survived Ravensbrück and Auschwitz and to a father who was murdered in Dachau—Schindel acknowledges about the novel in a 1992 *Profil* interview: "*Ich wollte mir die Toten vom Halse schaffen, die Toten sollten mit dem Roman begraben werden, damit ich mich den Lebenden zuwenden kann.*" (I wanted to get the dead off my back, the dead were supposed to have been laid to rest with the novel so that I could shift my attention to the living.) He adds in the same interview: "*Endlich hab' ich zu einer Normalität gefunden, wo man sich die Partner nicht mehr nach der Herkunft, sondern nach dem Gefühl aussucht.*" (I've finally arrived at a sort of normality where you can choose your partner according to feeling rather than origin.)[15] To be sure, both the novel and the film adaptation that appeared some ten years later seem to bear out what Eva Hoffman recently observed of children of the second generation: "Just as for some survivors only full remembering could bring about some catharsis, so for the second generation, only a full imaginative confrontation with the past—however uncanny, however unknown—can bring the haunting to an end."[16] "Full imaginative confrontation with the past" or the transformation of post-traumatic absent yet present memories into art is, however, never a completed process; it never quite allows for harmony, transcendence of heritage, or a return to the *status quo ante*.

Normalcy and uninhibited relations between historically antagonistic ethnic identity groups remain rather tenuous in both film and novel. In order to come to terms with this inhibition, *Gebürtig* makes use of a strategy familiar to Freudians, that of "transference," in its depiction of the way loss and mourning are transmitted and experienced from one generation to another. In Dominick LaCapra's words, transference can manifest itself as "a form of repetition, both in relations among researchers . . ., and perhaps more interestingly—because less developed—in the relationship to the object of study. When you study something, at some level you always have a tendency to repeat the problems you were studying."[17] *Gebürtig*, the film adaptation in particular, seems both to represent and thematize the complex interrelation of "acting out" and "working through." LaCapra, adapting Freudian psychoanalysis, highlights these two ways by which one can attempt to make more transparent the relation between traumatic history and subjectivity—the ways by which one can come to terms with limited events such as the Holocaust, experienced firsthand or in a mediated secondary manner. For Freud via LaCapra, the compulsive reenactment or "acting out" reflects melancholia, "an isolating experience allowing for specular intersubjectivity that immures the self in its desperate isolation," a "state in which one remains possessed by the phantasmically invested past . . ."[18] By contrast, again LaCapra reading Freud, in mourning or "in working through [traumatic past], the person tries to gain critical distance on a problem and to distinguish . . . between past, present, and future. And working through is intimately bound up with the possibility of being an ethical and political agent, which . . . involves the arduous process of moving from victim to survivor and agent."[19] Working through and arriving at a complex and differentiated understanding of the Holocaust trauma experienced by children of victims and perpetrators is not a unidirectional linear process that can be completed quickly and efficiently once and for all.

By juxtaposing the novel with its film adaptation, we can explore the ways in which Schindel problematizes how the secondary witnessing of the Holocaust past is processed by both Jewish and non-Jewish Austrians and Germans in Austria of the 1980s, the decade in which, on a national level, Austria's culpability with regard to anti-Semitism and Nazi war crimes entered the public discourse through Kurt Waldheim's election campaign. Moreover, the film adaptation also represents a self-conscious reenactment of the novel, an artistic representation of the post-*Shoah* generation's coming to terms with its own Jewish identity in contemporary Vienna.[20] This self-actualizing process is enabled through a strategy of "acting out" and "working through" repressed Holocaust memories. The film, thus reflects on a doubled past—it self-consciously historicizes coming to terms with the Nazi past in Vienna in the late 1980s even as it seems to respond to the rise in popularity of Jörg Haider's Freedom Party.

The film begins where the novel ends with a *mise en abîme*, a film within the film, that draws attention to the necessity and significance of restaging Auschwitz and the Holocaust trauma in both European and American culture. Even among the next generation, secondhand survivor guilt seems to require this reenactment on film as "*die Buße der Lebenden*," an atonement on the part of the living that even after forty-five years is not yet complete. In the epilogue of *Gebürtig*, Schindel fictionalizes his personal experience of "acting out"—as an extra with forty other Jews from Vienna in ABC's "War and Remembrance" documentary series on the Theresienstadt concentration camp. (In Beckermann's 1987 film *Paper Bridge*, Schindel himself is among those extras in the "War and Remembrance" series; this "acting out" is hardly only commemorative in that Beckermann captures the actors—Jews from Vienna but of various ethnic origins—on break discussing heatedly with one another modes of resistance and collaboration during the Holocaust and what Jewishness means in their time.) For Schindel, Jewishness in Vienna in the 1980s entails the repetition or acting out of post-traumatic conditions in terms of theatrical performativity. Moreover, chosen to perform in a Holocaust documentary because of his stereotypical Jewish physiognomy, the narrator observes ironically in a familiar Viennese-inflected syntax that, as children of survivors compulsively perform or play roles of concentration camp inmates in documentaries, thereby acting out and repeating the traumatic experience of their dead relatives, the deadliness of the Holocaust is actually diminished somewhat in the present for millions of spectators: "*Hier können wir froh sein, weil wir den Vertilgten nachspielen können, a Glück, das wir haben, wir sinen bloß Komparsen in einem Film, in einem Spiel, Millionen werden können sehn vorm Fernsehschirm, dass mer leben, a Glück. Wir spielen und wahrlich, das müssen Verzweifelte nur.*" (Here [in the performance] we can be happy because we can replay the exterminated ones. How fortunate that we are simply extras in a film, in a game. Millions of spectators can see on the television screen that we are alive. How fortunate. We perform, and truly only desperate ones do that.)[21] Indeed, having stereotypical-looking Jews perform the persecuted, murdered generations of Jews in a contemporary documentary film represents a triumph over the catastrophic destruction. It also signals a cathartic moment for viewers, who are reassured of their own safety and good fortune despite the very real and dehumanizing brutality and genocide of the Third Reich. While constructive of Jewish identity, however, this act of performance for Jews in Vienna, according to the novel, does not necessarily check the need for compulsive repetition and lead to potential transformation. Significantly, the film adaptation seems to promise this initially.

If we now return to the opening scene of *Gebürtig*, the film, too, self-consciously reflects on actor and spectator as it evokes the brutal concentration camp experience. In contrast to Beckermann in her post-memorial film *Paper Bridge*, Schindel begins his film with footage of camp inmates intent on keeping their footing on icy terrain, forced to march through a bleak snow-blown landscape under the supervision of a group of SS officers with menacing, barking German shepherds. As one of the inmates slips on the ice, an SS officer approaches and makes a grand theatrical gesture; the SS officer ceremoniously extends his hand to the fallen inmate and helps him up, thereby effectively disrupting the familiar scene of vicious perpetrators and helpless victims. The surprising slippage from apparent reality to reenactment, from dehumanizing brutality to humane decency, unsettles the spectator and creates an imaginative space for "working through" the traumatic secondary memory, and the necessary distance from the past for reflection in the present. This prologue scene of the film signals the potential for moving beyond a compulsive reenactment of trauma or "acting out" (which constrains Jewish identity as we see in the novel) to a repetition with change, an attempt to work over the past in a present where formerly fixed roles might be transformed.

The scene change in the next frame to a contemporary Viennese apartment is facilitated by a voice-over from the main character, Danny Demant. In his role as narrator in the film, he thus connects the reenactment scene that played in the concentration camp with the reality of 1980s Vienna. Moreover, in this contemporary setting, Demant as narrator seems to articulate the quandary that is raised by both the novel and the first scene of the film: how can children of Holocaust survivors shift their perspective from the past toward the future in an attempt to transcend or at least transform their inherited Jewish identity, still equated with persecution and victimhood in 1980s Vienna? "*An mir ist nichts echt*" (Nothing is real about me), Demant observes with regard to his relationships: "*ich spiele bloß den Getöteten hinterher*" (I just play at being the casualty in the end). Just as his relationship with his girlfriend is on a slippery slope, *Glatteis* as he calls it, so, too, his present reality is "*ein einziges Geröll*," as slippery as loose gravel. The film explores how Danny and members of the Jewish community in Vienna attempt to keep the past from dogging their every step forward, thereby trapping them in a melancholic post-memorial state of paralysis, and to finally arrive at "repetition with alteration."

The film adaptation, reduced to three intersecting plotlines, is clearly a more visually dramatic, direct, and distilled version of the complex novel as it explores individual alternatives to repetition compulsion, or melancholic paralysis—a condition that afflicts not only Jews of the second generation in Schindel's story but also the son of a perpetrator as well. The trajectories of Danny Demant, son of murdered Holocaust victims, Konrad Sachs, son of a Nazi war criminal, and Hermann Gebirtig, a Holocaust survivor whose family was murdered in Auschwitz and who, as a New York émigré, abhors the idea of returning to Vienna, are tightly interwoven in the film. Demant's voice serves as the omniscient narrator who reveals the psychological twists and turns of the other two main characters even as they interact with one another. There are also a number of small yet significant changes in the film. For instance, Danny Demant is a cabaret artist rather than an editor of Holocaust texts, Konrad Sachs is the son of an SS concentration camp doctor (rather than a lawyer in the novel) condemned to death at Nuremberg, and Hermann Gebirtig is a successful composer of American musicals rather than plays. Danny and Konrad, one Jewish and the other a gentile, ironically enough, share a kinship throughout the film via their noses; the stereotypical anatomical feature, his nose in profile, gets Danny the part of an extra in an American Holocaust film for which the American filmmaker is looking for "authentic-looking" Jewish actors. Upon seeing Danny's profile, the film-maker exclaims in English: "Now that's what I call Jewish." Jewishness for Austrians and Americans, then, is inscribed in the body, a racialized projection of both difference and authenticity.[22] Konrad Sachs, on the other hand, regularly experiences nosebleeds in the film whenever the revenant of his ominous father emerges in his present—a subconscious point of connection with racialized Jewish difference perhaps.

All three characters ultimately move from restrictive "acting out" or compulsive reenactment and attendant melancholia to "working through" the past by publicly staging their stories, by outing themselves in variations of bearing public witness. In this process and in contrast to the novel, the context of Waldheim's Vienna is even more firmly established just as Waldheim's rhetoric is more directly criticized. Protagonist Demant, for instance, is engaged in a ritualized repetition of his experience as an extra on the set of a Holocaust documentary in his cabaret "*Mischpoche*."[23] Particular, thus, to the film is that Demant reclaims cabaret, an entertainment genre consisting of political and social satire that flourished during the Weimar Republic but was censored by the Nazis. On stage, he can not only satirize his hometown Vienna, "the city of memories and amnesia," the "capital of anti-Semitism" and the city of "barbarism and music" but he can also restage the disturbing reenactment of the camp scenes using wit and black humor as a distancing device. In the course of the film, Demant, inserted back into the camp set of the American Holocaust film surrounded by masses of dead inmates as doll props and facing the gallows with dogs barking around him, abruptly stops the scene because it simply becomes too unbearable for him. In the cabaret setting, however, this unsettling reenactment can be processed on stage in terms of a communal virtual experience, a mode of working through in which the performance of past trauma always includes an awareness of its distance from the present. "*Sch'ma Jisruel*," he has the Jewish camp inmate whom he performs as intone in the blistering cold of the camps. The prayer never gets beyond the physical sensory reality of the freezing inmate, who simply repeats in the appropriate solemn tone of a prayer: Hear oh Israel "*kalt is ma in die Fiß, schm'a, di Fiß so kalt*" (a Yiddish variant of "My feet are freezing"). While Demant is able to work through and reshape his traumatic secondary memories, the heavily armed security guard stationed outside the cabaret at all times is, of course, a troubling reminder of the reality of anti-Semitism in Vienna in the 1980s.

Hermann Gebirtig's response to and experience of Austria in the 1980s again heightens the film's very direct attack on the Vienna of the Waldheim era. When initially asked to testify in person against the infamous concentration camp "Skull Cracker" Pointner, he rejects the idea of returning to this "snake pit," this *Naziland*, as he calls Austria. "Three words keep me from returning to Vienna," he adds, "three words that Waldheim uses in his election ads: now, more than ever." For Gebirtig, however, "working through" his post-traumatic stress entails revisiting the sites of his family memory in Vienna after decades of self-imposed exile. He agrees to testify against the war criminal Pointner, who had been a brutal camp officer at Ebensee. Bearing witness in the public forum of the court allows Gebirtig to experience a sense of liberation from the constraints of the past (*"vielleicht bin ich erst jetzt aus dem Lager heraus"*—I've finally made it out of the camp, he sighs after his testimony). The experience is dissatisfying and thwarted, however, for working through and mourning, as LaCapra and others have observed, requires a "supportive or even solidaristic social context."[24] Gebirtig's precise and clear testimony and incontestable identification of Pointner in a court of law, rendered even more convincingly in the film adaptation, is not enough to bring about justice. Pointner is released. If, as W. James Booth argues in *Communities of Memory: On Witness, Identity and Justice*, "doing justice and bearing witness are at their heart an expression of our memory-laden moral relation to the past . . ."[25] and "justice as the institutionalized remembrance of the past" must be understood as "a duty to the dead and as a condition of reconciliation,"[26] then Vienna of the 1980s, where crime and its victims are still enveloped in silence, does not grant Jews a space for working through secondary traumatization. The limits of working through extend from the public forum to the private space. The Austrian neighbors, too, who with initial surprise and even relief recognize Gebirtig upon his return to Vienna after forty years, manifest no shame or complicity, no deep feelings of contrition for the genocide of their Jewish compatriots. Their utter dissociation from the crimes and from a clear sense of culpability, empathy, or responsibility, and their self-identification as victims then and in the present disturbs and resonates now, just a few years after the end of the right-wing nationalist coalition of Schüssel and Haider.

Konrad Sachs, too, chooses to bear witness—i.e., go public—as a means to "work through" the debilitating shame of being a Nazi criminal's son. Interestingly, he is German not Austrian. He comes to Vienna because, for him, there are no psychoanalysts left in Germany with whom he can work through his troubling memories. In the film, it is Gebirtig who suggests that Sachs document the life of his father, that he "out himself" as the son of a war criminal by publishing a biography of his father that might act as an antidote to the inherited poison of his father's crimes. Sachs's story in the film emphasizes "acting out" and "working through" less in terms of its political and ethical implications of bringing about political agency and more in terms of the attempt to achieve redemption through mourning.

All three characters of the film adaptation emphasize that "working through" traumatic experience as a memory modality consists of bearing witness, and, as Danny remarks at the end of the film: *"Spuren müssen her."* Every trace must be documented—*"Ich muss es aufschreiben."* Writing as the means to connect secondhand experience with the legacy of the Holocaust for the second generation is, thus, ultimately privileged in the film, leading us as the spectators of the film back to the novel itself Danny's testimony about "a legacy that for him is not lived experienced" is, as McGlothlin has described it regarding the novel, "at moments both impossibly outrageous and outrageously impossible."[27] In other words, the difficult experience of personal agency, made possible through staged testimonial as a form of "working through," remains incomplete, especially without acknowledgment within a larger social context—whether this takes the form of a sociocultural (public) process of mourning or even of the capacity to recognize the traumatic burden of the Holocaust, as it reaches into the contemporary frame. Nonetheless, the novel and especially the film adaptation of *Gebürtig* represent a public process of "working through" or mourning that performatively opens an alternative space to the experience and heritage of victimhood, a place for critical judgment and ethical agency to develop.

NOTES

1. Robert Schindel, *Gebürtig* (Frankfurt am Main: Suhrkamp, 1992).

2. In a 2003 interview with the *Tiroler Tageszeitung* 15 (January 20, 2003): 12, Schindel insists that the film is not a *"Literaturverfilmung"* [literary film version of the book] because he and fellow director Lukas Stepanik *"den Stoff für den Film geändert haben"* [changed the material for the film]. Nonetheless, the film can be considered an adaptation of the novel.

3. "Österreich *wurde anders: Das blieb vom Wendejahr 1986,"* *Salzburger Nachrichten*, February 25, 2006, 2. In this issue, this article together with a second entitled *"Das Ende des Schweigens"* by Andreas Koller covered the entire second page.

4. Marianne Hirsch, *Family Frames: Photography, Narrative and Postmemory* (Cambridge, MA: Harvard University Press, 1997), 22.

5. Eva Hoffman, *After Such Knowledge: Memory, History, and the Legacy of the Holocaust* (New York: Public Affairs, 2004), 72–73.

6. See Michael Roloff's translation of Robert Schindel's *Gebürtig* (Riverside, CA: Ariadne Press, 1995).

7. While most critics hailed this as an intelligent film, the first to deal with coming to terms with the past "with the help of a homogenous and excellent ensemble of actors" (Ulrike Steiner, *Oberösterreichische Nachrichten*, April 5, 2002), it was also criticized for its form, for its being a bit too epigonic and conventional (Claus Philipp, *Der Standard*, March 19, 2002).

8. *"Die unterste Falte der Seele," Profil* 18 (April 18, 1992): 88.

9. *Die papierene Brücke*. Directed by Ruth Beckermann. Vienna: Aichholzer Film, 1987.

10. In addition to Ruth Beckermann's 1987 film *Paper Bridge (Papierene Brücke)*, see also her *Unzugehörig: Österreicher und Juden nach 1945* (Vienna: Löcker Verlag, 1989), 119.

11. Schindel, *Gebürtig*, 12. All translations from the novel or the film are mine.

12. Thomas Freeman emphasizes the novel's preoccupation with Jewish self-hatred in contemporary Vienna, a Jewish identity that stems from a sense of "community which shares the experience and memory of suffering," "Jewish Identity and the Holocaust in Robert Schindel's *Gebürtig*," *Modern Austrian Literature* 32, no. 2 (1999), 118. For Michael Ossar, Jewish *"Befangenheit"* or self-consciousness resulting from Austrian anti-Semitism prevents a positive self-identification in the present or future. See Ossar, "Austrians and Jews at the Turn of the Century: Robert Schindel's *Gebürtig* and Arthur Schnitzler's *Der Weg ins Freie*" in *Jews in German Literature Since 1945: German-Jewish Literature?*, ed. Pol O'Dochartaigh (Amsterdam: Rodopi, 2000), 35–44. Hildegard Kernmayer observes that Schindel's novel illustrates that Jewish identity is constructed from the outside, not from the inside—an identity constructed in response to anti-Semitism. See "Gebürtig *Ohneland. Robert Schindel: Auf der Suche nach der verlorenen Identität*," *Modern Austrian Literature* 27, nos. 3/4 (1994): 173–91. Peter Arnds emphasizes fragmentation of Jewish identity in the novel and that "for the sake of love and understanding" individuals must transcend their inherited cultural and ethnic margins. See Arnds, "Robert Schindel's Novel *Gebürtig* (1992) in a Postmodern Context," in *Towards the Millenium: Interpreting the Austrian Novel 1971–1996*, ed. Gerald Chapple (Tübingen: Schauffenberg, 2000), 217–39.

13. See Hildegard Nabbe's discussion of Dan Diner's "negative symbiosis" in *"Die Enkelkinder des Doppeladlers: Einblendung von politischer Vergangenheit in den Alltag der Gegenwart in Robert Schindels Roman* Gebürtig," *Modern Austrian Literature* 32, no. 2 (1999): 113–24.

14. Erin McGlothlin, *Second Generation Holocaust Literature: Legacies of Survival and Perpetration* (Rochester: Camden House, 2006), 91–124, 230.

15. Dagmar Lorenz, "Emancipation from the Past. From Group Identity Toward an Integrated Self: Robert Schindel's *Gebürtig*," in *Modern Austrian Prose: Interpretations and Insights,* ed. Paul F. Dvorak (Riverside, CA: Ariadne, 2001), 316.

16. *Profil* 12 (March 16, 1992): 88.

17. Hoffman, *After Such Knowledge*, 73.

18. "An Interview with Professor Dominick LaCapra," by Amos Goldberg, June 9, 1998, Shoah Resource Center, 32–33, http://www.yadvashem.org.

19. Dominick LaCapra, *History and Memory After Auschwitz* (Ithaca: Cornell University Press, 1998), 183.

20. Dominick LaCapra, *History in Transit: Experience, Identity, Critical Theory* (Ithaca: Cornell University Press, 2004), 103.

21. The ten-year delay in making the film certainly must have been due to a problem in financing.

22. Schindel, *Gebürtig*, 343.

23. Sander Gilman draws attention to another segment in the novel in which another character is identified via his nose in terms of a *Rassenmerkmal* (racial characteristic) by his gentile girlfriend. See *Jews in Today's German Culture* (Bloomington: Indiana University Press, 1995), 99.

24. A Jewish cabaret in 1980s Vienna was itself somewhat unusual even if a variegated Viennese Jewish community is once again emerging today. See "Shalom Wien: *Aufbruchstimmung in der jüdischen Gemeinde Wiens*," *Profil* 8 (February 20, 2006): 86–94. To this day, a venue of this type does not exist in Vienna.

25. LaCapra, *History and Memory*, 184.

26. W. James Booth, *Communities of Memory: On Witness, Identity, and Justice* (Ithaca: Cornell University Press, 2006), 112.

27. Ibid, 119.

28. McGlothlin, *Second Generation Holocaust Literature*, 124.

BIBLIOGRAPHY

Arnds, Peter. "Robert Schindel's Novel *Gebürtig* (1992) in a Postmodern Context." In *Towards the Millenium: Interpreting the Austrian Novel 1971–1996*, edited by Gerald Chapple, 217–39. Tübingen: Schauffenberg, 2000.

Beckermann, Ruth. *Die Papierene Brücke*. Video. Vienna: Filmladen, 1987.

———. *Unzugehörig: Österreicher und Juden nach 1945*. Vienna: Löcker Verlag, 1989.

Booth, W. James. *Communities of Memory: On Witness, Identity, and Justice*. Ithaca: Cornell University Press, 2006.

Freeman, Thomas. "Jewish Identity and the Holocaust in Robert Schindel's *Gebürtig*." *Modern Austrian Literature* 30, no. 1 (1999): 117–26.

Gilman, Sander. *Jews in Today's German Culture*. Bloomington: Indiana University Press, 1995.

Hirsch, Marianne. *Family Frames: Photography, Narrative and Postmemory*. Cambridge, MA: Harvard University Press, 1997.

Hoffman, Eva. *After Such Knowledge: Memory, History, and the Legacy of the Holocaust*. New York: Public Affairs, 2004.

Kernmayer, Hildegard. "*Gebürtig Ohneland. Robert Schindel: Auf der Suche nach der verlorenen Identität*." *Modern Austrian Literature* 27, nos. 3/4 (1994): 173–91.

LaCapra, Dominick. *History and Memory After Auschwitz*. Ithaca: Cornell University Press, 1998.

———. *History in Transit: Experience, Identity, Critical Theory.* Ithaca: Cornell University Press, 2004.

Lorenz, Dagmar. "Emancipation from the Past: From Group Identity toward an Integrated Self: Robert Schindel's *Gebürtig.*" In *Modern Austrian Prose: Interpretations and Insights,* edited by Paul F. Dvorak, 300–24. Riverside, CA: Ariadne, 2001.

McGlothlin, Erin. *Second Generation Holocaust Literature: Legacies of Survival and Perpetration.* Rochester: Camden House, 2006.

Nabbe, Hildegard. *"Die Enkelkinder des Doppeladlers: Einblendung von politischer Vergangenheit in den Alltag der Gegenwart in Robert Schindels Roman* Gebürtig." *Modern Austrian Literature* 32, no. 2 (1999): 113–24.

Ossar, Michael. "Austrians and Jews at the Turn of the Century: Robert Schindel's *Gebürtig* and Arthur Schnitzler's *Der Weg ins Freie.*" In *Jews in German Literature Since 1945: German-Jewish Literature?,* edited by Pol O'Dochartaigh, 35–44. Amsterdam: Rodopi, 2000.

Schindel, Robert. *Gebürtig.* Frankfurt am Main: Suhrkamp, 1992.

Schindel, Robert, and Lukas Stepanik. *Gebürtig.* DVD. Vienna: Cult-Film Produktion, 2002.

Chapter Two

From *le génocide* to *la shoah*

Changing Patterns in Documentary Representations of the Holocaust in France

Ferzina Banaji

> What is remembered of the Holocaust depends on how it is remembered, and how it is remembered depends in turn on the texts giving them form.[1]

The above epigraph goes straight to the heart of the investigation that I shall carry out in this chapter. I intend to examine the interface between the historical event of the Holocaust and its representation in French documentary cinema as a means of gauging its status in French cultural or national memory at large.

Omer Bartov offers a linguistic analysis of the terms used to describe the Holocaust, and observes that the French word *génocide* reflects a precise but still somehow unsatisfactorily cerebral expression of the actual events, one that does not necessarily reflect the human element. He suggests that the unsentimental and dispassionate nature of the term may reflect a French fear of accepting their own role in events and the concern that to speak of the Holocaust on a more emotional level might somehow diminish the role and sacrifices of the Resistance.[2] This chapter will plot the trajectory of representations of the event: from *génocide* to *l'univers concentrationnaire* (concentration camp universe) to *la shoah*, reflecting the change in national memory and memorialization by returning to the films in question. These films are Alain Resnais's *Nuit et Brouillard* (1955, released as *Night and Fog* in English), Marcel Ophuls's *Le Chagrin et la pitié* (1971, released as *The Sorrow and the Pity* in English) and Claude Lanzmann's *Shoah* (1985, title unchanged in English). These films have been chosen because of their exceptional status in, and their role in the transformation of, French culture and national memory, to suggest how they have literally, both linguistically and visually, altered the inheritance of the Holocaust in France. In recognition of the fact that *Le Chagrin et la pitié* is not a film that explicitly focuses on the Holocaust, the examination of the film will be less detailed than for *Nuit et Brouillard* and *Shoah*. As my argument will illustrate, however, Ophuls's film played a significant role in allowing for the emergence of Holocaust memory in France. The three films remain to this day moving and powerful, and they tell us about the events of the Holocaust or French Collaboration while vigilantly maintaining an ethical responsibility to the subject, bending, as this article will suggest, cinematic conventions in order to do so.

These introductory comments will set out the theoretical framework that will be employed in order to examine the network of relations that emerge between historical event, filmic representation (here specifically, documentaries), and cultural memory. As a caveat, it is necessary to stress that to look at the events themselves is to realize the immense difficulties inherent in their depiction, and there continues to be a troubled relationship between film and an event of the magnitude of the Holocaust. It is also necessary to draw a distinction here between the broader state-sponsored systematic persecution of and the annihilation of European Jewry by Nazi Germany, both of which comprise the entirety of what we refer to as the Holocaust. Of the latter, there exists only one known piece of motion picture footage, which lasts a scant two minutes, of the actual act of genocidal murder. Shot in 1941 by Reinhard Wiener, a naval sergeant stationed in Latvia, it shows people running into a pit and being shot by a firing squad.[3] We may, nonetheless, compare this to the proliferation of films on the subject that have returned relentlessly to cinema screens ever since, films that with very few exceptions rarely take us to the very heart of the darkness that was the Holocaust. This ever-growing corpus of films is reaching spectators who are historically and geographically moving further away from the event itself. As a consequence, we are obliged to consider cinema as a medium that alters, influences, or even forms our memory of the past, a past to which we may not even necessarily lay claim. The American philosopher Richard Rorty claims that "the novel, the film and the TV program [sic] have, gradually but steadily, replaced the sermon and the treatise as the principal vehicles of moral challenge and progress," suggesting therefore that the filmic medium may legitimately assert itself as a crucial creator and disseminator of memory.[4] Furthermore, in the context of France and the Holocaust, French historian Henry Rousso identifies cinema, along with official commemoration and scholarly discourse, as one of the decisive vectors of memory, particularly in the cultural sphere where it draws on both artistic and emotional views of the past.[5] It is from this nexus between film, historical event, and cultural memory that I shall begin my analysis of the three documentary films that shaped the memory of the Holocaust in postwar France.

Key to this examination of representations of the Holocaust is the interplay between ethics and identification. These two concepts, the one philosophical (and arguably critical in an engagement with a past not necessarily our own) and the other psychological and cinematic, constitute the theoretical essence of this chapter. On one level, this is to allow for a more thorough critical engagement between philosophy and film, drawing on the considerable privileging accorded psychoanalytic and psychological elements of film analysis in the past. It is also to further facilitate a reading of Holocaust films through an ethically rigorous framework. This is a necessary engagement given the fundamental importance accorded issues of ethical responsibility in the Holocaust genre at large. From Theodor Adorno's early (albeit much misinterpreted) dictum against poetry after Auschwitz to the mapping of rules of the Holocaust genre by Dominick LaCapra, Lawrence Langer, and Terence des Pres among others, there is a considerable amount of scholarship on issues of representation. Bearing these issues in mind but not limited by them as points of departure for my analysis of these films, I propose to draw on the ethical philosophy of the Lithuanian-born philosopher Emmanuel Levinas, privileging an ethical responsibility to alterity in my analysis of these key filmic texts.[6] In particular, I will draw on the dynamic between Self and Other and the strict ethical injunction against possessing or understanding alterity.[7]

A fruitful point of contrast may be observed if the Levinasian ethical imperative is juxtaposed against the key notion of cinematic identification, specifically as it refers to the perceived similarities between spectator and onscreen character. In any kind of film, documentary or otherwise, identification processes are believed to impact a number of reactions including, but not limited to, catharsis and empathy. Cinematic identification is supposed to trigger a learning process, and consequently allows for film to assume a potentially didactic role.[8] Precisely this traditional identification process may be seen to transgress a Levinasian ethical engagement, which posits that a cohesive understanding of the Other remains unattainable. Hence, I posit a refashioning of the way in which identification processes are seen to work in film. Bearing in mind the strict command that identification with the Other must be impossible, I propose to work instead with an ethical process of identification that takes into account an opposing notion of dis-identification. This term interrogates the traditional meaning of cinematic identification via the inclusion of a distance between Self (spectator) and Other (filmic subject). The viewer of these films is not allowed identification with the subject of the Holocaust, but rather is kept at a distance. This distance, which constitutes an important factor of cinematic examination in this chapter, adheres to the ethical imperative to respect the inviolability of the Other, and the term of interrogation that I shall employ is dis-identification, marking an oscillation between identification and the disallowing of identification. Drawing on the historical context for each film, it will be possible to open up the forum to include an examination of filmic and philosophical issues through ethical dis-identification, and bearing this base in mind, it is to the first of these films, Resnais's *Nuit et Brouillard*, that we now turn.

NUIT ET BROUILLARD (1955)

With reference to Bartov's comments on the difficulties of naming an event, discussed at the start of this chapter, this analysis of *Nuit et Brouillard* will begin with an examination of the issues of naming the filmic text itself, leading to a brief commentary on the French cultural context at the time of its making. It will then be possible to map the Levinasian structure of dis-identification onto the film, focusing primarily here on Resnais's use of archival footage and the subsequent ethical implications for the spectator.

Multiple meanings have been attached to the title of Resnais's landmark Holocaust documentary. It literally refers to the *Nacht-und-Nebel-Erlass* (the Night and Fog Decree) of December 7, 1941, which in turn had been inspired by Alberich, a Wagnerian character loosely based in German mythology who would invoke the night and fog before disappearing into thin air—the phrase resonated in Nazi philosophy as it tied in with the idea of Jewish populations disappearing without a trace.[9] *Nuit et Brouillard* can also be taken to mean the everlasting night that the deportees are taken to, the complete and utter lack of information regarding them after they left their homes, and the complicit silence that accompanied their disappearance from the fabric of daily life. Resnais's film reminds us that it was also a phrase used to classify incoming deportees, those classified as *Nacht und Nebel* (*Night and Fog*) who constituted the lowest rung in the hierarchy of camp society, even below the common criminals. Eventually, the phrase came to represent the horrors suffered by all the deportees regardless of the reasons for their incarceration. Jean Cayrol, the poet who scripted the film, had titled his book *Poèmes de la nuit et du brouillard* (*Poems of the Night and of the Fog*), which was published in 1946, soon after his return from Mauthausen.[10] The film cemented the posterity of the phrase *nuit et brouillard* and it became representative of simply those who bear witness against inhumanity. It reappeared in a 1963 song by Jean Ferrat, "*Nuit et Brouillard*," and features in the inscription on the *Monument aux Déportés on the Ile de la Cité* in Paris, which reads: "*Pour que vive le souvenir des deux cents mille français sombrés dans la nuit et le brouillard, exterminés dans les camps nazis.*" (Dedicated to the living memory of the two hundred thousand French deportees sleeping in the night and the fog, exterminated in the Nazi concentration camps.)[11]

The preceding discussion on the nuances attached to the title of the film are intended to highlight both the difficulty inherent in naming (a representation) of the Holocaust as well as the specific controversy that surrounded Resnais's film. It has been oft noted that *Nuit et Brouillard* never explicitly draws a connection between the anti-Semitism of the Nazis and the largely Jewish identity of the victims.[12] The occasionally visible stars sewn onto coats and camp uniforms and the labeling of the new deportees as those that disappeared into the night and fog of those years are the only clues we have as to a religious or an ethnic identity. Critical discourse on the matter has invariably argued that this either acts to erase the Jewish identity of the victims or to underline the larger humanity that was involved in the genocide. Resnais's reluctance to "name" the victims has been largely attributed to a desire to provide a warning to a global society, particularly to the French in light of their troubled relationship with Algeria. As the following discussion will demonstrate, Resnais's motivation can be linked to provoking a realization, namely that, while the victims of the entire genocide may or may not have been Jewish, the perpetrators could have, and may well have been, French. Indeed, this warning in relation to Algeria reiterates more strongly Resnais's preoccupation with the French Self and its relation to a general alterity.[13]

His reticence takes us to the heart of the general perception of the Holocaust in France during this period, one that bears closer examination—not in order to exonerate or adjudicate Resnais but, at the very least, to contextualize his representation of the Holocaust. Just after the end of the war, a French writer, David Rousset, published a book entitled *L'Univers concentrationnaire*, popularizing a blanket term that elided differences between the specific and the universal.[14] As the title suggests, the entirety of what we now understand as Nazi war crimes overwhelmed, and therefore included, what we would now call crimes against humanity. Furthermore, the term ignores the crucial distinction between concentration camps—such as Dachau or Buchenwald—that served in the extraction of labor from all kinds of prisoners of war, and were scattered all over the Third Reich—and the extermination camps of Treblinka, Sobibor, or Chelmno, that received primarily Jewish deportees headed for immediate extermination and were located in Poland. The importance of this distinction was not brought to national attention until 1966 with the publication of *Treblinka*, a book by Jean-François Steiner.[15] The book was eventually supported by one of France's leading classical historians and public intellectuals: Pierre Vidal-Naquet. While many questioned the authenticity of Steiner's lurid, sensationalizing book, Vidal-Naquet affirmed its contribution in highlighting the need for a differentiation in the general understanding of *l'univers concentrationnaire*.[16] The predominant idea of the Holocaust at the time of the making of *Nuit et Brouillard*, was, however, Rousset's, which suited very well the French political and intellectual establishment, and as Samuel Moyn comments, "struck a continuity with interwar fascist discourse, notably important in French politics, reviving its themes without allowing the novelty of genocide the force of interruption."[17] It does not follow, however, that Resnais's film was without controversy, as apparent in the debate that arose about a still shot Resnais wanted to include in the film that depicted a Vichy officer guarding a detention center while wearing his *kepi* or military headgear. The questioning of the distance or difference between the general identity and the Jewish specificity of the victims, which began in Resnais's *Nuit et Brouillard* in 1955, arguably only reached fruition in Steiner's *Treblinka*, over a decade later.

Beyond the linguistic register, the interplay between the historical and ethical also may be mapped onto the visual elements of the film. I suggest here that the complexity of the filmic images, both the archival footage and the contemporary filmed sequences, are skillfully manipulated by Resnais, reiterating the questioning of identification that I argued for in the previous section, making *Nuit et Brouillard* ethical within the Levinasian framework. This is no ordinary world that Resnais presents to his viewers—it is a shadowy world of fading film reel, some of which is quite obvious propaganda from Nazi archives. Let us first think about the ethical concerns at stake in this use of "tainted" footage originally filmed by the Nazis merely as a means of documenting their actions. As spectators, we are obliged to consider that by sharing the point of view of the perpetrators' camera we may also be encouraged to share their guilt, a concern that gains particular relevance for spectators increasingly distant, temporally and spatially, from the Holocaust. Rather than suggest that all viewers are necessarily implicated by this tainted gaze, Resnais compels us to question who we are and what responsibility we have to the victims. The viewer must strive against identification, away from the gaze of the camera and the gaze of the Nazis. Dis-identification, here, comes from within the viewer. The realization that we cannot consider the art of the perpetrator as a simple tool with which to examine their crimes works to challenge the easy link presented by traditional notions of cinematic identification. But while retaining the images, Resnais refashions the narrative, and this, in part, alters the meaning we may now choose to attribute to these images. Each image points beyond its specificity. It is precisely because we know, even if only vaguely, the horrors that transpired that each scene with a figure of a victim becomes all the more horrifying. Consider the image of a man pushing his wife, who sits on a makeshift trolley laden with suitcases, looking impatiently for a seat on the long train journey ahead, unaware of its fatal destination. This destination is one that the spectator already anticipates, since we know where the train is headed and what the likely end of these people will be. The brief presence of their images caught eternally in this moment on an obscure film reel, points grotesquely to their absence. By taking secondhand images and making something original out of them, Resnais does not only shatter identification processes—he also challenges art itself.[18]

Resnais's use of archival footage makes *Nuit et Brouillard* both beautiful and terrible, as he himself pointed out: "*si c'est beau ce ne peut être que plus efficace*" (the more beautiful [the image] is the more efficient it will be).[19] The intermingling of black and white and picture-postcard color marks a change in the perspective of the camera, and therefore, in the identification process. The grey, unfocused images of the past belong to the eyes of the Nazis, the bright color to Resnais. Cayrol's words, the words of survivors, straddle both these worlds, as does the music. By linking both worlds contrapuntally, Resnais creates the necessary space for dis-identification within the viewer, reiterating the sense of distance between viewer and subject. The impact that the very texture of *Nuit et Brouillard* had on subsequent filmmakers was dramatic—the shadowy black and white past contrasts with the barren but colored present. Even subsequent audiences, it seemed, imagined the Holocaust in black and white, leading Lance Morrow to write: "If any world needed to be filmed in black and white, it was . . . *l'univers concentrationnaire*. All that obscenity transpired in an absence of colour: the ashes and smoke were grey, the SS uniforms black, the skin ash white, the bones white."[20] As though trying to capture the memory of the past through photographs and images that were black and white by dint of the technology, or lack thereof, of the times, Holocaust representations continue to be clothed in a colorless garb. Steven Spielberg, whose hugely successful *Schindler's List* arguably brought the Holocaust (albeit a Hollywood version) to the contemporary global community, stated: "I've never seen the Holocaust in color. I don't know what Auschwitz looks like in color. Even though I've been there, it's still black and white in my eyes."[21] But Resnais does not leave us in the grey shadow world of the past; he brin̨s us back constantly to the present, to a benign sun shining over now calm fields and disused train rails. This return to the present is tinged with horror. We are meant to return to color and see beyond the image on the screen, to remember the nightmare of the past in the colors of the present. It is the constant back and forth motion of traveling between black and white and color, the shuttling of the spectator between identifying with the colorfully barren, empty camps today and dis-identifying with the world of the past populated with grey figures, that heightens dis-identification.

This mapping of distances may also be read into the dynamic of Self and Other in *Nuit et Brouillard*. The process begins with identification between the viewer and the victims, and then, as our horror and outrage grows, links impassivity with the perpetrators, until the climax of the film and the implicit caveat to be alert and moral. It is here that an oscillation becomes apparent between identification, suggested through the proximity between positions of spectatorship, and dis-identification, or the distance between these positions. The Levinasian edict regarding the unknowable nature of alterity is maintained through the reiteration of the aforementioned distance between (French) Self and Other, reinforced through the images of barbed wire, a particularly striking leitmotif throughout the film.[22] First, as we watch the camps go up, the barbed wire forms a barrier between our world and that of the camp. Then we find a world hemmed in by the wire and begin the journey to the spaces of unspeakable horror. The barbed wire represents the boundary between these two worlds and serves, in Resnais's film, to constantly remind us of, and more importantly maintain, the ethical distance that Levinas argues must exist between Self and Other. Critically, though, while preserving the unknowable and irreproachable nature of the Other, Resnais's film offers no such restraint in his condemnation of the Self, a process of self-interrogation that Ophuls continues, as will be discussed more fully in the following section.

Resnais's use of archival footage also inevitably encourages questions on the nature of memory itself—the fading film reel acts as a stand-in for our waning recollections of the event itself. It is by making the distinctions between past and present as interlinked as possible that Resnais achieves this in *Nuit et Brouillard*, since what is important for him is not the inevitability of forgetting, but a realization of that inevitability, an understanding that forgetting is essential, since it is linked to remembering specifics of historical time and place. Memory, however, is a deeper and continually changing process, one that constantly reiterates the links between the individual and a greater, shared history. While distancing the viewer from the subjects of the documentary, I would argue that Resnais is, in fact, presenting the viewer with an ethical framework with which to view the horrors of *l'univers concentrationnaire*. Resnais's film makes apparent the shift from *génocide* to *l'univers concentrationnaire*, leaving a more specific engagement with the Holocaust for a future generation. He replaces the distance to a remote past, toward which a viewer might not feel an ethical bond, with the more implicit distance to what is a living collective memory, which obliges the viewer to undertake the Levinasian imperative of responsibility to the Other. Resnais's film does not simply commemorate the Holocaust in a war memorial, but rather questions the notion that these terrible events were a part of the past and would never be repeated. While people built *those* camps, and while *that*

war may be over, it is the ability to build the camps that counts, and that is
still a very real and present talent.

The centrality of the two themes commented upon—the questioning of
the (French) Self and the recognition of the fallibility of memory—marks a
turning point in new emphases in representations of the Holocaust and Collaboration in France. It is to the further maturation of these themes in the
more specific framework of France—the core of Ophuls's *Le Chagrin et la
pitié*—to which we now turn.

LE CHAGRIN ET LA PITIÉ (1971)

While not explicitly dealing with the Holocaust, Ophuls's film positions itself
symbolically at the heart of the controversy that Resnais was forced to obscure in *Nuit et Brouillard*—that of the *képi* (military cap), and the nationality, of a guard watching over a camp—by questioning exactly how the French
had behaved under the Occupation.[23] This discussion of the film introduces
new elements into the general understanding of how the Holocaust would
come to be remembered in France, but the film will be treated in this chapter
as a link between Resnais's *l'univers concentrationnaire* and *la shoah* of
the subsequent section and, therefore, this examination is intentionally less
detailed here, in terms of both filmic analysis and the Levinasian engagement
I have employed so far. Where Resnais's film interrogates identification
between a generic audience and the victims of *l'univers concentrationnaire*
without necessarily provoking a tangible recognition of the guilt of French
anti-Semitism, Ophuls's film obliges an acknowledgment of precisely that
guilt. Instead of the discovering gaze of Resnais's camera, looking at that
which took place somewhere in the "barbaric East," even with the caveat that
it could occur in France, Ophuls's camera is rediscovering that which was
very much present in France. It is an acknowledgment not of potential, but
of guilt. In Ophuls's film, the French Self is more explicitly questioned, thus
defining an emerging contrast between the more personal approach to memory, as seen above in the discussion on Resnais, and the collective memory
contested in Ophuls's film. Ophuls's film does not question forgetting, but
rather the rewriting of memory, and for this reason it is relevant to consider
the context that immediately preceded *Le Chagrin et la pitié*.

Official discourse until well into the late 1960s referred back to the war
years through the lens of the Resistance. The privileged status accorded the
memorialization of the Resistance appeared to overshadow and occasionally
marginalize the legacy of the Holocaust.[24] This chapter would stress that

there was no active policy to negate or ignore the legacy of the Holocaust, but rather that the memory of the Holocaust in France was inextricably linked to the memory of the Resistance and thereby dependant on several variable factors. As a starting point, we may consider that, in the De Gaulle era, no fewer than sixty films were made extolling, either directly or indirectly, the role of the French in the Resistance, as against a scant eleven films post-De Gaulle under Giscard d'Estaing.[25] Ophuls's film is crucial to this debate precisely because of its role in shifting cultural memory away from that of the Resistance, and it remains worthy of closer analysis. The enormous scandal surrounding the release of the film suggests that it is almost impossible to separate a meaningful reading of the theme of memory within *Le Chagrin et la pitié* from the film's own subsequent impact on collective memory. Paradoxically, in fact, for a film that supposedly changed the collective memory of France, comparatively few people actually saw it when it was first released. The public controversy around the decision not to air it on television, however, triggered an outpouring in other cultural arenas leading to the "de-mythification" of the memory of the war in France.[26] Certain other contextual details further strengthen this reading of the film—the political turmoil of the late 1960s questioned De Gaulle not just in his present day, but also in his version of the past, one that defined his own role and that of the French nation through the idea of Resistance.

Fuel to the process of remembering and confronting official memory was added post-*Le Chagrin et la pitié* through books, newspaper articles, and films that increasingly reminded the French that millions of people had revered Philippe Pétain; that Vichy laws, not German laws, had been responsible for the deaths of thousands of French Jews; that French policemen, not German ones, had arrested Jews and Communists and sent them to their deaths. Ophuls's film set off these investigations in other cultural areas that were to further contribute to shattering the mythic status of the Resistance. Robert Paxton, an American historian, published a history of the four-year Vichy regime, citing previously unseen archives, in 1974.[27] After *Le Chagrin et la pitié*, the violation of the *lieu de mémoire* (site of memory) of Resistance becomes more obvious, more blatant, and more commonly depicted in narrative cinema, now itself a medium at the forefront of popular culture.

Thematically, through the 1970s it is possible to discern an explicit shift toward a more critical stance vis-à-vis the role of the Resistance in film. In 1973, Michel Drach's *Les Violons du bal* went so far as to not depict any cruelty on the part of the Germans, but presented all its villains as French. The extraordinarily successful 1974 film *Lacombe, Lucien*, directed by Louis Malle, is exemplary in this context: a young French peasant joins the Vichy police after being rejected by the Resistance. His choice was portrayed as one essentially made in a moral void, a vacuum, highlighting the ambiguity about why people become Fascists.[28] Similar questions were posed in films such as François Truffaut's *Le Dernier Métro* (1980) and in such documentaries as André Halimi's *La Délation sous l'Occupation* (1998). These films enjoyed considerable success and brought preoccupations that were emerging in other fields to the arena of popular culture and memory.

In terms of the (French) Self as it relates to alterity, we may also consider a specific religious element that emerged in the context of the *lieu de mémoire* of the Resistance and De Gaulle. The specific status accorded De Gaulle and, by implication, the Resistance, fulfills a certain basic need to "sanctify," a trend already strong in the French Catholic context.[29] What is more, this so-called cult develops a longevity that defies history, remaining outside of time, and, having survived intact for a certain number of years, it establishes an unassailable continuity. The memory of De Gaulle and the war years enters the myth of Resistance, in a quasi-religious context. This religious myth reiterated the notion of the Catholic French Self and served to further distance Jewish alterity from mainstream Resistance memory, prior to the shattering of the *lieu de mémoire* triggered by Ophuls's film.[30] Thus it is no understatement to refer to the seminal impact of *Le Chagrin et la pitié* as Jean Tulard does, in terms of literally shattering taboos: "*Cet esprit nouveau a bousculé les consciences, de nouvelles questions se sont posé: Que voulait dire être résistant, que voulait dire être collaborateur? L'Histoire officielle était égratignée, les tabous s'effondraient.*" [A new ethos has altered our awareness, new questions are being asked: what did it mean to have been a Resister? What did it mean to be a Collaborator? Once the surface of official history is scratched, taboos collapse.][31]

Ophuls's goal was to present the audience with images of the varying levels of attitudes and choices that allowed for Collaboration and, we can extrapolate, led to broader French complicity in the Holocaust. By confronting his viewers with a French Self, Ophuls, in fact, strengthens the need for dis-identification, which is rooted in their opposing desires to forget the war years and to remember their myth.

Nuit et Brouillard was made at a time when the memory of the Holocaust was largely repressed in France by the myth of the Resistance, which, as I have argued, was shattered by various assaults on memory, such as those performed by Ophuls's film. In fact, *Le Chagrin et la pitié* allowed for the Resistance myth to weaken to the extent that Holocaust memory was able to surface in France. Among the more popular films to tentatively engage with the Holocaust in the aftermath of the shattering of Resistance memory were Michel Mitrani's *Les Guichets du Louvre* (1974) and Joseph Losey's *Monsieur Klein* (1976), both of which make reference to the infamous roundup of Jews in Paris in 1942. This entry of the Holocaust into the French public domain arguably reaches artistic fruition in the film I now turn to: Lanzmann's *Shoah*. A further critical link between the three films provided by *Le Chagrin et la pitié* is that of point of view toward the subject matter. Resnais's film deals largely with anonymous victims, describing their journey to the camps, the horrors that awaited them there, and their ultimate and gruesome deaths. There is little mention of the perpetrators, leaving the film to provide a general warning against tyranny. Crucially, his film did not give a voice to Jewish victims of the Holocaust. Ophuls chose to show us largely the perpetrators, or more accurately, those who were in a position to act in some form against or with the Nazi Occupation. He rarely allows the focus of the camera to proceed beyond this point, to view the results of that action or inaction. It is to Lanzmann's *Shoah* that we now turn in order to see a representation of the Holocaust and the Occupation that encompasses both victims and perpetrators, one that explicitly names the victims and restores to them a voice, albeit a fractured one. This journey from *l'univers concentrationnaire* to *la shoah*, however, is not redemptive, as the process of rethinking a *lieu de mémoire* takes us from *Le Chagrin et la pitié* to the heart of absence, to a *non-lieu de mémoire*.

SHOAH (1985)

Returning to the Levinasian engagement with alterity for my analysis of Claude Lanzmann's *Shoah*, I shall first examine the implications of the name of the filmic text, an issue of some significance when juxtaposed against the French national context under consideration thus far. It is relevant to consider the film, therefore, as situated both within and outside of French culture and, drawing on dis-identification, to make explicit the ways in which alterity is negotiated in the national (namely French) and meta-national frames (referring here to the broader Holocaust genre).

Shoah, the title of Lanzmann's 1985 documentary, refers to the Hebrew word meaning chaos or annihilation, and is the name that Israelis in particular have given to the Holocaust. Lanzmann insisted that there was a basic impropriety in the term "Holocaust," with its connotations of religious sacrifice, and conspicuously chose the word *shoah* instead. *Shoah* is amongst the finest attempts at discussing but, crucially, not representing (or refashioning for cinema), the Holocaust, and was widely praised as a masterpiece, sometimes even as *the* cinematographic documentary masterpiece. The praise accorded *Shoah* parallels that of Resnais's *Nuit et Brouillard* in this respect: central to *Shoah* is the notion that recreation of any kind in a film about the Holocaust is a sort of transgression, as Lanzmann commented: "*Je pense profondément qu'il y a un interdit de la representation*" (I firmly believe there is a limit to representation).[32] The emphasis Lanzmann places on avoiding a visual transgression further strengthens the applicability of reading this film via Levinasian ethics, since it forcefully reiterates the need to retain ethical distances by respecting the unknowable nature of alterity. Dis-identification, as I will argue here, is brought about by the contrast between the reality that the film offers and the images it evokes but, crucially, does not reenact. Indeed, at no point does the film stop being reality. It never moves to the realm of imitation, but rather always returns to the theme of lived and remembered reality. This is, in part, due to Lanzmann's refusal to use archival footage or actors to restage events, referring back to his notion of a serious transgression. And it is a considerable and rare achievement that the film contains no music, no voice-over narration and no stock images—just questions, answers, and places evoking the horrors of the past—of what Annette Insdorf described as "horror recollected in tranquillity."[33] I read this lack of footage as part of the creation of a *non-lieu de mémoire*: it is the absence of images that serves as a reminder of the absence of the people, an absence of understanding, and an absence of a site of memory. The physical presence of sites of destruction act against sites as memory, negating their remembered or "mythic" essence by obliging us to consider them as "non-sites."

In order to maintain the inviolate status of alterity, Lanzmann's project is about the inability to understand, as he commented: "*il ya bien une obscénité absolue du projet de comprendre*" (There is indeed an absolute obscenity in the project of understanding).[34] Therefore, as a starting point, the film's imperative is not knowledge, but a recognition of the obscenity involved even in the attempt to gain that knowledge: an obscenity of understanding. Further, the publicly acknowledged fact of the hidden store of as-yet-unseen footage that Lanzmann filmed, the remainder of 300 hours, adds to the spectators' guilt, and, as Slavoj Žižek concludes, this is "the equivalent of our guilt at not being able to see the entire horror of the Holocaust."[35] The Holocaust remains ever outside our vision, eternally external to our comprehension. The "unknowability" of the *shoah* is reflected in that of *Shoah* the film, revealing a repetitive pattern of the lack of knowledge. Not only will we never know the entirety of the Holocaust, we are also excluded from the entirety of Lanzmann's unseen footage. We are at a further remove from the Holocaust than Lanzmann and, by reminding us of this, Lanzmann adds a new layer of dis-identification—namely, one between filmmaker and viewer. *Shoah*, therefore, threatens identification at a deeper level from what we have considered thus far, taking away even the possibility of a connection between viewer and filmmaker. Therefore, Lanzmann's own alterity would seem to remain inexplicable to the viewer. Indeed, if Resnais and Ophuls presented us with the image of the flawed French Self, then Lanzmann transcends national boundaries, disintegrating the viewing Self in the face of multiple fragmented Others. Lanzmann's meta-national narrative of the Holocaust will now be analyzed (and problematized), beginning with the linguistic register, before moving on to the visual aspects of the film.

A particularly noteworthy feature of *Shoah* is that Lanzmann has created a testament to the Holocaust that does not belong to a single language. From the beginning, it is clear that Lanzmann's film is not going to be a strictly visual documentary, but one that will oblige the viewer to listen, to hear. Subtitled *An Oral History of The Holocaust*, the witnesses are all asked to speak and the film is composed of a mixture of languages and dialects. It is precisely by presenting a multiplicity of languages, what has been referred to as "enacting the rebuilding of a shattered Tower of Babel,"[36] that Lanzmann is able to present us with an event located so far outside of the realm of human comprehension and discourse. The confusion produced by the different languages and dialects leads first to the inescapable conclusion that even if one were to speak all the languages in the world, the Holocaust would still remain inexplicable, marking a crucial point of distinction from the somber French narration of *Nuit et Brouillard*, and suggesting a shift in the locus of Holocaust memory beyond nation-specific borders. Further, the babble of languages remains unintelligible to those who do not speak Polish or German or Hebrew and it is through Lanzmann, and occasionally his interpreter, that the questions asked are met with answers. The presence of the interpreter further heightens the sense of distance between the viewing self and the interview subject on the screen, the Other.

Moreover, the traditional identificatory position suggests that speech presupposes the existence of the Other by positioning the Self in a place from which it can be heard or recognized by the Other. In *Shoah*, however, speech is restricted to being a function of the Other, and rather than consolidate the position of the Self, speech serves precisely to trouble the notion of the Self. This is due to the disturbed notions of duality that Lanzmann presents his viewers with: the impossibility of naming and the impossibility of understanding. This first impossibility is reflected in *Shoah* from its very outset.[37] The film begins silently with a written document that tells us of the number of Jews gassed at Chelmno, a place whose name the Germans changed to Kulmhof, mapping (and remapping) layers of languages and drawing attention to the German appropriation of language. We may consider, in this context, that more than any other place, the German name of the small Polish town of Oswiecim—known to the world as Auschwitz—has come to symbolize absolute evil. The names that Lanzmann introduces to his spectator: Chelmno,

Treblinka, Sobibor, are even more terrifying than that of Auschwitz, since the lack of survivors from those camps underlines more strenuously the horrific meaning behind their names. Chelmno is not Auschwitz, it is not a place remembered in multiple testimonies, but rather, it is a place recreated through the testimony of one person, one of only two survivors. It is the embodiment of the *non-lieu de mémoire*.

It is relevant, therefore, to note that, in *Shoah*, it is only the language of the victims that has changed. Polish bystanders still speak Polish, and former Nazis speak German. The victims, however, speak for the most part in a language other than their own. This reflects the difference in the sense of pain for the Poles, who witnessed their lands being annexed and given German names, and for the Jews for whom these new words came to represent destruction and total loss. Language, in fact, follows a geographically linguistic trajectory, from Poland at the start, through Germany, and ending in Hebrew in Israel. This motion across Europe toward Israel forms a motif throughout the film, linguistically mapping the geographical path of the Jewish survivors in the film.

If the impossibility of understanding, a marked feature of *Shoah*, is certainly evident in the linguistic element, it is also possible to analyze it on the visual register, reflecting that the hopelessness of comprehending is attached to the filmic image as much as to the verbal arena. *Shoah* presents us not with a chronological or factual record of the Holocaust, but rather with a kind of mosaic of interviews of survivors, perpetrators and bystanders. This mosaic reminds us that there is no singular answer to explain what the Holocaust was and further reminds us of the obscenity of attempting to find such any such simple answers. To approach this visual impossibility, we may draw on the Levinasian notion of the *visage*, which refers to the moment of encounter between the Self and alterity and both does and does not occupy a physical presence. For purposes of this chapter, I will consider Colin Davis's explanation as a working definition of the term: "The term *visage* encapsulates the problems raised by the paradoxical nature of the self's encounter with the infinite: it is something that is not available to vision but described as if it were, signalling an encounter which is not an event and an experience which does not occur in the consciousness of any subject."[38] The *visage* that we face in *Shoah*—the physicality of the faces on the screen—presents us literally with measurable features. The multitude of faces, the often-distorting close-ups that Lanzmann presents us with, the fractured stories, fractured identities and lives, however, oblige us to consider a *visage* that is beyond the features on the screen. By doing so, we grant the Other its infinite status since we are unable to contain it within the confines of our own singular capacity to understand.

The talking faces of Lanzmann's film present us with images too horrible to imagine—a particularly striking example being the interview of Professor Jan Karski, a former courier for the Polish government in exile. Thirty years on, Karski, who lives in the U.S., begins his interview by walking out of the room, unable to speak of the things he has witnessed, leaving the viewer to gaze at an empty chair and fearfully to attempt conjecture of the grotesque memories that continue to haunt his mind. Time has not succeeded in healing these wounds for they are too deep, too fundamental. Fillip Müller, a former *sonderkommando* in Auschwitz, who survived five liquidations, describes the gassing as a scene where the primary bond between parent and child disintegrates completely. It is the image of a terrifying struggle for hope, at the cost of any recognizable social or biological responsibility or obligation between parents and children, between the Self in its basic primeval state and the most fundamental of Others—one's own family. Abraham Bomba, now a retired barber, describes with great difficulty and with gentle, but constant, prodding from Lanzmann, incidents when women he knew from his village met him on their way to the gas chambers. The scene was filmed in a barbershop, but the client is an extra and, on close observation, Bomba is not cutting any hair, but merely staging a haircut. The physical motion, the reenactment of cutting hair, acts as a trigger to take the viewer back to the terrible scene he describes. The spectator is invited to see beyond the customer in a Tel Aviv barbershop and is, in fact, drawn to the past and to imagining the pandemonium of a tiny room packed with over sixty naked and petrified women, five SS guards, and sixteen barbers. The cutting of the hair in the present begins to slow down as Bomba relates the incident in which he saw a friend's farewell to his wife and sister as they entered the gas chamber. The image loses its primacy to Bomba's words, as the spectator realizes that the unfolding aural story will be unimaginably terrible. Eventually, even the words give way to silence, which acts as the final disconnection between barber and spectator. By the end of his interview, we struggle with this palimpsest of the past glimpsed through Bomba. Our encounter with alterity is here characterized by the inevitability of seeking the images described in our own mind and finding instead our own inability to fully understand.

Lanzmann's film questions how the Holocaust took place, following through events and details with a cold precision. If Resnais's film reflected on the artist in Resnais, then Lanzmann's film reflects on the engineer in Lanzmann, and is a testament to the vast bureaucracy needed to create and conduct an industrialized genocide. Lanzmann is not concerned with the ideas that led to the Holocaust, but rather with the people and the seemingly insignificant details that contributed to the working Nazi death machine. His film does not aim to give us answers about the Holocaust, but rather works to provoke questions of how the Holocaust took place. Indeed, while *Shoah* indicates that there are no answers to the Holocaust, only questions, the discerning viewer must nonetheless consider the questions that Lanzmann does not pose. By engaging with these questions, we may finally evaluate the significance of *Shoah*, and indeed the status of Holocaust memory, in postwar France.

For instance, it is a sign of some concern that Lanzmann does not turn his gaze onto France and the role played by Vichy in the Holocaust. His almost obsessive focus on the role played by Polish bystanders overshadows an apparent lack of concern with the Germans and his almost total lack of interest in his own compatriots. Critics, such as André Pierre Colombat, argue against this criticism, saying that the specificity of Lanzmann's film is not for France but for Jews, and that the film "is not a general presentation of the Holocaust . . . Its subject is the *Shoah* of the Jewish people, the extermination process itself and the people who directly witnessed it."[39] I would contend, however, that this is too limiting a model. While Lanzmann's stated aim was to apparently approach those who were closest to the extermination process, such as Auschwitz *sonderkommandos* or the scant handful of survivors from the death camps, he does also venture into Jewish communities and ghettos across Europe. And indeed, Jews from all over Europe perished in the death camps in Poland, their deportations often organized by compatriots in their countries of origin. The events that constitute the entirety of the Holocaust are not only to be found in the crematoria of Auschwitz, but in cities, towns, and villages across the continent, where a centuries-old anti-Semitism was allowed to reign free. Lanzmann's focus on the regions east of France allows for the presence of a geographical distance that effaces or compromises a French-specific ethical obligation to the memory of the event.

It is important to problematize this meta-narrative of the Holocaust even further since, upon closer examination, a more complex interplay of geopolitics and ethics emerges. *Shoah* is a film that subtly privileges Western Europe, and possibly Western viewers, over their Central and East European counterparts. The only people interviewed in the West are Lanzmann's avowed mentor, the noted historian Raul Hilberg, and Professor Karski, who is of Polish origin. Thus, symbolically, the West comes to represent a world that is intellectually superior to and more sensitive than the barbaric East. The privileging of Western over Eastern Europe, manifested here in terms of the omission of France's role in the Holocaust (and arguably that of the other Allied powers), is naturally a troubling one. In an interview, Lanzmann confessed: "*La circularité du film tient au caractère obsessionnel de mes questions, à mes propres obsessions: le froid, la peur de l'Est (l'Ouest, pour moi, est humain, l'Est me fout la trouille).*" [The circularity of the film comes from the obsessive nature of my own concerns. It comes from my own obsessions: the cold, the terror of the East (the West for me is human, the East terrifies me)].[40] The privilege accorded Western Europe marks a questionable point of contrast with the precise warning proffered by Resnais in *Nuit et Brouillard* that no one country or one people—and certainly not a post-Algerian War France—is any less susceptible to similar crimes against humanity. While it may be argued that Resnais's universalized moral message detracts from the specificity of the Holocaust, it is pertinent to note that Lanzmann's particularized focus on the Holocaust in Eastern Europe ignores the broader pan-national dimension in which it took place.

The politico-ethical dimension is also echoed in the conclusion of *Shoah*. Lanzmann was supposed to have commented that he knew that he could not have a happy ending to a film on the Holocaust, and at first glance it appears, in fact, not to have a "happy ending" at all.[41] The final words of the film are uttered by Simchah Rotem, one of the fighters in the Warsaw Ghetto Uprising, who describes his last night in the ghetto—the fear, the sense of complete isolation and loneliness: "*je me suis dit 'Je suis le dernier Juif, je vais attendre le matin, je vais attendre les Allemands.'*" ("I said to myself, 'I am the last Jew, I am going to wait for morning, I am going to wait for the Germans.'") It is a somber note to end the film on, but also one through which a sense of resolution emerges. As he speaks, Rotem is standing in the Ghetto Fighters Kibbutz in Israel, where we realize he evidently did survive the final Nazi onslaught on the ghetto, that he was not, in fact, the last Jew, and even that in due course he found his way to Israel. While it is particularly contentious to suggest that this may be read as a signal of some form of redemption coexisting with the destruction engendered in the Holocaust, *Shoah* may implicitly suggest that the Jew of Europe is not really safe until he or she discovers the safety offered by the state of Israel. It is no coincidence that Lanzmann also made a documentary called *Tsahal* on the Israeli Defense Forces, clearly emphasizing his preoccupation with what Israel has represented to the European Jew. This reading of Rotem's symbolic status as a survivor now living in Israel must, nonetheless, be juxtaposed with the contradictory final images of the film: that of a train rattling along the countryside. The contradiction between a survivor in Israel and the trains of Europe reiterates the inevitable rubric of the historical trajectory of the memory of the Holocaust, which has seemingly moved beyond Europe.

The aim of this chapter has been to examine representations of the Holocaust and Collaboration in French documentary films—from *l'univers concentrationnaire* to *la shoah*, as it is increasingly referred to in France today. As the epigraph to the article noted, a film on the Holocaust is, by necessity, one that engages not only with the historical fact of genocide, but rather with a living history. Such a film is one that allows for questions beyond the specificity of the past, actively interrogating the "present-ness" of the past. Common to my reading of all the films discussed here is the central position offered by an ethical engagement with alterity. Consequently, these films question and trouble the status of the Self embodied in the viewer. *Nuit et Brouillard* marks the starting point of the trajectory of the representation of the Holocaust in French cinema, and has the oracular tone of a warning to French society at large, issuing that warning to the French Self as well as to an entire society. The scrutiny accorded the French Self in *Le Chagrin et la pitié* demonstrates the need for an ethical encounter with alterity in a nation-specific historical context. As a result of the questioning of Resistance memory triggered by Ophuls's film, it was possible for a more explicit engagement with the Holocaust to emerge in French culture, once again referring and relating to a national audience. From the notion of a site of memory to that of a *non-lieu de mémoire*, Lanzmann's *Shoah* further cements the inviolate and unknowable nature of the Other by reducing the audience to each single viewer, who must engage ethically with a multiplicity of fragmented alterity on the screen. Lanzmann's audience is not anticipated to be largely, or only, French, and therefore the film does not question the specifics of the French Self. Instead, it seeks to renegotiate the ethical encounter between Self and Other from within the context of a Holocaust genre, recognizing no limiting national boundaries and instead seeking to represent the disembodied and unknowable alterity of the Holocaust itself. The construction of Holocaust memory has inevitably gone beyond national and linguistic borders, finding roots far away from the spaces (and non-spaces) of the past, but its resolution in France and French culture is still far from complete.

NOTES

1. James Young, *Writing and Rewriting the Holocaust: Narrative and the Consequences of Interpretation* (Bloomington: Indiana University Press, 1990), 1.

2. See Omer Bartov, *Murder in Our Midst: The Holocaust, Industrial Killing, and Representation* (Oxford: Oxford University Press, 1996).

3. The uniqueness of the Wiener footage is examined by Joshua Hirsch, who cites Zoe Burman, formerly of the Film Department of the United States Holocaust Memorial Museum, in making the above claim. For a more detailed discussion, see Joshua Hirsch, *Afterimage: Film, Trauma and the Holocaust* (Philadelphia: Temple University Press, 2004), 1–3.

4. Richard Rorty, *Contingency, Irony and Solidarity* (Cambridge: Cambridge University Press, 1989), xii–xiv.

5. See, for instance, Henry Rousso, *The Vichy Syndrome: History and Memory in France since 1944*, trans. Arthur Goldhammer (Cambridge, MA: Harvard University Press, 1991).

6. For the detailed theoretical framework of Levinas's philosophy, see Emmanuel Levinas, *Totalité Et Infini* (The Hague: Martinus Nijhoff, 1961). In the context of *Shoah*, this article will also specifically refer to Levinas's "*La Réalité et son ombre*," *Les Temps Modernes* 38 (1948): 769–89.

7. In this article, Self refers to the French viewing Self (nevertheless bearing in mind an implicit caveat that such a national identity may be said to exist at all and those who partake of it may be assumed to share some common cultural or ideological contexts) and Other refers to the specifically cinematic alterity of the Holocaust.

8. The working definition of how identification processes work has been drawn from Jean Laplanche and Jean-Bertrand Pontalis, *Vocabulaire de la Psychanalyse* (Paris: Presses Universitaires de France, 1967).

9. The full text of the decree may be sourced online at The Avalon Project, Yale Law School, 1997, accessed July 2005, http://www.yale.edu/lawweb/avalon/imt/document/l-90.htm.

10. The critic John Francis Kreidl argues that the meaning of the title of the film is linked only to its connotations with Nazism, the category of prisoner, and, according to him, "is *not* a poetic metaphor for the murkiness of the concentration camps." See John Francis Kreidl, *Alain Resnais* (Boston: Twain Publishers, 1977), 47. I would suggest, however, that there is a poetic intention in the reuse of the title, one that acts as a counterfoil to the promises of peace. Cayrol commented that one should read *Nuit et Brouillard* as a poetic appeal, a warning device against all the nights and all the fogs that may yet come to pass. See ibid, 41.

11. All translations from French are the author's own.

12. See, for instance, Robert Michael, "A Second Look: Night and Fog," *Cinéaste* (1984).

13. The troubled status accorded the French Self in Resnais's film can also be seen in the controversy surrounding the issue of the *képi*: *Nuit et Brouillard* includes footage from the camp of Pithiviers, one of two concentration camps for foreign-born Jews arrested in France, specifically a frame of an officer watching over the camp whose *képi* (military hat) identifies him as French. This provoked a controversy between Resnais and the censor board, who demanded the image be cut—it was retained in the film, but "doctored" by Resnais to hide the *képi*, and so too the complicity of the French state. Specifically, the questioning of the Self/viewer, imagined to be French, is a theme returned to in, and is indeed vital to, Ophuls's *Le Chagrin et la pitié*.

14. David Rousset, *L'univers Concentrationnaire* (Paris: Editions du Pavois, 1946).

15. Jean-François Steiner, *Treblinka: La Révolte D'un Camp D'extermination* (Paris: Fayard, 1966).

16. See, for instance, Pierre Vidal-Naquet, "*Le Défi De La Shoah À L'histoire*," *Les Temps Modernes* 507 (1988): 62–74. For a more detailed discussion of the Rousset-Steiner-Vidal-Naquet affair, see Samuel Moyn, "From *L'univers Concentration-*

naire to the Jewish Genocide: Pierre Vidal-Naquet and the Treblinka Controversy," in *After the Deluge: New Perspectives on the Intellectual and Cultural History of Postwar France*, ed. Julian Bourg (Lanham, MD: Lexington Books, 2004), 277–99.

17. Moyn, "From *L'Univers Concentrationnaire* to the Jewish Genocide," 282.

18. Indeed, the mistrust of art Resnais exhibits here finds echoes in Levinas's opinions on art: "*[L'Art] est l'*événement même de l'*obscurcissement, une tombée de la nuit, un envahissement de l'ombre*" (Art itself obscures, it is the falling of night, serving only to darken the shadows). Emmanuel Levinas, "*La Réalité Et Son Ombre*," *Les Temps Modernes* 38 (1948): 773. Art, which for Levinas represents a "non-truth," allows for Resnais's journey into the past, making possible this descent into the obscurity of night and fog.

19. Marcel Oms, *Alain Resnais* (Paris: Editions Rivages 1988), 14.

20. Lance Morrow, quoted in Jeffrey Shandler, "Schindler's Discourse: America Discusses the Holocaust and Its Mediation, from NBC's Miniseries to Spielberg's Film," in *Spielberg's Holocaust: Critical Perspectives on Schindler's List*, ed. Yosefa Loshitzky (Bloomington: Indiana University Press, 1997), 157.

21. Shandler, "Schindler's Discourse," 156.

22. Early on in the film, Resnais's camera pans over a series of pictures taken from outside the barbed wire fence, of a corpse perched on the electrified fence, then to a still from within the camp of the same corpse, and then to corpses lying near the fence, presumably shot down as they attempted to scale the fence. A fence, which at once holds death at bay from us, also invites us to watch death, presenting already a disconnection between viewer and those behind the fence.

23. This incident is referred to in note 13.

24. Rousso comments on this duality in a public lecture held at the Institut Français in London, on November 11, 2003, suggesting somewhat problematically that each "side," namely, French Holocaust survivor and French Resistant, possessed "spokespersons," who represented cultural symbols or sites of each group. According to Rousso, the French Holocaust survivors tended to be more emotional and, as they were invariably immigrants, spoke French with an accent. The French Resistants were perceived as more "French" and able to control their emotional outbursts. Perceptions of Frenchness aside, I would argue that the distinction between the two groups is strengthened if one considers the context of the struggle for each; so, while for Holocaust survivors, persecution was linked to their Jewishness, and was therefore out of the realm of their own control, for Resisters there was an active psychological decision made by them to resist the Occupier.

25. Resistance-themed films ranged from the lyrical (such as Robert Bresson's 1956 film *Un condamné à mort s'est echappé*) to the farcical (Gérard Oury's 1966 box office success *La Grande vadrouille*) highlighting that, conventions of genre notwithstanding, whether these films were complex narratives exploring the nuances of hidden meanings and moral ambiguity or more comedic fare, they revisited the memory of the war primarily through the lens of the Resistance.

26. Although initially commissioned by the television channel ORTF, the film was considered too incendiary to be shown to the national television audience. It could

initially only be seen in the small art house cinema Studio Saint-Séverin, in Paris, near St. Michel, causing daily queues of hundreds of curious Parisians to gather outside. It moved later to the larger and more accommodating Paramount-Elysées, before finally reaching its national television audience in 1981, attracting 15 million viewers.

27. See Robert O. Paxton, *Vichy France: Old Guard and New Order* (New York: Columbia University Press, 2001).

28. For a detailed discussion on the themes of these films, see Annette Insdorf, *Indelible Shadows: Film and the Holocaust*, 3rd ed. (Cambridge: Cambridge University Press, 2003).

29. For a detailed examination of the process of social sanctification undergone by De Gaulle (and Charlemagne and Charles Martel before him), see Alphonse Dupront, "Religion and Religious Anthropology," in *Constructing the Past: Essays in Historical Methodology*, ed. Jacques Le Goff and Pierre Nora (Cambridge: Cambridge University Press, 1985), 123–50.

30. It is no coincidence that the spirit of 1968 also sought to resist the opposing dualities of French Catholic Self and non-French Jewish Other: *"Nous sommes tous des Juifs allemands"* (We are all German Jews) being one of the rallying cries when student leader Daniel Cohn-Bendit's non-French origins were highlighted.

31. Jean Tulard, ed., *Guide Des Films: A-K* (Paris: Editions Robert Laffont, S.A., 1990), 362.

32. Claude Lanzmann, *"Holocauste, La Représentation Impossible,"* *Le Monde* 3 (March 1994): 7.

33. Insdorf, *Indelible Shadows: Film and the Holocaust*, 254.

34. Claude Lanzmann, *"Hier Ist Kein Warum,"* in *Au Sujet De Shoah: Le Film De Claude Lanzmann*, ed. Michel Deguy (Tours: Editions Berlin, 1990), 279.

35. Slavoj Žižek, *The Fright of Real Tears: Krzysztof Kieślowski between Theory and Post-Theory* (London: British Film Institute, 2001), 197.

36. Nelly Furman, "The Languages of Pain in *Shoah*," in *Auschwitz and After: Race Culture and "the Jewish Question" in France*, ed. Lawrence D. Kritzman (New York: Routledge, 1995), 299.

37. Shoshana Felman points out that the title of the film itself "without the article, enigmatically and indefinitely . . . names the very foreignness of languages, the very namelessness of a catastrophe which cannot be possessed by any native tongue," in Shoshana Felman, "In an Era of Testimony: Claude Lanzmann's *Shoah*," *Yale French Studies* 79 (1991): 47.

38. Colin Davis, *Levinas: An Introduction* (Cambridge, MA: Polity Press, 1996), 46. See Levinas, *Totalité Et Infini*, 177–78, for the philosophical examination of the term.

39. André-Pierre Colombat, *The Holocaust in French Film* (Lanham, MD: Scarecrow Press, 1993), 299.

40. Claude Lanzmann, *"Le Lieu Et La Parole,"* *Cahiers du cinéma* (July–August 1985): 21.

41. See Tim Cole, *Selling the Holocaust: From Auschwitz to Schindler: How History Is Bought, Packaged and Sold* (New York: Routledge, 2000), 85.

BIBLIOGRAPHY

Bartov, Omer. *Murder in Our Midst: The Holocaust, Industrial Killing, and Representation.* Oxford: Oxford University Press, 1996.

Bounoure, Gaston. *Alain Resnais.* Paris: Editions Seghers, 1974.

Bruzzi, Stella. *New Documentary: A Critical Introduction.* London: Routledge, 2000.

Cole, Tim. *Selling the Holocaust: From Auschwitz to Schindler: How History Is Bought, Packaged and Sold.* New York: Routledge, 2000.

Colombat, André-Pierre. *The Holocaust in French Film.* Lanham, MD: Scarecrow Press, 1993.

Davis, Colin. *Ethical Issues in Twentieth Century French Fiction: Killing the Other.* London: Macmillan Press, 2000.

———. *Levinas: An Introduction.* Cambridge, MA: Polity Press, 1996.

Deguy, Michel. *Au Sujet De Shoah: Le Film De Claude Lanzmann.* Tours: Editions Berlin, 1990.

Dupront, Alphonse. "Religion and Religious Anthropology." In *Constructing the Past: Essays in Historical Methodology,* edited by Jacques Le Goff and Pierre Nora, 123–50. Cambridge: Cambridge University Press, 1985.

Felman, Shoshana. "In an Era of Testimony: Claude Lanzmann's *Shoah.*" *Yale French Studies* 79 (1991): 39–81.

Furman, Nelly. "The Languages of Pain in *Shoah.*" In *Auschwitz and After: Race Culture and "the Jewish Question" in France,* edited by Lawrence D. Kritzman, 299–312. New York: Routledge, 1995.

Hirsch, Joshua. *Afterimage: Film, Trauma and the Holocaust.* Philadelphia: Temple University Press, 2004.

Insdorf, Annette. *Indelible Shadows: Film and the Holocaust.* Cambridge: Cambridge University Press, 2003.

Kreidl, John Francis. *Alain Resnais.* Boston: Twain Publishers, 1977.

Lanzmann, Claude. "*Hier Ist Kein Warum.*" In *Au Sujet De Shoah: Le Film De Claude Lanzmann,* edited by Michel Deguy. Tours: Editions Berlin, 1990.

———. "The Obscenity of Understanding: An Evening with Claude Lanzmann" (public lecture, Western New England Institute for Psychoanalysis, New Haven, CT, April 1990). In *Trauma: Explorations in Memory,* edited by Cathy Caruth, 200–220. Baltimore: Johns Hopkins University Press, 1995.

———. "*Holocauste, La Représentation Impossible.*" *Le Monde* 3 (March 1994).

———. "*Le Lieu Et La Parole.*" *Cahiers du cinéma* 374 (July–August 1985): 18–23.

Laplanche, Jean, and Jean-Bertrand Pontalis. *Vocabulaire de la Psychanalyse.* Paris: Presses Universitaires de France, 1967.

Le Chagrin et la pitié. Directed by Marcel Ophuls. Switzerland/France: NDR/Télévision Rencontre/TSR, 1971.

Levinas, Emmanuel. "*La Réalité Et Son Ombre.*" *Les Temps Modernes* 38 (1948): 769–89.

———. *Totalité Et Infini.* The Hague: Martinus Nijhoff, 1961.

Michael, Robert. "A Second Look: Night and Fog." *Cinéaste* (1984): 36–37.

Moyn, Samuel. "From *L'univers Concentrationnaire* to the Jewish Genocide: Pierre Vidal-Naquet and the Treblinka Controversy." In *After the Deluge: New Perspectives on the Intellectual and Cultural History of Postwar France*, edited by Julian Bourg, 277–99. Lanham, MD: Lexington Books, 2004.

Nora, Pierre. *Les Lieux De Mémoire: La République, La Nation, Les France*. Manchecourt: Editions Gallimard, 1997.

Nuit et Brouillard. Directed by Alain Resnais. Paris: Argos Films, 1955.

Oms, Marcel. *Alain Resnais*. Paris: Editions Rivages, 1988.

Paxton, Robert O. *Vichy France: Old Guard and New Order*. New York: Columbia University Press, 2001.

Robbins, Jill. *Altered Reading: Levinas and Literature*. Chicago: University of Chicago Press, 1999.

Rorty, Richard. *Contingency, Irony and Solidarity*. Cambridge: Cambridge University Press, 1989.

Rousset, David. *L'univers Concentrationnaire*. Paris: Editions du Pavois, 1946.

Rousso, Henry. *The Vichy Syndrome: History and Memory in France Since 1944*. Translated by Arthur Goldhammer. Cambridge: Harvard University Press, 1991.

Shandler, Jeffrey. "Schindler's Discourse: America Discusses the Holocaust and Its Mediation, from NBC's Miniseries to Spielberg's Film." In *Spielberg's Holocaust: Critical Perspectives on Schindler's List*, edited by Yosefa Loshitzky, 153–68. Bloomington: Indiana University Press, 1997.

Shoah. Directed by Claude Lanzmann. Paris: Les Films Aleph/Historia, 1985.

Steiner, Jean-François. *Treblinka: La Révolte d'un camp d'extermination*. Paris: Fayard, 1966.

Tulard, Jean, ed. *Guide Des Films: A-K*. Paris: Editions Robert Laffont, S.A., 1990.

Vidal-Naquet, Pierre. "*Le Défi De La Shoah À L'histoire*." *Les Temps Modernes* 507 (1988): 62–74.

Young, James. *Writing and Rewriting the Holocaust: Narrative and the Consequences of Interpretation*. Bloomington: Indiana University Press, 1990.

Žižek, Slavoj. *The Fright of Real Tears: Krzysztof Kieślowski between Theory and Post-Theory*. London: British Film Institute, 2001.

Chapter Three

Death in Vienna

Horrible Modernity in Michael Haneke's The Seventh Continent

Jennifer Taylor

Austrian filmmaker Michael Haneke's 1989 film, *The Seventh Continent* (*Der Siebente Kontinent*), which the director calls a depiction of a "terrible utopia," is intended to be an irritating and provocative critique of modern day Austria's denial of its own complicity in Nazism and of the continuities that still exist between that violent past and the bleak, numb present the director portrays here. In Haneke's portrait, Austria has allowed itself to become anesthetized and stupefied by modern technology in order to cling to an idealized postwar identity in which its own role under Nazism is ignored. The direct linkage between modern technology and national forgetting leads to some rather interesting issues, however. First, Haneke must acknowledge that his medium, film, is part of the modern and thus part of the object of his critique. He succeeds in large part here by being very highly self-referential; the viewer never forgets that the film is simultaneously an object of and a vehicle for critique. A greater challenge for the film, however, is to offer an alternative Austrian identity narrative to the anesthetized, repressed story of passivity and victimization that is exploded here. We are left to wonder if *Continent* is calling for some kind of idealized (premodern?) community while at the same time trying to maintain a distance from Nazi rhetoric, which also advocated rejecting the modern for a utopian community of an unspecified "Golden Age" (even as the Nazis amassed the technology to perpetrate the most hideous modern crimes in history). While the film both succeeds and fails at times to distance its voice from the antimodern voices of the Nazis, *Continent* ultimately provides an honest and provocative reflection of Austria's struggles with the legacy of its Nazi past.

The film begins with a portrait of a "typical" Austrian family living a "typical" Austrian postwar existence. We see a series of long takes of the middle-class family with one child, one car, two incomes, and an electric garage door.

They commit suicide after (and only after) we have been subjected to two relentless hours depicting three years in their cold and sterile modern world. Haneke's point—that modern technology and gadgetry alienate humans from each other and themselves—is well-taken though predictable (*Village Voice* critic Georgia Brown called the film "more didactic than spiritual").[1] The many close-ups of beepers, alarm clocks, electric fish tank contraptions, blinking lights, and sterile, orderly spaces all irritate the film audience just as these objects tend to irritate us outside of the cinema. *Continent* successfully captures, as if under a microscope, the irritatingly fragmented life of the protagonists, who are lost in a technological and unfeeling world. Nevertheless, there is something more problematic about this film than Haneke's intended provocation of middle-class Austrian society. *Continent* is a virulent and totalizing critique of modern society, which is shown to be doomed to end in an agonizing *Götterdämmerung*, a catastrophic, violent downfall much like the death the protagonists experience. This demonization of technology/modernity links the film dangerously with other antimodern texts, particularly with cinematic images of "degenerate" modernity depicted in such Nazi films as Fritz Hippler's *The Eternal Jew* (1940). Despite Haneke's often subtle and convincing attempts to avoid linking his critique of the modern with the Nazis, his anti-utopian vision appears nevertheless to elicit and even to embrace a nostalgic yearning for a lost "golden age," a premodern or at least pre-industrial age of community and belonging promised in Leni Riefenstahl's *Triumph of the Will* (1934).

Continent strongly links loneliness and isolation with mechanization and shows us a world utterly polarized between cold, steely technology and a human community only hinted at by omission. In the film, the alarm clock goes off at six every morning, waking the protagonists for another day of isolation and monotonous routine; the kitchen appliances fizzle and whistle, preparing breakfast as wordlessly as it is eaten; body parts, in fragmented close-ups, move mechanically through the yellow and deep blue spaces; and all the while the blackouts between scenes underline the discontinuity and isolation of the characters' lives. There is no community here, no warmth, no contact with other humans. A dystopic vision of modern life as hell, *Continent* echoes very closely the absolute critique of modernity associated with the far right in recent European history.

This is not to say that antimodernist sentiment belongs solely to the Nazis or even to the right in general; critics and thinkers on the left, too, have rejected the "modern" as cold and alienating. While members of the Vienna Secession, the Bauhaus, or early twentieth-century Marxists embraced modernity to create the *Gesamtkunstwerk* or the new modern Communist state, the later writings of leftist thinkers such as Theodor Adorno and Max

Horkheimer in fact reflect a heavily antimodern sentiment, more reminiscent in style of Heidegger's work than of anyone else's.[2] Haneke is, then, not alone as a leftist critic of the modern, nor is he the only filmmaker to take up the issue of technology and modernity critically in his films. Cinema is itself a very modern, technological art form and has reflected on its own ambiguous relationship to technology since its inception. Robert Wiene's *The Cabinet of Dr. Caligari* (1919), with its focus on the power of the tyrant with new technology in his hands (in this case, the ancient and modern art of hypnosis) and Austrian-born Fritz Lang's *Metropolis* (1928), which stirred up debate because of its apparent defense of capital against labor, are but two examples of film's obsession with technology and its own role in creating it.[3]

In the post-World War II years, the "New" German and Austrian filmmakers—including Haneke, Franz Novotny, Peter Patzak, Rainer Werner Fassbinder, and others—have explored the role of film and technology in manipulating society. Their films are usually marked by an awareness of the complexity of modern society, but occasionally one sees an unabashed nostalgia for a pretechnological society, as in Werner Herzog's *Where the Green Ants Dream* (1985) or even to some degree in Wim Wenders's *Wings of Desire* (1988). Such a totalizing damnation of modernity as *Continent*, though, is rare in the postwar period, given the explosive nature of European debates about modernity. As historian Stephen K. White points out, "the stakes involved with totalized critiques of modernity are very high for a German, who . . . has historically rooted worries that certain figures of thought may either lend themselves (even if unwittingly) to desperate forms of politics or provide insufficient resources for effective resistance to them."[4] The fact remains that Germans and Austrians have a highly traumatic recent history to contend with that makes it impossible and even dangerous to ignore the political and historical context of ideas. Haneke is then in a particularly difficult position as a leftist to avoid aligning himself with tainted ideas or images, such as those produced by Nazi filmmakers Leni Riefenstahl and Fritz Hippler.

Despite the left's occasional ambivalence about modernity and technology, the Nazis, and not the left, produced the famous film images and rhetoric that simultaneously engendered both an absolute critique of modernity as evil as well as a desire for a pre-enlightened, Germanic-Medieval world. These are two sides of the same cinematic coin. On the one hand, Hippler's anti-Semitic pseudo-documentary *The Eternal Jew* (1941) depicts the "modern" as foreign and thus dangerous to a "healthy" German identity. The film similarly depicts Jews as foreign and "degenerate" and then conflates these anti-Semitic images with what are shown to be the illnesses of "modern" society—the democratic nation-state, international trade, modern art, theater, and music.

Riefenstahl's *Triumph of the Will* (1934), on the other hand, celebrates the concept of the "simple" idealized life of the Germans, not constrained by this "modern plague." The film shows smiling peasants in folk costumes, and young healthy soldiers working together to cook breakfast on an open fire. All of this takes place against the background of carefully selected medieval streets in Nuremberg, a landscape that is remarkably premodern. In fact, it is highly ironic that a film made specifically to celebrate and promote Germany's military machinery employs rhetoric and imagery that are absolutely unmodern, if not antimodern. There is not a single shot of a factory, a modern building, or a piece of modern artwork here. *Triumph* is driven by a continuous desire for a return to "simpler" times, a need for what Susan Sontag has described in her essay "Fascinating Fascism" as "community." Sontag points out that *Triumph* succeeds because fascism was (or is) appealing to large masses of people. In films such as *Triumph*, fascism depicted itself not as brutality and terror, but rather as:

> an ideal or rather ideals that are persistent today under other banners: the ideal of life as art, the cult of beauty, the fetishism of courage, the dissolution of alienation in ecstatic feelings of community; the repudiation of the intellect . . . Riefenstahl's films are still effective because, among other reasons, their longings are still felt, because their content is a romantic ideal to which many continue to be attached.[5]

Sontag defines this desire as "the fascist longings in our midst," implying that this desire for community and human contact is still very much alive. In the end, though, Sontag ultimately exposes Riefenstahl's appealing image of "community" as one that depends on exclusion and on denial of the real world. In Riefenstahl's world, according to Sontag, only the young, the healthy, and the whole have a place. All that is disturbing, complex, ambiguous, fascinating, sick or in any way "other" has no place in this "community." As a result, all that is modern, both the bad and the good, is thrown out in this utopian vision.

What, though, of Haneke's utopian vision? To what degree is the implicit longing for community we see in *Continent* similar to what we see in *Triumph*? Certainly, he would want to distance himself completely from Riefenstahl's ideological stance. He explains in an interview, for instance, that he does not rely on images of beauty but rather on those of our ugliness to "provoke" the audience and to show the possibility of transcendence for humanity through ". . . the exact description of misery and the radical depiction of our 'desolateness.'" The film is supposed to elicit in the audience what he calls ". . . the desire for the possibility of a presence of transcendence."[6] What is this transcendence he is describing and how is it different from the transcendence promised in *Triumph of the Will*? Is it enough of a difference that he is showing the "exact description of misery" while Riefenstahl's project is supposed to depict the (exact?) details of utopia? And to what extent is Haneke's depiction of technology as evil the same or different from *The Eternal Jew*'s representation of modern jazz as "degenerate"?

As I mentioned above, Haneke's film appears well aware of the troubling questions it opens up and works hard to distance its critique of the modern (as well as its desire for transcendence) from both the antimodern rhetoric of the Nazis as well as that of the Hapsburg Empire, though with limited success. There are, for instance, several important political signposts in the film that give a political and historical context to what would otherwise seem a nameless, faceless portrait of the modern malaise. These signposts help the audience to understand that the quandary the protagonists find themselves in has real historical causes—namely the Nazi past and Austrian society's inability to deal with it. Over and over in this film, the very technology that is destroying Georg's, Anna's and Eva's humanity is linked strongly to the Nazi past, underlining the continuities that exist between past and present in the story. In one scene, for instance, Eva, the daughter, claims to be blind while at school. As the other children look on with a mixture of glee and terror, a teacher tricks her into confessing that she has only been pretending. That night, Anna confronts her daughter with the teacher's report, promising she will not punish her if she just tells the truth. When Eva does confess, her mother slaps her. The scene has several levels of significance: Eva's name reminds us of the biblical Eve and thus of innocence as well as the impending Fall of Man, while her blindness is associated with repression, a desire to forget about the "real" world (Adam and Eve "see" that they are naked only after the Fall). It is in the context of the scene immediately following it, though, that Eva's blindness takes on a specific political meaning.

There is a quick cut from little Eva at the school to her mother Anna's optometry practice (Anna and her brother have inherited it from their parents). Anna is examining the eye of an elderly woman, who is telling a story about her own childhood and school days (the scene takes place in 1987, and the woman is in her early to mid-sixties, thus making her a schoolgirl during the Nazi period). During her story, the camera cuts back and forth between close-ups of the woman's eye under the optometrist's lens and close-ups of Anna's face, showing that she is disturbed by what she is hearing. The focus on lenses, cameras, and watching all serve to reinforce the self-reflective nature of the scene; we are forced to confront our own role as viewers here. During the eye exam, the woman is recounting an incident from her elementary school in which another little girl, a German, peed on the floor one day because she had been teased too much about her very thick glasses. After her humiliation by the other children, the German girl had announced her wish that they all would have to wear such glasses. By the time they were in high school, the woman concludes, they were in fact all wearing those same ugly thick glasses.

This scene, in conjunction with Eva's feigned blindness, underlines the continuity between the cold institutions of the Nazi past and those of the present, where children like the old woman and Eva learn only humiliation and subordination to arbitrary authority. Eva, like her biblical counterpart, sees all too clearly now, but we are led to believe that she, like the old woman and all other adults in this world, will also need thick glasses by the time she is older and truly "blind" to the world around her. These scenes appear to explain if only partially the coldness in Anna's, Eva's, and Georg's world; the senseless authority (closely linked to the Nazis) that humiliated the young German girl is now working on Eva, and all of the characters appear to be victims of a history over which they feel they have no control.

There are other political signposts as well. Georg, the father, gets a promotion at his factory, a huge, *Metropolis*-like cavernous space filled with machinery and engines that dwarf the figure of Georg as we watch him cross the floor. The man he replaces, who is in his sixties like the woman in the optometry shop and thus linked to the Nazi past in some way, is forced into "early retirement" by the very institution he has helped to create. Georg, we are shown, is a willing replacement, ignoring the fact that he, too, will someday be replaced by a newer model. The factory, like the school and like every other aspect of Haneke's depiction of Austrian middle-class life in this film, has existed from the Nazi and Hapsburg past and will continue to exist through the present and beyond. Nothing has changed in Austria, Haneke seems to be arguing.

Yet another compelling scene illustrates this continuity between past and present in a manner that borders on the comic. Before the family's decision to commit suicide, Anna's voice is heard reading a letter she had written to Georg's parents describing to them that the family was doing very well financially, due in part to the inheritance she had received after the recent death of her mother. Later, Anna and Georg take all of their money, a very large sum, out of the bank, telling the bank teller they plan to move to Australia. In fact, they take the money home and flush it down the toilet in one of the longer scenes of the entire film. We watch from above as the couple stuffs the colorful bills into the bowl over and over, flushing and flushing until it all goes down the pipe. With this scene, Haneke intends to expose bourgeoisie Austrian attachment to money and material goods (in an interview he has said that middle-class sentiments would be injured most by this scene as well as the one in which Eva's goldfish dies a slow and painful death after the family takes sledgehammers to their orderly, middle-class house, before taking the poison). The scene depicting money being flushed down a toilet, while perhaps upsetting to middle-class Austrians (or Americans, for that matter) is radically disturbing in ways that go beyond a critique of middle-class materialism.

Georg and Anna are not just throwing money in the toilet. This money symbolizes both a monetary inheritance (*Erbschaft*) as well as the cultural, spiritual, and political heritage (*Erbe*) from the mother, a woman who would have to have been an adult during the Nazi period (the protagonists of *Continent* are, like many in the New German and Austrian Film community—including Haneke—postwar babies whose parents were young adults during the Third Reich). Flushing the "Nazi" inheritance/heritage down the toilet seems to be a more than symbolic act of rejection and rebellion against society for Georg and Anna (and, perhaps, for Haneke). Ultimately, though, this fails to save Georg and Anna from death and is revealed to be an act, not of rebellion, but rather of repression, in which they flush away an unexamined (and literally undigested) burden from the past.

Who is to blame for the state of modern Austria in Haneke's *Continent*, though? In an interview with WEGA-Film Publishers, Haneke playfully suggests that asking who is to blame for the society depicted in *Continent* is naive, but then goes on to answer the question himself with "The Devil, perhaps," referring to a title of a movie by his lifelong model, the French filmmaker Robert Bresson. We might conclude that *Continent* is a portrait of Haneke's modern Devil, but who is he and what does he look like? Is the monster a mixture of Nazi schoolteachers and electric garage doors, a creature who represents capitalism gone crazy, the Fascist past, and the ubiquitous droning of televisions in every house? Certainly, the film points an accusing finger at Austria's refusal or inability to address the continuities between the Nazi past and the present, which account for modern society's alienation from its human side. One particular continuity is of special interest to Haneke here—namely that modern media, especially the "seamless" narrative style of the dominant cinema—continues to manipulate and control human lives just as it did under the Nazis.

Continent is most subtle and compelling when it takes on the manipulative qualities of cinema itself and points to the continuities between Nazi cinematic style and modern day film and advertisements. More than the political signposts, this self-reflexive quality of the film gives credence to Haneke's idea that modern society is in deep trouble. From the beginning of the film, there are intercuts of a billboard depicting a deserted beach scene, with the words "Welcome to Australia" written across the top. At first, the billboard is a diegetic prop in the story, a roadside advertisement the family drives by after washing their car in a drive-through car wash. As the film progresses, however, the billboard begins to take on a non-diegetic role as it becomes more and more of a symbol of escape than a real prop. The billboard often appears without warning between scenes, set off by blackouts. In one scene, we see the billboard before the characters awaken, implying that they have been dreaming about Australia and its significance as an escape. Each time it appears, the billboard takes on more of the cinematic qualities of sound, light, and movement; we begin to hear the rush of the waves, for instance, and the light begins to move in the picture. It never looks like "real" cinema, but it is a self-reflexive symbol of the cinema. The film is reflecting on the qualities that make cinema function while exposing it as constructed.

The billboard is, then, more than the advertisement for a vacation; it also represents the cinematic promise of redemption and transcendence for the protagonists, who are caught in a sterile and alienating world. *Continent* thus links this promise of transcendence, embodied in the paradise-like empty beach of the "Welcome to Australia" billboard, with the trappings of the seamless narrative style of both Nazi-era and Hollywood dominant cinema. Initially, the family is shown to have bought into this vision of escape; they take their money out of the bank, sell their car, and quit their jobs—all supposedly to "emigrate" to Australia. Georg's voice-over reads the final letter written to his parents explaining their decision as a family to "be consistent and make this move together." One expects the move to be to Australia; instead it is, of course, the destruction of their home and their suicide. The billboard's, and thus cinema's, promise of escape and transcendence is thus exposed to us (and to Georg and Anna) as a lie; the cinematic promise of transcendence found in utopian films such as *Triumph of the Will* is shown to be a false one.

Haneke must confront the utopian ideology informing *Triumph* if he is to be able to formulate his own critique of modernity and his own vision of transcendence. It is hard to imagine making a dystopic postwar film without referring in some way to *Triumph*, one of the only truly utopian films ever made. *Continent* does refer explicitly to *Triumph* and works to expose the falsity of Riefenstahl's vision by establishing itself as a counter-text in its ideology, editing, imagery, and rhythm. There are interesting similarities too; both films are aesthetically appealing, rendering the familiar unfamiliar through close-ups and unexpected montages—such as Haneke's long shot of loaves of bread wrapped in cellophane or Riefenstahl's focus on the many arms of men working together to cut wood (it is as if Haneke were trying to reclaim the right to art from its tainted Nazi past).

Triumph, however, emphasizes community and harmony through fast cuts between groups of humans moving as one and a relatively still close-up of Hitler, stressing his individual power as well as the subordination of the crowd to the leader. The smooth, "seamless" cutting and quick rhythm work to pull the audience into its ideological viewpoint, that the world of the Nazis is harmonious, communal, and under the fatherly control of a good leader. *Continent*, on the other hand, labors to undermine this harmonious vision, highlighting a broken society through long takes of fragmented body and machine parts. Haneke's slow, deliberate editing, with long blackouts between scenes, underscores his vision of humans as machines, living without community, isolated from each other and themselves. The only father figure here is directionless until his eventual suicide. The audience is confronted with a disquieting and frustrating visual experience that is supposed to lead to a productive reevaluation of postwar society.

In the end, though, it remains unclear whether *Continent* achieves the goal Haneke articulates in an interview, in which he says he wants to create a shock that is ". . . big enough that there will perhaps be a little bit of change in (the audience's) life."[7] In spite of the film's intense engagement with the political and historical roots of its protagonists' quandary, *Continent*, in fact, never escapes from the same polarizing critique of modernity it claims to be attacking, and it ends up posing questions that are, ironically, answered best by the utopian vision at the heart of *Triumph of the Will*. While the film goes to elaborate lengths to mark the dominant cinema represented by the billboard and the TVs as manipulative, there are no such markers when we see the long shots of the electric garage door, the coffee maker, or the fish tank. The same holds true when we watch the long take of a hand working the cash register; we are supposed to be critical of the way human life is fragmented, but not necessarily of the cinematic power of the shot itself (one could argue that the aestheticized nature of these shots calls attention to them, but this is still an entirely different kind of self-reflection than one sees in the film's treatment of the billboard). In other words, there is an inarticulated normative standard that the film presupposes—namely that the third person narrator (the camera) is right, good, even morally superior.

The omniscient and unnamed narrator appears to be telling this story from a critical standpoint outside the narrative system, a standpoint that is beyond critique. As such, the film sets up a world polarized between the "false" modernity of the billboard and the "real" utopian space occupied by the narrator (toward which we are asked to strive). To avoid this polarizing effect, Haneke would have to have marked even his own critical point of view as cinematic (and thus constructed), a difficult feat. Fassbinder's *The Marriage of Maria Braun* (1979), Pedro Almodóvar's *What Have I Done to Deserve This*, as well as Haneke's later film, *Benny's Video* (1992), are a few films that successfully reflect on their own complicity in the problem of modernity while nevertheless critiquing modern society. In postwar Austria and Germany, the stakes are too high—the debate about modernity has too much baggage attached to it—for such apparently unselfconscious yearnings for transcendence.

NOTES

1. Georgia Brown, review of *The Seventh Continent*, directed by Michael Haneke. *The Village Voice*, March 27, 1990.
2. See Stephen K. White, ed., *The Cambridge Companion to Habermas* (Cambridge: Cambridge University Press, 1995), *3ff.* for a detailed discussion of the intense debate about modernity among Horkheimer, Adorno, Heidegger, and Habermas in the postwar years.
3. See Andreas Huyssen, "Technology and Sexuality in Fritz Lang's *Metropolis*," in *New German Critique* no. 24–25 (Fall/Winter 1981–82), for an excellent treatment of this film.
4. White, *The Cambridge Companion to Habermas*, 5.
5. Susan Sontag, "Fascinating Fascism," in *A Susan Sontag Reader* (New York: Farrar, Straus, Giroux, 1982), 320.
6. Stefan Grissemann and Michael Omasta, *"Ein Gespräch mit dem Regisseur,"* in *Der siebente Kontinent: Michael Haneke und seine Filme*, ed. Alexander Horwath (Vienna: Europaverlag, 1991). Haneke begins the interview: *"Was mir wichtig wäre ist, durch die genaue Beschreibung des Elends und die radikale Schilderung unserer 'Verlassenheit,' das Gefühl der Sehnsucht nach der Möglichkeit einer Anwesenheit von Transzendenz zu stärken. Der Film versucht zu provozieren."* [What is important to me is the exact representation of misery and the radical depiction of our "desolation," to strengthen the feeling of desire for the possibility of the presence of transcendence. The film is attempting to provoke.]
7. Ibid., 203. Haneke is quoted in the interview as saying: *"Wenn der Schock gross genug ist, wird es vielleicht ein bisschen Veränderung in seinem Leben geben können."* [If the shock is great enough, perhaps there can be a little bit of change in one's life.]

BIBLIOGRAPHY

Brown, Georgia. Review of *The Seventh Continent*, directed by Michael Haneke. *The Village Voice*, March 27, 1990.
The Eternal Jew. Directed by Fritz Hippler. Berlin: Terra, 1940.
Grissemann, Stefan and Omasta, Michael, *"Ein Gespräch mit dem Regisseur."* In *Der siebente Kontinent: Michael Haneke und seine Filme*, edited by Alexander Horwath. Vienna: Europaverlag, 1991.
Huyssen, Andreas. "Technology and Sexuality in Fritz Lang's *Metropolis*." *New German Critique*, no. 24–25 (Fall/Winter 1981–82), 221–237.
The Seventh Continent. Directed by Michael Haneke. Vienna: Wega Film, 1989.
Sontag, Susan. "Fascinating Fascism." In *A Susan Sontag Reader* (New York: Farrar, Straus, Giroux, 1982).
Triumph of the Will. Directed by Leni Riefenstahl. Berlin: UFA, 1935.
White, Stephen K., ed. *The Cambridge Companion to Habermas*. Cambridge: Cambridge University Press, 1995.

Chapter Four

Lithuanian Nationalism
and the Holocaust

Public Expressions of Memory in Museums
and Sites of Memory in Vilnius, Lithuania

Edna Kantorovitz Southard and Robert Southard

Dedicated to Robert Southard
July 27, 1945–November 6, 2007
of blessed memory

The annihilation of the Jews in Lithuania was so successful that 96 percent of the Jewish population was killed, and that was achieved by outright murder in public view and without concentration camps. Hitler was delighted with this success and cited it as an example of how inciting local populations was a most effective way to achieve Nazi goals.

How are these and other historical facts publicly acknowledged in Lithuania today? The Holocaust is a difficult subject in Lithuania, and this difficulty is strikingly and interestingly visible in the historical museums in and around Lithuania's present capital, Vilnius. In other chapters of our study, we will examine museums in other Lithuanian cities, because just as each country in Europe has a different history in terms of the Holocaust, so each city in the Baltic countries has its own history, public monuments, and museums.[1]

The difficulty in discussing the Holocaust in current Lithuania is so great that Lithuanian and Jewish public presentations of the documented historical past hardly seem to refer to the same events. Of course, we all understand that different peoples have different experiences and see matters differently, but the presentations in Vilnius are more than merely differences of perspective. Each seems to be a counter-history to the other's history, although that formulation is not adequate because it presents an illusion of symmetry in which each version appears a little right and a little wrong. Although it is comfortable and easy to view the differences this way, it is also irresponsible because it obscures the most successful work of genocide in European history while concealing the culpable, and popular, role of Lithuanian nationalists in its perpetration.

Some history and statistics strengthen this contention and may begin to answer the complicated question about why this brutal legacy exists and is denied.[2] Interwar Lithuania was a small state whose independence in the wake of Russian collapse and German military defeat in World War I came as a surprise even to Lithuania's nationalists, who, before 1914, hoped only for some cultural autonomy and land reform within the Russian Empire. By 1923, this peasant state had lost Vilnius and its environs to Poland but had seized the German Memelland on the coast. There was a separate Jewish geographic imagery at work throughout the region. Few Jews would have understood themselves, certainly before the end of World War I, as "Lithuanian Jews," but many would have considered themselves as Jews from the territory of *Lite*, the Yiddish term for Lithuania, which referred to the eastern regions of the old Polish-Lithuanian Commonwealth (dismembered in 1772–1795 during the three partitions of Poland). However, the geographic boundary of *Lite* did not map onto the post-World War I Lithuanian state, creating a dissonance between what Jews meant when they spoke of *Lite* and what Lithuanians meant when they spoke of the Lithuanian nation after the establishment of independent Lithuania in 1918. This helped to cultivate anti-Semitism and promote a conception of Lithuanian citizenship that excluded Jews. Before World War II, Lithuania had 21,489 square miles and a population of 2,421,570. Of this population, 84 percent were Lithuanian and 7.6 percent were Jewish—that is, Jews who lived in Lithuanian territory and were never granted rights of citizenship because of the Judeophobia that eventuated their annihilation.

The German division of Poland with the Soviet Union in August 1939 and the related awarding of Lithuania to the Soviet sphere of influence resulted in the granting of Vilnius to now Soviet satellite Lithuania. This placed Vilnius's many Jews and additional Jews from elsewhere in Poland within Lithuania's new frontiers in October 1939. Desperate to improve its strategic position before the German Army—after its shocking victory in France—could turn east, the Soviet Army occupied all of Lithuania in June 1940. The Soviet occupation led to deportations in which Jews (who were more urban and commercial than Lithuanians) were deported at a higher percentile rate than Lithuanians. Nevertheless, a few Jews took positions in the occupation government and many Jews, although not comfortable with Soviet rule and arrested by the occupiers more often than Lithuanians, understandably felt safer than they had under German rule. According to Lithuanian perception, however, the Jews were pro-Soviet. Before this time, Lithuania had not been an overtly anti-Semitic country. Jews and Lithuanians lived apart from each other, Jewish assimilation was infrequent, and for diplomatic reasons, Lithuania granted

Jews cultural and political autonomy until the dictatorship of Antanas Smetona in 1926.[3] The belief that Jews were Soviet collaborators brought threats and taunts during the months of Soviet rule.

In the immediate aftermath of the German invasion, it brought rapes of Jewish women, torture of rabbis, and mass killings of Jews by their Lithuanian neighbors. In the Kaunas suburb of Slobodka, 1,200 men, women, and children were killed on June 25, 1941, and another 2,300 were killed during the following days. This sparked similar killings in Vilnius and Siauliai. Lithuanian paramilitaries began to imprison Jews in sites that later served for mass killings. Paneriai outside Vilnius is a case in point.[4]

The German *Einsatzgruppe A* soon took over the supervision and execution of these killings with considerable and enthusiastic local help from Lithuanians. The Final Solution had not yet become policy for other areas of German occupation, but it was already operating doctrine in Lithuania.[5] These killings occurred so quickly that by December 1941, deaths amounted to 180,000 (72 percent) of the Jews present in Lithuania including Vilnius but not Memel (which Germany had reannexed in March 1939). Of the 250,000 Jews in Lithuania when the Germans invaded, about 17,000 escaped into the interior of the Soviet Union. Some lived in hiding, some fled to become partisans in the forests, and a very few survived German mistreatment. Of Jews who did not escape Lithuania immediately after the invasion, a stunning 96 percent—the highest kill rate in Nazi-occupied Europe—were murdered by Germans but also with persistent and substantial Lithuanian collaboration. The strong association in Lithuanian minds of Jews with Soviet rule meant that, after the Germans fled in July 1944, neither returning Jews nor their few local rescuers were safe from attack.

Before World War II, the city then called Vilna, or Vilne in Yiddish, was the world's largest and most culturally productive center of Jewish life in the Russian Empire and then the Soviet Union.[6] Called "Jerusalem of the North," Vilna was a major locus for pre-Holocaust Jewish history. In 1918, Lithuania declared independence and the name "Litvak" came to apply to the learned Orthodox but anti-Hasidic Jews. Lithuania tried to gain Vilna from Poland by professing philo-Semitism, yet anti-Semitism persisted and was commonplace after Vilna was annexed by Poland and many Lithuanians blamed Jews for Soviet depredations. This legacy continues today.

During World War II, more than 200,000 Jewish people in Lithuania were murdered—and not in concentration camps. The Jews in Lithuania were massacred, burnt in synagogues, or bludgeoned to death in public town squares. Germans did not have to do all of the work; the local Lithuanian population willingly obliged. Today there are some Jews living in Lithuania, mainly from Russia, but there are few Jews whose origins are in Lithuania. Active

Jewish life is struggling and is generally ignored by the Lithuanian populace, but as a former Jewish partisan fighter, now a librarian at the Yiddish library, said poignantly during a conversation with us in Vilnius in 2005, "There are worse things for Jews than being ignored." But ignorance and casual hostility exist—from a whispered, "Are you Jewish?" to stony silence when asking directions to Jewish sites, swastikas painted on the sides of buildings, Jewish cemeteries now serving as overgrown needle parks, and Jewish tombstones used for road paving and for walls in public squares.

The quiet combat—more than sixty years after the Germans left Vilnius—between Lithuanian and Jewish museums, and the roles of silence and implication in their presentations and text panels, need to be considered with this history and this legacy in mind.[7] As destinations for cultural tourism, national museums display a nation's art and its historical prizes and become places where national pride can be expressed openly. Attention to museums must be paid because the past must be reconciled with the present and future. Such efforts are ongoing—with mixed success—in Washington, D.C., for example. What can the future look like when the past is ignored or distorted? What happens when narratives compete and collide? Who is included in a national identity justifies whose story gets told in the national narrative. The enslavement and murder of a group of people living in one's midst can be ignored and diminished if one denies them inclusion in the historical narrative—thus Jews never were viewed as Lithuanians; they were outsiders to the national narrative.

In July 2005, we, a professor of European and Jewish history and a museum curator/art historian, did collaborative research on site at three public museums in the city of Vilnius that receive public funding—The National Museum of Lithuania, the Museum of Genocide Victims, and the Vilna Gaon Jewish Museum—examining how history is presented and to whom, and looking at the ways in which national identities are expressed and understood. We studied the Vilna Gaon Jewish State Museum in its three buildings in Vilnius and its museum at Paneriai.

Although this chapter focuses on Vilnius, we visited more than thirty museums and sites of memory in the main cities of Lithuania and Latvia during July and August of 2005. In full disclosure, the paternal grandparents of one of us, Edna Kantorovitz Southard, were among those murdered in Lithuania. We looked at sites of memory, which are defined as public spaces, such as a museum or former killing field, that have been acknowledged and opened to visitors. More than 200 towns and fields in Lithuania were sites of massacres in 1941–1944 and could be sites of memory but are not acknowledged as such. An example is the popular lake area of Trakai with its picturesque castle, where there is no acknowledgment of the massacre of 2,500 Jews that occurred there. Sites of memory are not neutral or self-evident in significance because someone selects them for visits and viewing; someone guides the progress of visitors, and someone drafts and displays commemorative and explanatory texts and decides in which language or languages these should be presented. For these reasons, sites of memory inform us about the mentality of the presenters as well as about the events they commemorate.

Our method included speaking to museum personnel and docent guides, purchasing all of each museum's available written materials, and taking digital and film images of exhibition cases, wall labels, text panels, and installations. Museums use overt and subtle means—including lighting, type size and style, length of labels, and artifact selection and placement. We noted the languages used on labels and text panels and took into account the publicly acknowledged funding of the museums, and we tried to learn the mission, goals, hours of operation, and the funding sources, including donors, and budgetary priorities of each museum and site of memory. Who tells the story at each place and how do they tell it? What is told and what is omitted? Who decides?

A historical narrative that leaves out segments of history is a "narrative of omission." Simply leaving out parts of history is one way to change the understanding of the past. One set of facts or one group of people is marginalized, thus suggesting that they are not important, and this is accomplished by segmentizing both the history and the museum presentation. Our word for this concept is "segmentization" of the history, which can be achieved in a museum by the way in which walls divide thematic sections, using subtle museological practices to lead the viewer through the museum and by extension through the historical past. By contrast, at the U.S. Holocaust Memorial Museum in Washington, D.C., one room and one section leads to another, suggesting not only a flow through the museum but an ineluctable inevitability in the flow of history. One event leads inescapably to another. The victim (or the viewer) is trapped in the cause and effect of history which leads either to survival or death. The opposite of this approach is segmentization, examples of which abound in the Latvian and Lithuanian museums of Riga, Klaipėda, and Kaunas. This concept is important in understanding the museums of Vilnius, too.

In the post-Communist era, Vilnius is the capital of Lithuania, the center for tourism and entertainment, the showplace of Lithuanian museums and culture, and most clearly under the gaze of nationalistic museum culture. Much of the city has been restored to its baroque splendor, its buildings repainted to their original pastel colors, its old buildings in the central city gentrified and transformed into hotels, shops, restaurants, cafes, bars, and nightspots. Now liberated by the collapse of the Soviet Union, the city is richly endowed

Figure 4.1. National Museum, Vilnius. Photograph courtesy of Edna Kantorovitz Southard.

through capitalist enterprise. The economic future looks bright. Well-dressed, elegant people in their twenties predominate on the streets and in the shops and restaurants. Tourists and families flock to the Castle Museum on Gediminas Hill on Sunday afternoons to see shiny arms and armor of medieval Lithuania and to view the city's panorama.

The National Museum of Lithuania is located on Arsenalo Street, not far from the Cathedral in Vilnius. The museum is large, well-funded, and aims to survey the art and culture of Lithuania supposedly until World War II, but in fact, the work of late-twentieth-century artists is on display. The museum includes a sequence of buildings housing several sections, among them the Applied Arts Museum, with folk art and large wood carvings of crosses gathered from many villages throughout rural Lithuania.

An exclusionary historical point of view is expressed in many ways, including silence, and also by segmentization of the exhibition displays, so that the exhibition deals only with some parts of the narrative and displays other parts in a marginalized way, separately in a display case or by other means. An example of this narrative by omission is a text panel on the ethnic history of Lithuania that mentions warriors and peasants, Tatars and Karaites, but omits mention of Jews. A Jewish sect beginning in eighth-century Persia, Karaites follow the Bible literally and do not accept Talmudic traditions. A small and marginal group, they are given prominence in Lithuanian history out of proportion to the greater significance of the Jewish population in Lithuania.

This exclusionary perspective is contained within an otherwise comprehensive approach. Thus, in some of its exhibitions—such as in the ground floor exhibition of Semigallian archaeological sites—artifacts from 200 sites, from the ninth through the thirteenth centuries, are displayed. The installation itself is so artful and ingenious that the large number of objects displayed in glass cases does not give the visual effect of being overwhelming and presents the illusion of floating lightness. The craftsmanship of the installations is subtle and elegant, and the effective lighting that highlights curatorial selections testifies to the professionalism of the preparator and installation team.

Also highly professional by museum standards in its installation techniques was the Napoleonic exhibition then on the second floor. In 2001, during its construction, a mass grave was discovered on Verkiu Street in Vilnius. It contained the remains of 40,000 Napoleonic soldiers who died of starvation and typhus after their retreat from Moscow in November 1812. In July 2005, a temporary exhibition at the National Museum showed artifacts found in the mass grave, including fragmentary uniforms found on decaying bodies. Dramatically lit, a uniform with feathered cap hung from fishing wire seemed to float between two glass panels. Labels were in Lithuanian and English. A text panel in the two languages explained that 50,000 soldiers were killed on November 27–29 while crossing the Berezina River and 40,000 were killed in Vilnius.

Permanent exhibitions of much less fragile farm tools and reconstructions of rural life in Lithuania are displayed in a large exhibit space on the second floor of the National Museum. The hoes, hammers, plows, and other tools are artfully shown along with black-and-white photographs suggesting their use and relevance today. On an inside wall case, given little attention and without comment, are Shrove Tuesday masks with evident anti-Semitic stereotypes and caricatures that would, in museums in many countries, either have resulted in their removal from the national museum or in extensive commentary and explanation. Rooms of peasant huts are reconstructed as in American historical museums and black-and-white photographs from 1949 to 1969 show such huts existing even into the modern world. Photographs of wooden shrines are displayed in visual rather than chronological order. Dating from 1926 to 1995, they suggest a nationalistic agenda promoting the continuity, enduring faith, and good values of the rural life. In contrast with the exhibition on the Napoleonic soldiers, which gave the impression of having no emotional urgency, the displays of seventeenth- and eighteenth-through twentieth-century peasant life are vivid, well-installed, and emphatic.

The National Museum of Lithuania also included several temporary exhibitions of post-World War II artists, primarily of a traditional nature, in
July 2005. Two temporary exhibitions featured work by Lithuanian women
artists. A room of colorful paintings done in a naïve style by a woman artist
aged ninety-five was nostalgic in the manner of the American artist Grandma
Moses. A solo exhibition of the artist Elena Gaputyte (1927–1991) showed
sculptural installations and photographs of her minimalist installation work
involving the use of stones, rocks, lights, and natural phenomena. The introductory text panel, written by Dr. Laima Laučkaitéin in Lithuanian and
English, described the artist's life and included the following paragraph
(transcribed on July 16, 2005):

> While the people in the West knew what World War II was, they had little
> imagination of what happened in Lithuania during and after it. As celebrations
> and discourse surrounding 60th anniversary of the cessation of the war has
> shown this year, westerners still do not understand that the war did not end in
> Lithuania (and 'Eastern Europe') in 1945.

The problem of historical interpretation is basically summarized in those
sentences. Even in a museum whose mission statement clearly limits its
activities to the outbreak of World War II, the issue continues to be raised
emphatically.

The Museum of Genocide Victims at Aukų Street in Vilnius is a large,
patriotic, and pro-Lithuanian museum located in the former KGB Building.
The word "genocide" is used in the name of this museum both in English and
in Lithuanian. The use of this word in this museum refers to repression by
Soviet Russia against Lithuanians and does not refer to the systematic murder
of Jews. On the outside of the building is this statement in Lithuanian and
English: "1941–1944 headquarters of the German Secret Police (Gestapo)
and SD, its prison, barracks of special squad which carried out repression
against Jewish and other populations of Lithuania." The exterior of the building has memorial plaques dedicated to victims in 1945 and 1946.

The museum is associated with the Genocide and Resistance Research
Center of Lithuania and receives considerable funding by donation. The
Lithuanian-American Council headquartered in Chicago is acknowledged as
having funded the lower execution cell exhibitions. The Balzekas Museum
of Lithuanian Culture also funded the main publications that are available for
purchase at the museum shops at the Museum of Genocide Victims in Vilnius
and at the Balzekas Museum at 6500 South Pulaski Road in Chicago.

The building that houses the Museum of Genocide Victims is a "symbol
of the 50 year Soviet occupation in Lithuania" and the museum itself "has
already become the symbol of painful experience of the Lithuanian nation,"

Figure 4.2. Museum of Genocide, Vilnius. Photograph courtesy of Edna Kantorovitz Southard.

according to the catalog text strikingly designed in black and red type with texts in Lithuanian and English.[8] In the basement, the cells are "left as is" from when the KGB officers departed in August 1991. Open every day except Monday, the museum offers tours in Lithuanian, English, and Russian.

The upper floors use state-of-the-art modern exhibit display techniques with complete scenes, full panels, and Plexiglas labels. The full-length displays of texts and images are interspersed with holograms in the hallway. The holograms have the effect of reaching a wide audience and of inspiring identification with the victims. Even the most blasé museumgoer must be stunned for a moment by the sight of a gun aiming directly at his or her head, until—with shock at the realization—it is clear that it is a hologram of a hand aiming a gun.

In July 2005, the temporary exhibition space had a full-length panel exhibition about the Armenian Genocide, evidently an effort to universalize the concept of genocide—a safe subject because Lithuanians were not implicated in those mass murders in 1915–23. By contrast, there was no mention of the Jewish genocide in Lithuania that had considerable Lithuanian collaboration, although Hitler used the genocide of Armenians as a model for dealing with the Jews. Thus, the isolation of the Armenian Genocide exhibition, which has little to do with the Lithuanians and their history, is an example of segmentization, but the failure to mention anything about the genocide of the Jews in Lithuania in this museum is a case of narrative by omission.

In Lithuania, most Holocaust denial occurs by omission and silence. Lithuanian Fighters Union (LLA) atrocities against the Jews, for instance, are not mentioned. A text panel on the wall of the Museum of Genocide Victims gives these invidious statistics on the first—that is, the Soviet—occupation: 30,000 dead, "Lithuanians suffered the most 68.1 percent, Jews 8.9 percent." Stated this way, the panels invite the reader to think of Jews as an alien population in Lithuania, although the percentage figure of 8.9 percent is actually larger than the Jewish percentage in the total population. This example should make it clear that Jews today are not considered to be Lithuanians by those belonging to the dominant ethnicity of Lithuania. Another text panel gives this information on the Partisan War, 1944–53: the LLA (Lithuanian Fighters Union) "tried in every possible way to stop the disorder and excess." This defense raises unanswered questions: What "disorder?" Against whom? And most interestingly, in refutation of whose accusations?

In a subtle, unintentional way, the subsequent panels provide the answers. The viewer who reads carefully learns that 200 LLA members went to Germany for further training as guerillas, that they joined Lithuanian partisans from the forests after the German retreat in July 1944, and that for the next eight years they held out while waiting for war between the Americans and the Russians—in the course of which it was thought that Lithuania might, based upon the Atlantic Charter of 1941, at last regain its freedom. In the meantime, the LLA avoided open fighting with the Soviet Army. Instead, they attacked civilian administrators and "collaborators." In the Vilna Gaon Jewish Museum a half a mile away from the Museum of Genocide Victims in Vilnius, one learns that "collaborator" was a code word for Jews and for gentile Lithuanians who hid Jews during the German occupation. Presumably, the "disorder" and "excess" mentioned in the earlier panel refer to sweeping pogroms rather than to getting the right collaborators. The carefully phrased statement, then, is a defense that reveals knowledge of the accusation of Lithuanians siding with the Germans against the Russians and joining in eliminating the Jews before and after July 1944. The oral tour was more evenhanded than the written information. Visiting the cells in the lower floor, the tour guide told a large group of visitors that "94 percent of Lithuanian persons chose not to collaborate in mass executions of Jews," which is not only untrue but also an example of the continuing separation of the Jewish people as not Lithuanian.

The Vilna Gaon Jewish State Museum contains exhibitions in three separate buildings in Vilnius and in two other towns: in Paneriai, where 70,000 Jews and 30,000 non-Jews were killed; and in Druskininkai, where a small museum dedicated to the sculptor Jacques Lipchitz struggles for existence in the face of funding difficulties.[9] The history of the Vilna Gaon Museum reflects the vicissitudes of the tragic history of the region and of the Jewish people in particular. The first Jewish museum in Vilnius opened in 1913, but its collection was burnt during World War I. The museum was restored and rebuilt in the interwar period, but most of its collection was destroyed during World War II. The second Jewish museum was established in 1944 after Lithuania was liberated but was closed five years later by Soviet authorities. Its collection was dispersed. For the next forty years, Jewish art, books, and documents—and the subject of Judaism itself—were taboo. Plans for a new Jewish museum began in the Gorbachev era under the auspices of the ad hoc Jewish Cultural Society of Lithuania, which sought to establish a new Jewish museum in Vilnius. This happened with state funding in 1988 or, according to a brochure at the museum, in 1989. The handout obscures the role of JCSL by stating that the foundation was instigated "by a group of Jewish intellectuals at the Lithuanian Cultural Foundation."[10] Currently, the museum is under the direction of the Lithuanian Ministry of Culture. Some pre-World War II items were transferred there from the Ciurlionis National Art Museum in Kaunas. Today, the Vilna Gaon Jewish Museum collection includes some 5,000 objects in four locations.

Compared to the other two museums discussed here, the Jewish museum has limited funding and resources. Much of its energy is devoted to educational outreach and publications. The museum staff and docents are a small but devoted group, mostly Holocaust survivors or children of survivors. Their dedication to their task reflects their roles as members of the Second Generation and as "memorial candles."[11]

One part of the Vilna Gaon Jewish Museum is located in the Jewish Community Center on Pylimo Street. After passing the reception desk, one climbs a dark staircase to the exhibitions, which are divided into three sections. The first room includes an exhibition showing the 16th Lithuanian Red Army, in which 4,500 Jews served; the second section depicts struggle (that is, spiritual resistance) in the ghettos; the third section is devoted to Jewish partisans. There is also a section on Jews from Vilna in the U.S. Armed Forces and the British forces during World War II. A separate room is devoted to the musician Jascha Heifetz and another small room to writer Avrom Karpinowicz. On our second visit to the Jewish Community Center, after receiving an invitation from the Green House, we were guided to a room that is normally locked: the room of the Righteous Gentiles. This exhibition receives funding from Yad Vashem in Jerusalem. Here one learns—if one thinks to ask—why so many of the gentiles honored by portraits here died in July 1944 after the Germans fled: they were shot as collaborators by the partisans honored in the Genocide Museum across town.

Figure 4.3. Green House, the Vilna Gaon Jewish Museum. Photograph courtesy of Edna Kantorovitz Southard.

Devoted to the Holocaust in Lithuania, the Green House is a separate building of the Vilna Gaon Jewish Museum, located on Paménkalnio Street. This small, old, wooden building on a hill houses exhibitions in seven small rooms on one floor. The attic story is a conference room. The exhibition spaces start with maps of Lithuania and follow a sequential telling of discrimination against and ghettoization of Jews, and of partisan fighting, provides a model of the ghetto and its liquidation, and ends with a room of mural photographs of people in the ghettos and a modern abstract sculpture expressive of despair and hope. The amount of factual information on the Holocaust is extensive, with small photographs and long texts in Lithuanian and Russian and very little English, but with handouts of translations in English. Compared to the National Museum and the Genocide Museum, this museum is more like a book or poster display. The uniform lighting and tone of these texts recalls the unemotional monotone used by survivors when they describe the events of the Holocaust. Is it the numbness caused by trauma and the sense that the repetition of the facts will speak loudly for itself? Or is it an unconscious damming to prevent a flood of limitless and uncontrollable tears?

A tour of museum galleries by Rachel Margolis, a Vilna Ghetto survivor who was a Jewish partisan fighter during the war, continued that sense of monotone recitation of horrors. In Yiddish-German, she spoke eloquently about the exhibitions and her life to a group that included two Austrian museum interns—Johannes Langer, who was just finishing his year-long internship; and the new intern, who was just beginning his year. These internships, sponsored by the Austrian Gedenkdienst, part of the Austrian government, are offered as alternatives to military service. The plan is that, each year for ten years, one intern is sent to this Holocaust museum in Vilnius. The Anne Frank House in Amsterdam has also benefited from this exchange.

The Vilna Gaon Museum's educational outreach program tries to explain the Jewish component of the history of Lithuania to Lithuanian high school students. These students generally express little interest in the Holocaust, but they enjoy having a chance to practice English with people close to them in age. Sometimes accompanied by a museum assistant who spoke Lithuanian, Johannes Langer had visited fifteen high schools in twelve cities, towns, and villages in Lithuania, where he gave discussions and Microsoft PowerPoint presentations about the Holocaust to 475 eleventh and twelfth graders at no cost to the schools. He gave us a copy of his impressive final report, "Project: A Lecture about the Holocaust, Anti-Semitism as well as the EU," which documented how the small budget allotted to the program was spent and the anti-Semitic concepts expressed by the Lithuanian students—most frequently the concern that "the Jews" were only interested in restitution and this would cost the Lithuanians jobs and income. As the engaged and enthusiastic Austrian museum interns discussed the project, their fundamental sympathies became evident. We engaged the two of them in a frank discussion about this question and asked them directly about their identifications. They identified neither with victims nor collaborators, neither Jewish nor Lithuanian, but with the German or Austrian military—specifically with a German military officer whose story of righteous acts they had heard and whose morality they would have wished to emulate, if they had been alive then. We told the young Austrians that our identifications lay directly and consistently with the victims, as is entirely typical for the children of Holocaust survivors. While we admired the work of the Austrian museum interns and found them to be admirably sensitive, we also acknowledge that their limited sense of identification may be an impermeable barrier to true understanding.

The educational mission of the Green House museum includes not only significant work in the area of educational outreach to the schools but also publications. Since opening fifteen years ago, the museum has published an impressive twenty-six volumes.[12] An exhibition called "Jewish Life in Lithuania" has been prepared for travel to museums in other countries. Seminars and lectures are held in some of the smaller cities, such as Siauliai, where horrific slaughters of Jews occurred in 1941. The museum has had little success, however, in interrupting the dominant Lithuanian narrative in which the Holocaust receives only fleeting and ambivalent consideration.

Rachel Kostanian-Danzig, deputy director of the museum, pointed out that the educational and publication missions are particularly important because the vast majority of visitors to the museum are not local people. Seventy percent of visitors are American or from other parts of Europe, and most visitors are Jewish. An exhibition about Anne Frank in the 1990s was accepted by the Lithuanian public and began a discussion about the Holocaust. Despite lack of local support, the museum works hard to recall and explain the past with a view to shaping the future, to preventing another *Shoah*, and to arousing in visitors pride in Lithuania's Jewish past and confidence in Lithuania's Jewish future. The museum tells a difficult story clearly and forcefully, despite its limited exhibition spaces.

A few blocks from the Green House is the more visible and modern Tolerance Center, in a building renovated in 2004 and part of the Vilna Gaon State Jewish Museum. Because the Green House is a separate, partly hidden entity, the Tolerance Center does not need to discuss the Holocaust directly. Instead, it connects Jewish themes to a celebration of tolerance in general. Most museumgoers are safely in favor of tolerance and, suggestively, tolerance is visually associated by the museum with Jewish people and objects.

The museum is situated where the old Tarbut Theater of the Tarbut Gymnasium stood before the war. In interwar Lithuania, most Jewish students went to Yiddish language Socialist schools, to Hebrew language religious

Yavneh schools, or—by far the most popular—secular Zionist Hebrew language "Tarbut" schools, named with the Hebrew word for "culture." Our guide at the Museum of Tolerance was Violeta Palcinskaite, a popular writer of children's literature whose Jewish relatives were hidden by her Catholic relatives.[13] Although the museum was recently renovated, the air conditioning did not work and the broken alarm system rang constantly while we were there. The museum contains Jewish objects from pre-Holocaust Lithuania, including a plaque of the Ten Commandments in Hebrew that was preserved and displayed by the Museum of Atheism under the Soviets. There are paintings by Holocaust and post-Holocaust artists. One room is devoted to the cubist sculptor Jacques Lipchitz. A wall panel display presents the history of Jewish life in a format similar to the Armenian Genocide display at the Museum of Genocide Victims. Relentlessly factual, the format results in an experience comparable to reading a book while standing up. The point seems to be to establish what happened to Lithuania's Jews. The lesson is basic: we must not allow this to happen again.

The Vilna Gaon Museum offers tours not only of its three exhibition parts but also of the Old and New Ghettos, where Jews were forced to reside during World War II.[14] Stone wall plaques were recently installed on buildings on the streets that are the boundaries of the ghettos. These signs are mostly in English and Yiddish, but there are also some signs in Lithuanian. The language choices show that the ghettos are presumed to be of interest to Jewish tourists rather than to the Lithuanian- and Russian-language speakers who live in this country. The many antique shops in this area of the old town are filled with fine antiques, including, unsettlingly, a number of Jewish ritual objects, such as menorahs.

From 1941 to 1944, Jews in the Vilna Ghetto were transported by train to the nearby Paneriai Forest (Ponary in English), where they were rounded up into pits and murdered. Today, the short train ride from Vilnius follows the same train tracks to Ponary. Upon arriving, one walks along a road to the killing site. The way to the site of memory of Ponary, the killing fields, is unmarked. On the train from Vilnius, we met an American scholar who gave us directions and told us that we would certainly not find a taxi, as the concierge at our hotel had said. Although the concierge was usually so helpful with information, it became clear that he had never been to Ponary. This dying industrial town had been a resort and was readied by the Red Army for aviation fuel, which is why the round pits were there, convenient for the killings. Here 100,000 people were killed—70,000 Jews and 30,000 non-Jews. The sight of many Christian monuments featuring large crosses compared to the lone Jewish monument does not reflect that 70 percent to 30 percent ratio. On the Jewish stone monument, a swastika had been ineffectually cleaned off. The unmarked round pits were covered with newly mowed grass.

Figure 4.4. Entrance to the Paneriai museum. Photograph courtesy of Edna Kantorovitz Southard.

A small triangular building has a large map of the killing fields at the entrance and a stone sign that reads "Paneriai Museum: A Department of Jewish State Museum of Lithuania," in English, Yiddish, and Lithuanian. Connected administratively to the Vilna Gaon Jewish State Museum, it was guarded by M. Gantaros, who spoke only Lithuanian. The museum is arranged with tall glass vitrines containing long texts, small black-and-white photographs, and objects that had been found in the killing pits: watches, cups, silverware, glasses, and shoes. The first panel on display is labeled "Paneriai 1941–44" and indicates the numbers of people killed here and how they arrived at this destination. The sequence of the cases, with English titles, is: "Killed War Prisoners"; "Hitlerites—Children Murderers" with pictures of children being tortured and killed; "Vilnius Dwellers Killed in Paneriai in 1941"; "Dwellers Killed in Paneriai 1942"; "Dwellers Killed in Paneriai 1943" with letters and lists: and "The Intellectual Polish People Killed in Paneriai in 1941–44" with text in Polish and Lithuanian.

A full-length diorama shows a burner—that is, a reconstruction of the burning of the corpses. Another panel, "Escape of the Burners Brigade," includes a photograph of three Jewish men—Dovid Kantorovic, Morduch Zaidel, and Ichak Dogin—who were corpse burners, escaped from Paneriai, and moved to

Israel after the war. It is striking that so much emphasis is given to the fact that the corpse burners were Jewish, when so little attention is given to other activities of the 70,000 Jewish victims. Jewish fatalities are underplayed throughout and are presented as only one of several categories of the dead, which include Russian POWs, Polish intellectuals, and residents of Paneriai.

Sometimes Jewish victims can be supposed in a larger panel that deals more generally with victims, as in "Dwellers Killed in Paneriai in 1944," which includes a picture of Samuel and Emma Margolis—relatives of Rachel Margolis, the partisan fighter and Vilna Ghetto survivor. Another panel is entitled, "Lithuanian Local Troops Murdered in Paneriai on May 17–21, 1944." The last panel deals with the Jews killed in Ponary.

A panel of images of the other Lithuanian killing sites universalizes the murders, as in "50,000 people of different nationalities were killed here," referring to the First Fort of Kaunas. Elsewhere, Jews are identified in smaller numbers, such as "Eisiskes: There were killed 2,500 Jews." Six Jewish sites are identified, and only the Ukmerge pine forest in Pivonija has a large number (10,239). "Locality of Mass Massacre in Lithuania" lists Kaunas IX Fort, Klaipėdos; Utena; Kaunas IV Fort, VII Fort; Alytus; Svencionys Ghetto; Forest Velruchronys: 1,159 Jews; Nemenchine: 403 Jews, 446 Jews, 25 Lithuanians; Forest in Gubernija Siauliai: 1,000 Jews; Merkine 4; Karaimai: 1,600 Jews. In Soviet times, Jews could not be identified as the victims, even though 70 percent of the dead at Paneriai were Jewish. Instead, all victims were labeled "Soviet Citizens." This euphemism has been replaced in Yiddish- and English-language panels near the museum, but the Russian- and Lithuanian-language panels still avoid accurate ethnic identification.[15]

"The Diary of a Witness to Events" panel concerns a journal kept in a buried bottle. This text is in Polish and English: "The inhabitants do not dare to go to the forest now. Ravens above are flying there. Many ravens, an entire cloud. Ravens and shots in the forest. Murderers are raging there." The narrator, Kazimierz Sakowicz, refers only to "people" being killed—not to Jews.[16]

Two Israeli flags hang in this gallery. There are fragments of a "Book of Experts in Forensic Medicine" and a section with books and photographs from the Special Commission in Paneriai. The "Trial of the Warcriminals [sic]" panel includes a picture of the war criminals who worked in Paneriai and in Vilna. There is a listing of those killed in the Vilna Jewish Ghetto.

In the grassy "park" of the killing pits, we encountered only one other visitor. Despite its difficult accessibility and its mystifications, the museum at Paneriai gives a powerful sense of the horrors that occurred in its woods. There were other mass murders near many other Lithuanian towns and cities. They are usually unmarked. To take a case in point, a Sunday afternoon visitor to Paneriai might choose not to wait three hours for a local train back to

Vilnius and choose, instead, to take an earlier train in the opposite direction to the nearby tourist destination of Trakai, from which there is an express train to Vilnius in the early evening.

In sharp contrast to the desolation of Paneriai with so few visitors, Trakai is crowded with visitors on Sunday afternoons in summer. In post-Communist, capitalist Lithuania, Trakai makes a perfect picture postcard with its red medieval castle against a deep blue lake and white sailboats, cafes and shops along the water's edge, perfect for fishing, boating, swimming, and picnicking. Trakai also has a museum established in the 1990s that celebrates the Karaites, who settled in Trakai in the late fourteenth century and had full free resident rights in contrast to the Jews. Rejecting rabbinic tradition and relying solely on written Torah, the few Karaites were spared the fate of the Jews in Lithuania. The history of Trakai in Lithuanian, or Troki in Yiddish, is that in September 1941, Lithuanians and Germans shot and drowned 2,500 Jews in the region, including all 300 Jews of Trakai.[17] There is no marker to remind visitors that the wooded island just across from the picturesque castle was a place where 2,500 people were shot and drowned in the lake in a massive ethnic cleansing. Prejudice begins with separating one group of people from the dominant culture, as the Lithuanians did by denying the Jews who lived within their borders rights of citizenship. Judeophobia culminates in murder, and it resulted in the annihilation of 96 percent of the Jews who lived in Lithuania. It continues in denial, perpetuated by the omission of the uncomfortable history and by the segmentization of that history so that it can easily be excluded from the dominant narrative, as we have seen in several examples in public museums in Vilnius. There is more striking evidence of this perspective in museums in Kaunas, Riga, and in other Lithuanian and Latvian museums of art and history.

The brutal facts, the unwillingness to accept or ascribe blame to the perpetrators of crimes against the Jews, the legacy of a complicated history and only recent release from Communist rule are all possible reasons for the resistance in Lithuania to acknowledging its complicity in the Holocaust far more so than is the case in Poland, France, Austria, and Germany today. Post-Communist Lithuania is discovering the economic benefits of capitalism, but its brutal past remains. Our observations about public acknowledgments of the Holocaust should be a caveat to all peoples that we all must acknowledge the history of the peoples in our nations. When a nation allows individual lives and stories, whole cultures, languages and literatures, customs and traditions—an entire people—to be obliterated both in fact and in memory, its national history becomes false and subjective. Can such a nation ever recover from historical amnesia? Is it possible to reconcile the past with the present and future?

NOTES

1. This chapter is part of a larger book project and represents the culmination of forty years of collaborative work on history and museums. The authors were both deeply grateful for research funding that enabled this joint project, to Edna Kantorovitz Southard from the Philip and Elaina Hampton Fund through the Office of International Education at Miami University, Ohio, and to Robert Southard through a Global Partners Mellon grant administered by the Associated Colleges of the Midwest for the Mellon Foundation, which funded research travel to Lithuania and Latvia, based on earlier travel to Poland and other parts of Europe. The research and writing were entirely collaborative. This chapter is dedicated to the memory of Robert Southard, whose sudden and untimely death prevented him from seeing it to publication.

2. The scholarly literature includes, most helpfully: Ezra Mendelsohn, *The Jews of East Central Europe Between the World Wars* (Bloomington: Indiana University Press, 1983), 213–39; Edvardas Tuskenis, Alfonsas Eidintas, Vytautas Zalys, and Alfred Erich Senn, eds., *Lithuania in European Politics: The Years of the First Republic, 1918–1940* (New York: St. Martin's Press, 1998); Joseph Rothschild, *East Central Europe between the Two World Wars* (Seattle: University of Washington Press, 1974); Dov Levin, "Lithuania," in *The World Reacts to the Holocaust*, ed. David S. Wyman (Baltimore: Johns Hopkins University Press, 1997), 325–53; Walter Lacquer, *The Holocaust Encyclopedia* (New Haven: Yale University Press, 2001); Lloyd P. Gartner, *History of the Jews in Modern Times* (Oxford: Oxford University Press, 2001).

The context and ethnic composition of this region are discussed in many scholarly works, such as the clear description in Jan T. Gross, *Revolution from Abroad: The Soviet Conquest of Poland's Western Ukraine and Western Belorussia*, expanded ed. (Princeton: Princeton University Press, 2002), 3–13; Dov Levin, *The Lesser of Two Evils: Eastern European Jewry under Soviet Rule, 1939–1941*, trans. Naftali Greenwood, (Philadelphia: Jewish Publication Society, 1995).

The paradigm for our research is indebted to parallel work on the Holocaust memory and contested memory, including recent work in other regions offering parallels and contrasts with the situation in Lithuania: Richard Ned Lebow, Wulf Kansteiner, and Claudio Fogu, eds., *The Politics of Memory in Postwar Europe* (Durham, NC: Duke University Press, 2006); Alon Confino, *Germany as a Culture of Remembrance* (Chapel Hill: University of North Carolina Press, 2006); Konrad H. Jarausch and Michael Geyer, *Shattered Past: Reconstructing German Histories* (Princeton: Princeton University Press, 2003); Lawrence L. Langer, *Holocaust Testimonies: The Ruins of Memory* (New Haven: Yale University Press, 1991); Jan-Werner Müller, *Memory and Power in Post-War Europe: Studies in the Presence of the Past* (Cambridge: Cambridge University Press, 2002); Jan T. Gross, *Neighbors: The Destruction of the Jewish Community in Jedwabne, Poland* (Princeton: Princeton University Press, 2001); Ben Shepherd, *War in the Wild East: The German Army and Soviet Partisans* (Cambridge, MA: Harvard University Press, 2004); Omer Bartov, *Germany's War and the Holocaust: Disputed Histories* (Ithaca: Cornell University Press, 2003); Leonard S. Newman and Ralph Erber, *Understanding Genocide: The*

Social Psychology of the Holocaust (Oxford: Oxford University Press, 2002); Joshua D. Zimmerman, ed., *Contested Memories: Poles and Jews during the Holocaust and Its Aftermath* (New Brunswick: Rutgers University Press, 2002) all with bibliographies of previous work.

On memorials and national identity, see John R. Gillis, ed., *Commemorations: The Politics of National Identity* (Princeton: Princeton University Press, 1994), which offers some parallels to our work on Lithuania presented here. The extensive literature on memorials still is indebted to the major work by James E. Young, *The Texture of Memory: Holocaust Memorials and Meaning* (New Haven: Yale University Press, 1993), which also examines the memorials in geographical context. See also Michael C. Steinlauf, *Bondage to the Dead: Poland and the Memory of the Holocaust* (Syracuse: Syracuse University Press, 1997); Svetlana Boym, *The Future of Nostalgia* (New York: Basic Books, 2001); Bill Niven, *Facing the Nazi Past: United Germany and the Legacy of the Third Reich* (London: Routledge, 2002).

The extensive literature in museum studies includes, relevantly, Victoria Newhouse, *Towards a New Museum*, rev. ed. (New York: Monacelli Press, 2006), and *Art and the Power of Placement* (New York: Monacelli Press, 2005). There is also extensive literature on exhibition techniques, which is consulted by curators, preparators, and other museum professionals in publications by the American Association of Museums, notably the journals *Exhibitionist* and *Museum*. Regarding the theoretical aspects of memorials in the United States today and elsewhere, in the wake of September 11, see Andreas Huyssen, *Present Pasts: Urban Palimpsests and the Politics of Memory* (Stanford: Stanford University Press, 2003), and the reaction of Erika Doss, "Memorial Mania: Fear, Anxiety and Public Culture," in *Museum* (March–April 2008), 36–43, which expresses a backlash to memorials that is further discussed in her book *Memorial Mania: Public Feeling in America* (Chicago: University of Chicago Press, 2010).

3. See especially Mendelsohn, *The Jews of East Central Europe*, 213–24. For a recent history of the invasions, see Geoffrey P. Megargee, *War of Annihilation: Combat and Genocide on the Eastern Front, 1941* (Lanham, MD, Rowman and Littlefield, 2006).

4. See Levin, "Lithuania," 333.

5. Christopher R. Browning, with contributions by Jürgen Matthäus, *The Origins of the Final Solution: The Evolution of Nazi Jewish Policy, September 1939–March 1942* (Lincoln: University of Nebraska Press, 2004), 268–78, 252–55, 244 *ff.*; Alan Palmer, *The Baltic: A New History of the Region and its People* (New York: Overlook Press, 2005), 351–52.

6. See Israel Cohen, *Vilna, 1943*, facs. ed. Esther Hautzig (Philadelphia: The Jewish Publication Society of America, 1992); N. N. Shneidman, *Jerusalem of Lithuania: The Rise and Fall of Jewish Vilnius* (Oxford: Mosaic Press, 1998); Herman Kruk, *The Last Days of the Jerusalem of Lithuania: Chronicles from the Vilna Ghetto and the Camps, 1939–1944*, ed. Benjamin Harshaw, trans. Barbara Harshaw (New Haven: Yale University Press, 2002).

7. See especially Stephen E. Weil, *Making Museums Matter* (Washington, DC: Smithsonian Institution Press, 2002); and his *Rethinking the Museum and Other Meditations* (Washington, DC: Smithsonian Institution Press, 1990); also Neil G.

Kotler, *Museum Strategy and Marketing: Designing Missions, Building Audiences, Generating Revenue and Resources* (San Francisco: Jossey-Bass Publishers, 2008).

8. The Museum of Genocide Victims, *War after War/Karas po Karo: Armed Anti-Soviet Resistance in Lithuania in 1944–53* (Vilnius: Genocide and Resistance Research Centre of Lithuania, 2004).

9. The museum is included in Grace Cohen Grossman, *Jewish Museums of the World* (Southport, CT: Universe Publishers, 2003).

10. Levin, "Lithuania," 343–44.

11. See Dina Wardi, *Memorial Candles: Children of the Holocaust*, Hebrew ed., trans. Naomi Goldblum (London: Routledge, 1992) and Edna Kantorovitz, "Rethinking the American Jewish Experience: Feathers and Other Memories of a Child of the Shoah," *American Jewish Archives Journal* XLVII, no. 1 (Spring–Summer 1995): 62–95.

12. A complete list is available at the museum. See, for example, the inspiring Rachel Kostanian-Danzig, *Spiritual Resistance in the Vilna Ghetto* (Vilnius: The Vilna Gaon Jewish State Museum, 2002).

13. An interview with Violeta Palcinskaite is published in *Jewish Renaissance* (July 2005): 21.

14. See N. N. Shneidman, *The Three Tragic Heroes of the Vilnius Ghetto: Witenberg, Sheinbaum, Gens* (Oaksville: Mosaic Press, 2002).

15. Levin, "Lithuania," 344. For complete details and pictures of the sites of mass massacre of Jews in Lithuania during the Nazi occupation, see the impressive and indispensable Yosif Levinson et al., *Skausmo Knyga: The Book of Sorrow* (Vilnius: The Vilna Gaon Jewish State Museum, 1997).

16. Kazimierz Sakowicz, *Ponary Diary 1941–43: A Bystander's Account of a Mass Murder*, ed. Yitzhak Arad (New Haven: Yale University Press, 2005).

17. Shmuel Spector and Geoffrey Wigoder, with foreword by Elie Wiesel, *The Encyclopedia of Jewish Life Before and During the Holocaust*, vol. 3 (New York: New York University Press, 2001), 1333–34.

BIBLIOGRAPHY

Adelman, Jonathan R. *Torrents of Spring: Soviet and Post-Soviet Politics*. New York: McGraw Hill, 1995.

Bartov, Omer. *Germany's War and the Holocaust: Disputed Histories*. Ithaca: Cornell University Press, 2003.

Boym, Svetlana. *The Future of Nostalgia*. New York: Basic Books, 2002.

Browning, Christopher R. With contributions by Jürgen Matthäus. *The Origins of the Final Solution: The Evolution of Nazi Jewish Policy, September 1939–March 1942*. Lincoln: University of Nebraska Press, 2004.

Cohen, Israel. *Vilna*. Edited by Esther Hautzig. Originally published as *Jewish Communities Series: Vilna* (1943). Philadelphia: The Jewish Publication Society of America, 1992.

Cohen, Norma. "Creativity Continues: Norma Cohen talks to Writers Marcus Zing-eris and Violeta Palcinskaite." In "The Jews of Lithuania," *Jewish Renaissance: Quarterly Magazine of Jewish Culture.* Vol. 4, issue 4, July 2005.

Confino, Alon. *Germany as a Culture of Remembrance.* Chapel Hill: University of North Carolina Press, 2006.

Doss, Erika. "Memorial Mania: Fear, Anxiety and Public Culture." *Museum* (March–April 2008), 36–43.

Gartner, Lloyd P. *History of the Jews in Modern Times.* Oxford: Oxford University Press, 2001.

Gillis, John R., ed. *Commemorations: The Politics of National Identity.* Princeton: Princeton University Press, 1994.

Gross, Jan T. *Neighbors: The Destruction of the Jewish Community in Jedwabne, Poland.* Princeton: Princeton University Press, 2001.

———. *Revolution from Abroad: The Soviet Conquest of Poland's Western Ukraine and Western Belorussia.* Expanded ed. Princeton: Princeton University Press, 2002.

Grossman, Grace Cohen. *Jewish Museums of the World.* Southport, CT: Universe Publishers, 2003.

Huyssen, Andreas. *Present Pasts: Urban Palimpsests and the Politics of Memory.* Stanford: Stanford University Press, 2003.

Jarausch, Konrad H. and Michael Geyer. *Shattered Past: Reconstructing German Histories.* Princeton: Princeton University Press, 2003.

Kantorovitz, Edna. "Rethinking the American Jewish Experience: Feathers and Other Memories of a Child of the Shoah." *American Jewish Archives Journal* XLVII, no. 1 (Spring–Summer 1995): 62–95.

Kjeld Boek, Esben, ed. *The Power of the Object: Museums and World War II.* London: MuseumsEtc., 2009.

Kostanian-Danzig, Rachel. *Spiritual Resistance in the Vilna Ghetto.* Vilnius: The Vilna Gaon Jewish State Museum, 2002.

Kotler, Neil G. *Museum Strategy and Marketing: Designing Missions, Building Audiences, Generating Revenue and Resources.* San Francisco: Jossey-Bass Publishers, 2008.

Kruk, Herman. *The Last Days of the Jerusalem of Lithuania: Chronicles from the Vilna Ghetto and the Camps, 1939–1944.* Edited by Benjamin Harshaw. Translated by Barbara Harshaw. New Haven: Yale University Press, 2002.

Lacquer, Walter. *The Holocaust Encyclopedia.* New Haven: Yale University Press, 2001.

Langer, Lawrence L. *Holocaust Testimonies: The Ruins of Memory.* New Haven: Yale University Press, 1991.

Lebow, Richard Ned, Wulf Kansteiner, and Claudio Fogu, ed. *The Politics of Memory in Postwar Europe.* Durham, NC: Duke University Press, 2006.

Levin, Dov. *The Lesser of Two Evils: Eastern European Jewry under Soviet Rule, 1939–1941.* Translated by Naftali Greenwood. Philadelphia: Jewish Publication Society, 1995.

————. "Lithuania." In *The World Reacts to the Holocaust*, edited by David S. Wyman. Bloomfield, MI: 1997.

Levinson, Yosif. *Skausmo Knyga: The Book of Sorrow.* Vilnius: The Vilna Gaon Jewish State Museum, 1997.

Megargee, Geoffrey P. *War of Annihilation: Combat and Genocide on the Eastern Front, 1941.* Lanham, MD: Rowman and Littlefield, 2006.

Mendelsohn, Ezra. The *Jews of East Central Europe between the World Wars.* Bloomington: Indiana University Press, 1983.

Müller, Jan-Werner. *Memory and Power in Post-War Europe: Studies in the Presence of the Past.* Cambridge: Cambridge University Press, 2002.

The Museum of Genocide Victims. *War after War/Karas po Karo: Armed Anti-Soviet Resistance in Lithuania in 1944–53.* Vilnius: The Genocide and Resistance Research Centre of Lithuania, 2004.

Newhouse, Victoria. *Art and the Power of Placement.* New York: Monacelli Press, 2005.

————. *Towards a New Museum.* Rev. Ed. New York: Monacelli Press, 2006.

Newman, Leonard S. and Ralph Erber. *Understanding Genocide: The Social Psychology of the Holocaust.* Oxford: Oxford University Press, 2002.

Nikžentaitis, Alvydas, Stefan Schreiner, and Darius Staliūnas. *The Vanished World of Lithuanian Jews.* Amsterdam and New York: Rodopi B.V., 2004.

Niven, Bill. *Facing the Nazi Past: United Germany and the Legacy of the Third Reich.* London: Routledge, 2002.

Palmer, Alan Warwick. *The Baltic: A New History of the Region and Its People.* New York: Overlook Press, 2006.

Rothschild, Joseph. *East Central Europe between the Two World Wars.* Seattle: University of Washington Press, 1977.

Sakowicz, Kazimierz. *Ponary Diary 1941–43: A Bystander's Account of a Mass Murder.* Edited by Yitzhak Arad. Foreword by Rachel Margolis. First English edition. New Haven: Yale University Press, 2005.

Shepherd, Benjamin V. *War in the Wild East: The German Army and Soviet Partisans.* Cambridge, MA: Harvard University Press, 2004.

Shneidman, N. N. *Jerusalem of Lithuania: The Rise and Fall of Jewish Vilnius.* Oaksville: Mosaic Press, 1998.

————. *The Three Tragic Heroes of the Vilnius Ghetto: Witenberg, Sheinbaum, Gens.* Oaksville: Mosaic Press, 2002.

Snyder, Timothy. *The Reconstruction of Nations: Poland, Ukraine, Lithuania, Belarus, 1569–1999.* New Haven: Yale University Press, 2003.

Spector, Shmuel, and Geoffrey Wigoder. *The Encyclopedia of Jewish Life Before and During the Holocaust.* 3 vols. New York: New York University Press, 2001.

Steinlauf, Michael C. *Bondage to the Dead: Poland and the Memory of the Holocaust.* Syracuse: Syracuse University Press, 1997.

Suziedelis, Saulius A. *The Lithuanian Peasantry of Trans-Niemen Lithuania 1807–1864: A Study of Social, Economic and Cultural Change.* PhD dissertation, University of Kansas, 1977.

————. "Memories of Destruction: Soviet Icons, Nationalist Mythology, and the Genocide of the Jews as Warring Narratives in Lithuania." Presentation at *Soviet Jewish Soldiers, Jewish Resistance, and Jews in the USSR during the Holocaust* international conference, Center for Jewish History and New York University, New York, NY, November 16–17, 2008.

Tuskenis, Edvardas, Alfonsas Eidintas, Vytautas Zalys, and Alfred Erich Senn, eds. *Lithuania in European Politics: The Years of the First Republic, 1918–1940*. New York: St. Martin's Press, 1997.

Wardi, Dina. *Memorial Candles: Children of the Holocaust*. Translated by Naomi Goldblum. London: Routledge, 1992.

Weeks, Theodore R. "A Multi-Ethnic City in Transition: Vilnius' Stormy Decade 1939–1949." *Eurasian Geography and Economics* 47, no. 4, March/April 2006, 153–175.

Weil, Stephen E. *Making Museums Matter*. Washington, D.C.: Smithsonian Institution Press, 2002.

————. *Rethinking the Museum and other Meditations*. Washington, D.C.: Smithsonian Institution Press, 1990.

Wyman, David S., ed. *The World Reacts to the Holocaust*. Baltimore: Johns Hopkins University Press, 1997.

Young, James E. *The Texture of Memory: Holocaust Memorials and Meaning*. New Haven: Yale University Press, 1993.

Zimmerman, Joshua D., ed. *Contested Memories: Poles and Jews during the Holocaust and Its Aftermath*. New Brunswick: Rutgers University Press, 2002.

Chapter Five

"Soil of Annihilation"

Czeslaw Milosz's Pastoral Poland and the Holocaust

Donna Coffey

While Czeslaw Milosz never envisioned himself as a writer of Holocaust literature, images of the Holocaust are scattered throughout his poetry and prose. Milosz, a Catholic Lithuanian/Pole originally from Vilnius, spent the war years in Warsaw and opposed the Nazis through underground publications. His opposition to the Nazis and his sympathy for the plight of Polish Jews never led him to hide or rescue Jews. He was a Holocaust bystander, and his references to the Holocaust in his writings explore the guilt, shame, and defensiveness associated with that role. Particularly after his return to Poland in the 1980s, facilitated by his status as Nobel laureate and by the collapse of Communism, Milosz was drawn into discussions within Poland regarding the complicity of Poles in the Holocaust.

Milosz's sense of national identity was never stable, given that Lithuania was his homeland, Polish was his mother tongue, and Vilnius had been claimed by Russia, Poland, Germany, and an independent Lithuania during Milosz's lifetime. Moreover, after his defection from Communist Poland in 1951, Milosz spent much of his adult life in the United States. Adam Michnik points out the irony that when Milosz won the Nobel Prize, "[a] writer who had struggled his entire life with Polishness became, at a specifiable moment, its most illustrious embodiment."[1]

Exile that he was, Milosz was preoccupied with exploring the history, landscapes, homes, and nations that shaped his identity. As Louis Iribarne comments, Milosz's "obsession with place is seen . . . in the titles of his works," such as *Native Realm*, *The Issa Valley*, *Continents*, *The Land of Ulro*, and *Unattainable Earth*.[2] In Milosz's writings about the Holocaust, there is almost always a collision between a nostalgic longing for an innocent time and place, couched in pastoral images, and a grieved acknowledgment that such a time and place, if it ever existed at all, has been irrevocably tainted by the fate of Lithuanian and Polish Jews.

Milosz earned the distinction of being hated equally by the leaders of Poland's Communist regime and by the right-wing Polish nationalists who became increasingly powerful and vocal after the fall of Communism. In retaliation for his defection to the West, the Communist regime never allowed his books to be published in Poland; he was described in Poland's *Universal Encyclopedia* as "an enemy of the Polish People's Republic."[3]

Yet when Milosz passed away in 2004, it was the right-wing All-Polish Youth who protested Milosz's burial in the abbey of Skalka, the resting place for notable Polish artists and writers. The League objected to Milosz's dual Lithuanian/Polish identity, as well as remarks Milosz, an otherwise devout Catholic, had made questioning certain Catholic orthodoxies, especially the Church's condemnation of homosexuality. Ironically, the right-wing Radio Maryja and its affiliated newspaper, *Nowy Dziennik*, also called attention to Milosz's supposed "communist sympathies," presumably because Milosz had worked for the Communist regime as an embassy official for several years before his defection.[4] After almost two weeks of arguments and negotiations, it required a telegram from the Pope in order for the burial of Milosz to take place at Skalka without disruption.

An additional issue for Milosz's nationalist opponents was Milosz's stance toward the question of Polish complicity in the Holocaust. The All-Polish Youth stated in one of its publications that it objected to Milosz's lines in the poem"My Faithful Mother Tongue" describing his Polish compatriots as "ill with their own innocence."[5] All-Polish Youth leader Jaroslaw Komorniczek stated that "[Milosz's] writing overflows with hatred for all that is Polish."[6]

Milosz's poetry had also figured in one of the key debates in Poland about Holocaust complicity, a firestorm of letters to the editor precipitated by Jan Blonski's article "The Poor Poles Look at the Ghetto" in the January 11, 1987 issue of the Catholic weekly *Tygodnik Powszechny*. Blonski drew the title of his article from Milosz's wartime poem "A Poor Christian Looks at the Ghetto"and used both that poem and Milosz's "*Campo dei Fiori*" to suggest that Poles carry within themselves a buried "feeling of guilt which we do not want to admit" in regard to the Holocaust, not because of direct complicity in most cases, but because of indifference and inaction.[7]

Of the nearly 200 letters that the editors of *Tygodnik Powszechny* received in response to Blonski's article, some supported Blonski's position, while others argued that Blonski had besmirched the honor of Poland and played into an international campaign to distort the role of the Poles in the Holocaust.[8] Milosz himself did not enter into the Blonski debate, but his sentiments on the subject may have been more complicated than the Blonski article suggests. As Blonski admits ("Poor," 36), Milosz himself was ambivalent about *"Campo dei Fiori,"* stating in *Conversations* that the poem "is a bit of a touchy subject for me" and that there was "no question of leveling any accusations" in the poem.[9] He seems to have objected to the poem being appropriated as evidence in debates about Polish complicity.

Blonski's article and other pivotal events of the past two decades, such as the debut of Claude Lanzmann's film *Shoah*, the debate about the Carmelite convent and commemorative crosses at Auschwitz, and the publication of Jan Gross's book *Neighbors*, describing how Poles massacred their Jewish neighbors in Jedwabne, have catalyzed a heated reckoning of Jewish-Catholic relations in Poland and impassioned debates about Polish guilt or innocence in regard to the Holocaust. As Antony Polonsky and Joanna B. Michlic describe in *The Neighbors Respond*, Poland in the past twenty years has undergone a "deconstruction of [its] dominant collective self-image" and of its "sanitized view of its history" as issues of Polish complicity in the Holocaust have been revisited.[10]

In the often bitter debates that have ensued, there is what Polonsky and Michlic describe as a "self-critical" faction of Poles who are willing to confront Poland's history of anti-Semitism and Polish indifference toward, or in some cases collaboration with, the destruction of the Jews. On the opposite end of the spectrum is what Polonsky and Michlic describe as the "apologetic" faction of Poles who maintain Polish innocence, emphasize Nazi destruction of Poles rather than of Jews, and view criticism of Poland as antipolonism (*Neighbors*, 33). The All-Polish Youth, the League of Polish Families, and other extreme nationalist groups form the radical end of the apologetic faction.

Clearly the All-Polish Youth who protested Milosz's burial at Skalka located Milosz within the self-critical faction. Yet their characterization of Milosz was (not surprisingly) an oversimplification. While Milosz was undoubtedly more self-critical than apologetic, his views on Polish and Lithuanian history and nationhood and on the role of Poles in the Holocaust were complicated.

Milosz's public statements about Polish complicity in the Holocaust are a mixture of self-accusation on the one hand, and defensiveness in regard to blanket condemnations of Poland on the other hand. He writes in *Native Realm*: "As an eyewitness to the crime of genocide, and therefore deprived of the luxury of innocence, I am prone to agree with the accusations brought against myself and others,"[11] and he refers in *Conversations* to the "sin of survival" (*Conversations*, 264).

Yet in his essay "Dialogue About Wilno with Tomas Venclova," he states, even as he acknowledges the history of Polish anti-Semitism, that he is "deeply offended and pained by Jewish hatred of Poles, despite their surprising forgiveness of Germans and Russians."[12] Moreover, he used the opportunity of his Nobel Prize lecture in 1980 to state that he felt "anxiety" that "the word holocaust undergoes gradual modifications, so that the word begins to belong to the history of the Jews exclusively, as if among the victims there were not also millions of Poles, Russians, Ukrainians, and prisoners of other nationalities."[13] Henryk Grynberg gently points out in his article "Appropriating the Holocaust" that Milosz, although "enlightened and well-intentioned," makes a "mistake" in universalizing the term "holocaust" in his Nobel speech, for the Jews in Poland were targeted and annihilated on a scale and in a manner altogether different from other groups.[14]

There is no question of Milosz's firm stance against anti-Semitism and of his revulsion against nationalist politics, dating back to his adolescence. His dual Lithuanian/Polish identity rendered him an outsider with a "distrust" of the nationalism of "'trueborn' Poles" (*NR*, 96). He describes in *Native Realm* his brief flirtation with and subsequent rejection of the anti-Semitism of a certain bigoted relative and his "allergy to everything that smacks of the 'national' and an almost physical disgust for people who transmit such signals" (*NR*, 95). At Stefan Batory University, he detested the right-wing fraternities for whom anti-Semitism was a rallying cry and gravitated toward the left-leaning Student Vagabonds Club. As Clare Cavanagh points out, in his poetry dating back to the 1930s, Milosz resisted the "nationalist religiosity" and "godandfatherlander" myths that have "persisted in Polish self-definition since Romanticism" ("Chaplain," 380).

Moreover, in post-Communist Poland's debates about Catholic-Jewish relations and about how the Holocaust is to be understood, Milosz used his status as a Nobel laureate to condemn anti-Semitism and to insist upon accurate and appropriate historiography and commemoration of the Holocaust. In 1997, when Father Henryk Jankowski made anti-Semitic remarks about author and political candidate Adam Michnik, Milosz objected publicly in the pages of *Tygodnik Powszechny* ("Farewell," 2). In September 1998, Milosz, along with several other Krakow intellectuals, wrote an open letter to Prime Minister Jerzy Buzek urging him to "stop the provocation" at Auschwitz, where radical Catholic groups were erecting hundreds of crosses accompanied by the distribution of anti-Semitic propaganda.[15] In 1999, Milosz signed a letter of protest to the Ministry of Education regarding the continued use of Andrzej Szczesniak's history textbooks, which explained to students that Poles were "sentenced to annihilation" by the Nazis, while Jews were merely "relocated."[16] Milosz himself wrote a history of Poland during the interwar period, *Wyprawa w Dwudziestolecie* (*An Excursion Through the Twenties and Thirties*, published in Krakow in 1999 and not yet available in English), in which he documented at length the Polish anti-Semitism of the 1930s (Polonsky and Michlic, *Neighbors*, 22). Moreover, he lent public support to the new Polish translation of the Torah by Rabbi Sacha Pecaric, who offered a eulogy at Milosz's funeral.[17]

While Milosz's activism in the last two decades of his life places him predominantly in the self-critical camp, his literary works reveal an internal struggle to come to terms with Polish and Lithuanian history, with his own role as Holocaust bystander, and with the fault lines in Christian European culture as a whole. As Stanislaw Baranczak has argued, Milosz was a "critical patriot" whose "vision of national questions does justice to both the dark and light sides of our history and of our collective character by emphasizing the profound contradictions created by the pressure of historical catastrophes."[18]

In some ways, Milosz acts out the dialogue between the self-critical and the apologetic within his poetry, and this dialogue often appears in his juxtaposition of pastoral images of bucolic Poland and Lithuania with brutal images of the Holocaust. Through this juxtaposition, he enacts the painful but ethically imperative leave-taking of a way of viewing the past, the land, and the nation, and of ways of writing about them, that could no longer be sustained. For Milosz, it is not, as Theodor Adorno suggested, poetry itself that is no longer possible, but rather a certain *kind* of poetry, a poetry that evades history in order to celebrate beauty.[19] As Terrence Des Pres notes, Milosz accepted the "terrible detour through history" that poetry had to take after the Second World War in order for "the authority of poetic affirmation" to remain plausible; Des Pres describes Milosz's style as a "poetics of aftermath."[20] Much of Milosz's poetry is an elegy to an illusion with which he reluctantly but definitively parts.

The pastoral has deep roots in Western culture, from the *Idylls* of Theocritus to the *Bucolics* of Virgil to the arcadian visions of Spenser and Shakespeare. The common theme of the pastoral is an idealization of rural life, often in an imagined golden age, in an edenic world peopled by shepherds and other rural folk living in imagined harmony with nature. The pastoral is often primitivist and nostalgic, contrasting the ills of "modern" and urban life with the imagined innocence and simplicity of earlier rural lifestyles.

Nazi ideology had drawn upon the pastoral tradition in its evocation of the innocence and purity of the Aryan folk, at one with nature. The antimodernism of the Nazis and the Nazi idealization of blood and soil were derived in large part from romantic versions of the pastoral. For these reasons, R. Clifton Spargo writes that the "the pastoral scene stands for a European tradition of poetry that had fostered the relationship between the land and the people only to be suddenly, perhaps permanently, interrupted by violence" and that "pastoral is a hypothesis of continuity, whether national, natural, or poetic, that quite possibly cannot survive the things done in its name or on its places."[21]

The relationship between the pastoral and the Holocaust is further complicated by the fact that in the tradition of European poetry, the pastoral has been intertwined with the genre of the elegy, the conventional mode for the expression of mourning. How can one write about the Holocaust without elegizing? Yet the elegy is simultaneously tainted and grossly inadequate in its reliance upon the cycles of nature for consolation. Jahan Ramazani points out in his study of twentieth-century elegy that "fierce moral objections to the compensatory imagination [of the traditional elegy] belong to a post-Holocaust vision of history." Holocaust elegies, argues Ramazani, "refuse the closure, rebirth and substitution traditional in the elegiac genre."[22] Susan Gubar, who devotes a chapter of her *Poetry After Auschwitz* to Holocaust elegy, notes that much literature of the Holocaust contains "rancorous satires against inadequate conventions of mourning"[23] and rejects the "ludicrously incommensurate elegiac tropes of consolation" (*Poetry*, 211).

Milosz's exposure and attraction to pastoral images stemmed from both his boyhood reading and his boyhood environment. As an adolescent growing up near Vilnius, Milosz was fascinated by the rural landscape and its flora and fauna. He explains in *Native Realm*: "The lakes and forests that surrounded the town gave one a sense of being constantly in touch with nature. And many times my father, whose passion for hunting provided an outlet for his excess energy, took me with him. So I was initiated early into the habits of animals and birds, into the species of trees and plants" (64). In college, he and his fellow Vagabonds reveled in outdoor adventures such as kayaking, canoeing, skiing, hiking, and camping in the lakes and forests of Vilnius and surrounding areas (*NR*, 110).

Milosz's active experience of the world of nature was framed by readings that taught him the conventional literary modes for the expression of nature's beauty. He writes in *Native Realm* about studying Latin in school, reading about the Golden Age and shepherds from the *Bucolics*, and translating the line from Ovid, "And golden from the green oak seeped the honey" (*NR*, 75). Milosz would later agree in *Conversations* that Ovid's line is echoed in his poem "Notes" in the line "Unbounded forests flowing with the honey of wild bees," a phrase that he identifies as "the archetype of all bucolic poetry" (261). Milosz was also deeply influenced by the Polish Romantic poet Adam Mickiewicz, whose narrative poem *Pan Tadeusz* shaped Milosz's perception of the Lithuanian landscape (*Conversations*, 4). As Aleksander Fiut points out, even though Milosz revolted in some ways against Mickiewicz, the "pressure of romantic tradition" and the "inheritance of national myths" had been ingrained in him since childhood.[24]

In *The Land of Ulro*, Milosz explains that the pastoral impulse was, since boyhood, a way for him to envision a better world. He writes that as a boy he:

> spent hour after hour filling his notebooks with the fantastic sketches of his ideal countries. Their borders, their lakes and rivers meant not only that I was organizing space but that I was surmounting the present tense, because they were countries as they ought to have been. They were, I must confess, not so much human habitats as secluded woodlands, sanctuaries of unspoiled wilderness, trackless, with only a network of waterways fit for canoe travel.[25]

Milosz argues as well for the political and ethical benefits of the pastoral in the section of his essay "A Semi-Private Letter About Poetry" entitled "The Arcadian Myth." This portion of the essay is a response to Kazimierz Wyka's article "Somnambulist Gardens and Pastoral Gardens," in which Wyka criticizes Milosz's Warsaw poems, especially "The World,""Voices of Poor People," and "Songs of Adrian Zielinski," for revealing an attraction to the arcadian myth and tending toward escapist aestheticism.[26] Milosz argues that "[f]aith in an arcadian myth is by no means a crime. If there were no poets to repeat continuously that humankind ought to live" in a better way, "we would turn into a species of reptiles."[27] He insists that the pastoral can function as "an indication that the world need not always be like this; it can be different" ("Semi-Private," 350). He argues that the pastoral almost always contains what he calls the "dynamism of contrast," an implicit criticism of the social order to which the pastoral provides an alternative.

The heart of Milosz's refutation of Wyka's criticisms is that there is irony in all of his pastoral moments, an irony that is sometimes a dramatic irony created by the time and place in which the poem is written and that is sometimes directly indicated in the poem. Milosz's practice of appending to each poem the place and date of composition, maintained from the Warsaw period until *From the Rising of the Sun* in 1974, creates a potential dramatic irony in every poem. Wyka had criticized Milosz's "Waltz," a poem written in Nazi-occupied Warsaw in which a woman dancing a waltz in 1910 has a prophetic vision of the Holocaust, because Milosz ends the poem by urging the woman to "Forget it. Nothing exists but this bright ballroom / And the waltz, the flowers, the lights, and the echoes."

Milosz responds to Wyka's criticism:

> Undoubtedly, dancing the waltz has more beauty in it than a vision of concentration camps. But if she weren't dancing the waltz in her delightful ignorance, there would be no dramatic conflict, there would be no poem. Was I really obligated to add a commentary with more or less the following content: "Ah, you pathetic creature, just wait, you'll get yours!"? ("Semi-Private," 346)

Milosz also points to his poem "In Warsaw," in which he writes:

> Was I born to become
> A ritual mourner?
> I want to sing of festivities,
> The greenwood into which Shakespeare
> Often took me. Leave
> To poets a moment of happiness,
> Otherwise your world will perish.

Milosz points out that the poem hinges upon the "artistic irony" that "the poet does not want to become a ritual mourner, but he is a ritual mourner" ("Semi-Private," 349). As Milosz admits in the poem "In Milan": "Yes, I would like to be a poet of the five senses, / That's why I don't allow myself to become one."[28]

His novel *Issa Valley* and the wartime sequence of poems "The World: A Naïve Poem" are the only examples within his oeuvre of a pure pastoral not directly contrasted with reminders of historical atrocity. Both present a nostalgic view of a pastoral world closely associated with the poet's childhood. Each of the twenty poems in "The World" is told from the point of view of a child living in a peaceful, secure rural environment with a sister, a brother, a nurturing mother and a wise, protective father. It is a prelapsarian world into which danger and doubt only intrude in the poem "Fear," which is followed by the reassuring poem "Recovery." Milosz says of "The World" in *Conversations* that he meant it to be a "calligraphic purification of the image free of any trace of the Nazi experience" (*Conversations*, 129) and a "creation of an artificial world as a defense against the horror" (*Conversations*, 128). The poem is a good example of the type of dramatic irony Milosz perceived in his "arcadian" moments, since the notation "Warsaw, 1943," appended to the end, reminds us that the world being described in the poem has already been destroyed.

The world described in *The Issa Valley*, written in 1955, had also been destroyed. The novel is loosely autobiographical, describing a boy growing up during the interwar period on a rural estate and glorying in his daily contact with the rivers, hills and forests surrounding Vilnius. It does seem almost Blood-and-Soil-ish in its evocation of rural life, and Milosz admits in *Conversations* to his discomfort with how popular the book became in Germany: "I thought: What the hell is this, is it the *Natur* that interests them so much?" (*Conversations*, 165). The only allusion to the Holocaust in the novel is an oblique reference at the beginning of the book to a time when "the earth was plowed up by the tracks of tanks" and "those who were about to be executed dug their own shallow graves by the river."[29]

Ewa Czarnecka, interviewing Milosz in *Conversations*, suggests to him that "the world [*The Issa Valley*] depicts is not Arcadian in the least" because "Thomas's realization of dearth and transience makes for painful initiation" (*Conversations*, 165), and Milosz agrees that "the problem of evil is there— the discovery of the world of murder, nature, the hunt" (*Conversations*, 167). As in his response to Wyka, Milosz emphasizes the irony of the novel, "irony in the sense that Blake is an ironic poet" (*Conversations*, 166). He refers to Blakean irony in discussing "The World" as well, commenting that "someone could be deluded into thinking that the entire cycle is sunny and childishly positive. That's why the date when it was written is important," like the "procedure William Blake used when juxtaposing *Songs of Innocence* and *Songs of Experience*" (*Conversations*, 128).

Ironic or not, there is something grotesque about a novel written in 1955 portraying the hills and forests around Vilnius in an idyllic light. Perhaps the most stark reminder of the uses to which the forests and hills idealized by Milosz were put during the Holocaust is the example of the Ponary forest, where some 60,000–70,000 Jews were killed and dumped in mass graves between 1941 and 1944. While Milosz does not mention Ponary by name in *The Issa Valley* (he fictionalized the names of places and people in the novel), he refers to it in several other works. In *The Land of Ulro*, he describes his boyhood self as "a romantic nature lover who in the Ponary Mountains collected specimens for a herbarium and who hunted with Józef Maruszewski on the outskirts of the Rudnicki Wilderness" (164). In *Szukanie ojczyzny* (*In Search of a Homeland*, published in Warsaw in 1992, not yet translated into English), he refers to "the petty and middle gentry of the Grand Duchy" who "attended Philaret and *Promienisci* picnics under the oaks of the Ponary Mountains."[30] In "City Without a Name," a poem to Vilnius, Milosz refers to Ponary using explicitly pastoral and elegiac imagery: "What shepherd's horn swatched in the bark of birch / Will sound in the Ponary hills memory of the absent— / Vagabonds, Pathfinders, brethren of a dissolved lodge?" (*NCP*, 214)

Surely any elegy to the "absent" of the Ponary hills should remember those who were massacred there, not just the "Vagabonds" and "Pathfinders," however "dissolved" their "lodge."[31] Milosz does include the Jews of Vilnius in his elegizing later in the poem, but it seems odd that one so attuned to the land should so bracket its transformation into a killing site. Milosz mentions his knowledge of the massacres at Ponary in passing in *Native Realm*: "I had already left my city when the Germans murdered its Jews. For that purpose they chose Ponary, a forest of oaks in the hills, the place where we went on school and university excursions" (107). Yet he never came to terms with the massacres at Ponary within his poetry. It is the poem that he *didn't* write.

"The World" and *The Issa Valley* in some ways reenact the "looking the other way" of the Holocaust bystander. Looking to the past can be a way of looking the other way, and nostalgia can be an act of denial, both because it ignores later atrocities and because it ignores the historical roots of atrocity. In many other poems, however, Milosz shows that he understands that the hills and forests and soil of Lithuania and Poland have been fundamentally altered by the Holocaust and that a nostalgic stance is no longer tenable. In the majority of his poems in which he invokes the pastoral, he does not settle for implied irony, but rather practices overt juxtaposition.

In many of Milosz's poems, he uses imagery of the soil being actually poisoned. Like Anne Michaels in *Fugitive Pieces*,[32] Milosz reverses the Nazi paradigm of Blood and Soil by literalizing it and depicting the presence of actual blood in the soil. He writes in the poem "Earth" of his "sweet European homeland": "A butterfly lighting on your flowers stains its wings with blood, / Blood gathers in the mouths of tulips . . . For one is served here a glass of poison liquor / With lees, the poison of centuries" (*NCP*, 102). The reference to "the poison of centuries" implies Milosz's awareness in 1949 not only that the soil of Europe was stained with recent blood, but also that it had been for centuries; it was *never* pure. The poison image recurs in the later poem "A Notebook: Bon by Lake Leman," in which he writes:

> And you, landscapes
> Feeding our hearts with mild warmth,
> What poison dwells in you, that seals our lips,
> Makes us sit with folded arms, and the look
> Of sleepy animals? (*Eternal*, vii)

The two poems seem to be contradictory, because in "Earth" the poison is memory, but in "A Notebook" the poison is forgetfulness. But beauty is poison because it invites an evasion of history and reduces humans to the status of "sleepy animals." In both poems, there is the insistence that human suffering outweighs natural beauty and that forgetting is neither possible nor ethical. In the poem "Legend," written in 1949, Milosz portrays the transition from historical unconsciousness to historical consciousness:

> We lived in this city
> Without caring about its past . . .
> Our age is better, we would say. No plague, no sword
> To pursue us, so why should we look back?
> Let the centuries of terror sleep in the hard earth.

Yet this lack of historical consciousness can persist only

Till that day arrived.
The makeup streamed down women's cheeks. Their rings
Rattled against the pavement. Eyes
Turned to the indifferent abysses of heavens
And accepted death. Foundations of ornate buildings
Burst, the dust of crushed brick
Rose with smoke to the sun.

From that moment, he writes, "in the sand we saw / [t]he ashes of centuries mixed with fresh blood" (*NCP*, 100) and "ever since / [w]e have had our home founded in history" (*NCP*, 101). Again, Milosz presents the insight that the land was never pure; "centuries of terror" and "ashes of centuries" were already present in the very soil.

The death of the pastoral is especially evident in the poem "Song on Porcelain" from Milosz's 1953 collection *Daylight*. In this poem, too, the soil itself has been tainted, in this case by the broken pottery crushed into the ground:

The earth wakes up, and moans.
It is the small sad cry
Of cups and saucers cracking,
The masters' precious dream
Of roses, of mowers raking,
And shepherds on the lawn.

The pastoral here is the pattern on the broken porcelain, the "masters' precious dream / Of roses, of mowers raking, / And shepherds on the lawn" (*NCP*, 81), but it is now irreparably cracked and broken. Its ahistorical and idyllic world has been shattered by history. The pastoral is the "masters' dream," perhaps a hint that Milosz associated the pastoral with Nazism, but the porcelain belonged to the masters' victims, who had literally bought into the dream. With the shattering of the porcelain's idealized depictions of nature, there is nothing to keep at bay the "black underground stream," "blackened plain," and "black loam" of new graves (*NCP*, 81); the landscape has become a wasteland. The speaker of the poem's refrain that "porcelain troubles me most" is a distancing device, a focus on things rather than people. Like some of Milosz's other poems about the war period, such as "Song of a Citizen," the poem dramatizes the bystander's attempts to detach himself from the fate of his fellow human beings. Perhaps the poem is an elegy to illusion more than it is an elegy to people.

While there are numerous other poems in which the juxtaposition of pastoral images and images of wartime destruction are present, especially "A Book in the Ruins" and "*Campo dei Fiori*," I will focus in the remainder of this chapter on the long poem *Treatise on Poetry*, written in 1955 and 1956. In this poem, Milosz returns to the subject of the war years and the Holocaust, especially in the third section entitled "The Spirit of History." In the *Treatise*, Milosz attempts to define how poetry should respond to historical events. "The Spirit of History" and the following section, "Natura," portray two temptations that Milosz ultimately rejects: the temptation to write political poetry and the temptation to evade history altogether in favor of nature. The Marxist "Spirit of History" is the scientific worldview applied to history; it is universal and deterministic, and individuals are not important in the greater and inevitable sweep of historical events. While the "Spirit of History" represents the dangers threatening Polish poetry, the "Natura" section represents the dangers Milosz identified with his own temptation to stay in America, forget about the historical traumas he witnessed, and write an essentially pastoral poetry.

In the *Treatise,* Milosz presents a choice between being, represented by Natura, and becoming, represented by the Marxist Spirit of History, and rejects both in favor of a poetry that neither evades nor subsumes human suffering. The fragmented, multi-voiced, and densely allusive structure of the *Treatise* models the type of poetry Milosz envisions. It is not a dialectic because there is no resolution, no synthesis of thesis and antithesis, whether between the Spirit of History and the Spirit of Nature or between the willfully ignorant voices of Polish peasants and the agonized voices of dying Jews. As Stanislaw Baranczak has pointed out, Milosz's technique comes close to what Bakhtin called Dostoyevskian polyphony, an attempt to "multiply testimonies belonging to various points of view, value systems, voices."[33] In some ways, Milosz might be aiming at what Shoshana Felman suggests that Claude Lanzmann accomplishes in his film *Shoah*: to "create a *connection* that did not exist during the war and does not exist today *between the inside and the outside*—to set them both in motion and in dialogue with one another."[34] Yet Milosz's *Treatise* is not really a dialogue, because the speakers do not listen to one another, or even see one another. The Poles in the poem act much like the Poles in Lanzmann's film, as described by Felman: "as bystanders, they do not quite *look*, they avoid looking directly, and thus they *overlook* at once their responsibility and their complicity as witnesses" ("Return," 208).

The *Treatise* is one of the few works in which Milosz touches upon the collective guilt of Poland in the Holocaust. In "The Spirit of History" section of the *Treatise*, he juxtaposes the voices of Jewish victims and Christian peasants. Pastoral motifs in this section are connected to what Milosz calls in the poem the "golden house of *is*."[35] He explains in his notes to the poem that as a reaction to the concept of evolution, both scientific and historical, "man started to look with nostalgia to a lost, golden house of being" (*Treatise*, 107).

In political terms, Milosz equates the house with Polish nationalism, and in the poem it emerges in evocations of traditional poetry, rural landscapes, and Polish folk traditions. He asks, "Lutes, arcadian groves, and leaves of laurel / Bright ladies, princes with consorts, where are you?" (*Treatise*, 31). In poetry of the time before, "[b]ooks were still governed by the old rule, / [b]orn of a belief that visible beauty / is a little mirror for the beauty of being" (*Treatise*, 35). This "golden house of *is*" is threatened by the Spirit of History, whose "face is the size of ten moons" and who "wears / [a]bout his neck a chain of severed heads" (*Treatise*, 31). The Spirit of History isn't bothered by the smell of the crematorium because "he likes these countries washed/ [b]y a deluge, deprived of shape and now ready" (*Treatise*, 30). As Milosz points out in *Conversations*, it was a Communist friend who had said to him, "What difference do a million people make, either way?" (177).

Yet even though the Spirit of History is the ostensible monster in the poem, its methodical impersonality is far less disturbing than the juxtaposed images of Jewish victims and Polish peasantry. One of the first images in the poem is of an "old Jew, tossed in a clay pit" whose "moans subside only when the sun comes up" (*Treatise*, 30). But no one else in the poem is listening, not the peasant woman smuggling butter or Stanislaw and Henryk navigating a steamer down the Vistula. Milosz alternates between the dying words of a man in a concentration camp and the "awkward speech of Slavic peasants" and their centuries-old "rustling rhymes" and Christmas carols (*Treatise*, 39). The invocation of Christmas carols can only be grotesque in such a context and forms an extreme example of the willful denial of bystanders.

The guilt of the bystanders emerges at one point in the poem, where Milosz writes that "[t]he survivors ran through fields, escaping / [f]rom themselves, knowing they wouldn't return / [f]or a hundred years" and that "[t]ill the end of their days all of them / [c]arried the memory of their cowardice" (*Treatise*, 35). Yet the words of the Jewish victims in the poems suggest their awareness that *they* will *not* be remembered. The man in the concentration camp carves words on the walls of his cell, beats a rhythm on an "empty can," and writes in a diary that is hidden between bricks and may only someday be unearthed.

The section about young Jewish girls who have died is a parody of traditional elegy. The narrator of the poem calls it a "song for ladies in a pretty season / [w]hose meaning time just happened to reverse" and lists their names, "Miriam, Sonia, Rachel," paralleling the list of names in Francois Villon's "Where are the snows of yesteryear," which Milosz invokes in the following section. Images of spring accompany the insistence that "[a]bove our bodies . . . [g]rass will thrive" (*Treatise*, 39–40). Yet this conventional mechanism of elegiac consolation cannot withstand the truth of how the girls died and the hideous irony of invoking cranes, rosy pebbles, tulips, and the "young leaves of the oak" accompanied by the statement that the girls' "only joy" is "vengeance" (*Treatise*, 39).

   While traditional elegiac consolation hinges upon the fact that nature is cyclical and the land will bloom again, Milosz implies in the poem that the land will not in fact ever be the same. Earlier in the poem, he had written that for the fleeing survivors, "[b]efore them were spread / [t]hose quicksands where a tree changes into nothing, / [i]nto an anti-tree" (*Treatise*, 35). Later in the poem he quotes a line from Mickiewicz, "a castle sits on the Nowogródek hill," but in the wasteland that the Holocaust has created there are only "[p]lains, empty and misty, to the Ural Mountains" (*Treatise*, 40-41). One of the narrators says that "[w]hat we do need are forests, clear waters. / [f]or there's nothing here to defend a man" from the "void of the horizon" (*Treatise*, 41). Indeed, the man in the concentration camp curses the very earth, proclaiming,

> Soil of annihilation, soil of hate,
> No word will purify it ever.
> No such poet will be born.
>
> For even if one had been called, he walked
> Beside us to the last gate, for only
> A child of the ghetto could utter the words. (*Treatise*, 38)

Milosz comments upon the poem in *Conversations*, "all that's left is an earth that is burdened, blood-stained, desecrated. . . . The crime burdening the land was the crime against the Jews" (178).

   It's ironic, then, that Milosz follows his most bitter indictment of the pastoral in "The Spirit of History" with the section "Natura," which contains his strongest temptation toward the pastoral. In this poem, nature is America, portrayed in positive images of beavers and roses. The temptation is to stay there, live on a farm, flee memories of the past and engagement with politics, and write contemplative poetry, the poetry of being rather than becoming: "Why not / Sit down at a rough country table and compose / An ode in the old manner?" (*Treatise*, 56). Milosz perceives America as historyless and memoryless, a blank slate. For a moment he seems almost Rousseauian, stating that his "covenant" with "society" has been "broken" (*Treatise*, 53) and presenting an image of "man, naked and mortal" (*Treatise*, 54). Yet he rejects the "peaceful silence" and "eternal moment" and chooses instead to write poetry that "rais[es] the dust of names and of events" even though "they disappear / [i]n a thousand sparks and we with them" (*Treatise*, 58). Poetry must incorporate history, not as impersonal necessity but as individualized memory, in order to "rescue human beings" (*Treatise*, 52). He ends the poem with the image of a voyage back to Europe, not to the "isles of bliss," for "storm winds have drowned" the stanzas of Horace that he learned in school (*Treatise*, 61), but rather to what the dying man earlier in the poem had called the "soil of annihilation."

Torn between the temptation to endorse an illusory and consoling version of home and history and a sense of moral responsibility to tell the truth about the "crime against the Jews" that "desecrated" his homeland(s), Milosz chose the latter, both in his poetry and in his public life upon his return to Poland. In his poetry, he does not attempt to ventriloquize Holocaust victims, but rather to portray the enduring and unresolved chasm between Jewish victims and Polish and Lithuanian bystanders. His purpose is neither to indict nor to defend himself and his compatriots, but rather to portray how things were at that time. The mixture of guilt, helplessness, denial, indifference, and grief experienced by the bystander is articulated in his poetry. His contrast of pastoral images and Holocaust images simultaneously elegizes the ideal of his country as he wished it could have been and the Jewish victims whose deaths have changed the land forever.

CODA: THE SQUARE ROOT OF GENOCIDE

In the years since Milosz's death, Poland continues to grapple with the legacies of World War II and the Holocaust. The election of the conservative nationalist Kaczynski brothers, Lech and Jaroslaw, as President and Prime Minister in 2005 and 2006, in a coalition with the far-right League of Polish Families and the leftist populist Andrzej Lepper, perpetuated a climate of intolerance toward minority groups, especially homosexuals, and led to an escalation of tensions with Germany regarding the repercussions and historiography of World War II and the Holocaust. In Summer 2007, three developments revealed the ways in which Poland continues to be haunted by its wartime experiences: a conflict with Germany over Poland's representation within the European Union (EU); a change in the nomenclature of the Auschwitz site; and the groundbreaking for the Museum of the History of Polish Jews on the site of the Warsaw Ghetto.

In June 2007, the Kaczynski brothers' invocation of Germany's devastation of Poland during World War II as an argument for greater voting rights for Poland within the European Union shocked the European community. Prime Minister Jaroslaw Kaczynski argued that, "If Poland had not had to live through the years of 1939–1945, Poland would be looking at the demographics of a country of 66 million," rather than the approximately 38 million that Poland had by that time, and thus should be granted votes in the EU proportionate to what its population *would* have been.[36]

The original plan in the proposed EU treaty was based on a "double major-ity" provision, in which decisions within the EU's governing council would require approval by 55 percent of all EU states representing 65 percent of the EU's total population. The Polish delegation argued for an alternative plan in which votes would be based on the square root of each country's popula-tion, a system that would lead to greater representation for smaller countries. Poland threatened to veto the new EU constitution if it included the "double majority" voting system. Indeed, President Lech Kaczynski declared his willingness to "die for the square root." After much negotiation, the crisis was averted by a compromise in which a new voting system would not be introduced until 2014 ("At Talks").

In many ways, the EU treaty crisis was a showdown between Poland and Germany, which Lech Kaczynski accused of "dictating" the direction of the EU.[37] In an interview after the compromise was reached, Prime Minister Ja-roslaw Kaczynski stated that

> I will never accept a situation where it is forbidden to mention Germany and allowed to mention Poland in the context of the Holocaust. This type of political correctness is simply destructive. Unfortunately, we have been forced by the cir-cumstances to remind everyone who was the victim and who was the oppressor during WWII. While we have to tackle property compensation claims resulting from the war, Poland cannot even say how things were back then."[38]

In alluding to "property compensation claims," Kaczynski may have been referring to the Polish government's plan to allot 65–70 billion zlotys (23.6–25.4 billion dollars) to settle the claims of people whose property was nationalized by the postwar Communist regime. Approximately 17 percent of these claims are from people of Polish-Jewish origin, a fact that prompted Father Tadeusz Rydzyk, the head of the right-wing, anti-Semitic radio station Radio Maryja, to proclaim that, "You know what this is about; Poland giving [the Jews] 65 billion dollars. They will come to you and say, 'Give me your coat! Take off your trousers! Give me your shoes!'" according to a recording obtained by the Polish weekly *Wprost*.[39]

Kaczynski may also have been referring to the claims pressed by Germans who were displaced from Poland at the end of World War II and who are still demanding compensation for lost property. Erika Steinbach, a member of the German parliament and the head of the German Federation of Expellees, has called for Poland to pay damages to Germans displaced from Polish and Czech territory after the war. Steinbach's proposal infuriated Poles, and an issue of *Wprost* in 2003 depicted Steinbach in Nazi garb sexually dominat-ing Gerhard Schroeder after the then-chancellor received a visit from her, although neither he nor present chancellor Angela Merkel have endorsed the group's claims ("German Report"). Another German group representing German expellees, the Prussian Claims Trust, filed for compensation from Poland with the European Court of Human Rights in Strasbourg, and a television series in Germany in summer 2007 about German postwar refugees was enormously popular among German viewers.[40]

The Kaczynski brothers' comments about Germany and Father Rydzyk's slurs against Polish Jews reflect Poland's continuing resentment toward both the Germans who decimated their country and the Jews for whose fate they wish to exonerate themselves. Both resentments were reflected in Poland's request that the name of the Auschwitz site be changed from "Auschwitz Concentration Camp" to "Auschwitz-Birkenau German Nazi Concentration and Extermination Camp (1940–1945)," a change approved by the UNESCO World Heritage Committee the same week that Poland almost scuttled the EU treaty with references to the German decimation of the Polish population.[41] Poland proposed the change in order to "remind future visitors and tourists that the Poles neither built nor had a hand in running the facility."[42] Poland's Deputy Minister of Culture, Tomasz Merta, argued that international news reports often refer to Auschwitz in terms that make the Poles seem responsible for it, such as "Polish concentration camp or Polish holocaust. And then, in the Polish foreign office, they tried to count how many of these terms were present in newspapers all over the world. And it wasn't 10 or 12, but it was two or three hundreds."[43]

The same week in June 2007 in which Poland bucked the EU and in which the Auschwitz name change became official, ground was broken for the new Museum of the History of Polish Jews on the site of the Warsaw Ghetto, with President Lech Kaczynski in attendance. The $65 million museum is financed in large part by public Polish funds and chronicles Polish Jewish culture over the course of its thousand-year history, with only about 15–20 percent of the exhibits focusing on the Holocaust. Barbara Kirshenblatt-Gimblett, an American scholar who led the international team to develop the exhibition, said that its goal is to show the "complex spectrum of relations" between Catholic Poles and Jewish Poles, ranging from tolerance to discrimination. Kirshenblatt-Gimblett commented that, "Polish-Jewish relations is [sic] usually understood as anti-Semitism, but the subject is much broader and we want our visitors to understand that range of interactions."[44]

Witold Zygulski, news editor for the English-language weekly *Warsaw Voice*, stated that he hadn't "heard about any controversy apart from the shouting of a very small group of nationalists" and that the broad public support for the museum showed "increasing awareness among Poles of the need to create an institutional memory of Poland's past."[45] Most Poles today continue to negotiate the delicate balance between the apologetic and the self-critical modeled by Milosz, who probably would have endorsed both the Auschwitz name change and the establishment of the Jewish museum in Warsaw. As Milosz wrote, "No word will [ever] purify" the soil of Poland, yet memorials such as the Jewish Museum are at least an attempt to remember the culture and contributions of Polish Jews, who were 3 million before the Holocaust, 300,000 after the Holocaust, and now number 30,000. But how can the lost ever be adequately represented, either politically or artistically?

NOTES

1. Adam Michnik, "Milosz Has Gone," *Common Knowledge* 11, no. 2 (February 2005): 176.

2. Louis Iribarne, "Lost in the 'Earth-Garden': The Exile of Czeslaw Milosz," *World Literature Today* 73, no. 4 (April 1999): 642.

3. Adam Michnik," A Farewell to Czeslaw Milosz," last modified 2004, www .newschool.edu/tcds/Milosz1, 2. In subsequent references, referred to as "Farewell."

4. Clare Cavanagh, "Chaplain of Shades: The Ending of Czeslaw Milosz," *Poetry* 185, no. 5 (May 2005): 380. In subsequent references, referred to as "Chaplain."

5. Tomasz Kitlinski, Pawel Leszkowicz and Joe Lockard, "Poland's Transition: From Communism to Fundamentalist Hetero-Sex," *Bad Subjects* 72 (2005): 8, http:// bad.eserver.org/issues/2005/72/kitlinskileszkowiczlockard.html.

6. Andrew Powers, "Hecklers Protest Nobel Winner's Funeral Plan," *New Warsaw Express* 34, no. 108 (2004): 2.

7. Jan Blonski, "The Poor Poles Look at the Ghetto," in *My Brother's Keeper?: Recent Polish Debates on the Holocaust*, ed. Antony Polonsky (New York: Routledge, 1990), 34. In subsequent references, referred to as "Poor."

8. Antony Polonsky, "Introduction," in *My Brother's Keeper?*, 1–33.

9. Eva Czarnecka and Aleksander Fiut, *Conversations with Czeslaw Milosz*, trans. Richard Lourie (New York: Harcourt Brace Jovanovich, 1987), 131. In subsequent references, referred to as *Conversations.*

10. Antony Polonsky and Joanna B. Michlic, *The Neighbors Respond: The Controversy over the Jedwabne Massacre in Poland* (Princeton: Princeton University Press, 2004), 33–34. In subsequent references, referred to as *Neighbors.*

11. Czeslaw Milosz, *Native Realm*, trans. Catherine S. Leach (London: Sidgwick and Jackson, 1981), 105. In subsequent references, referred to as *NR.*

12. Czeslaw Milosz, "Dialogue About Wilno with Tomas Venclova," in *Beginning with My Streets: Essays and Recollections*, trans. Madeline G. Levine (New York: Farrar, Straus, Giroux, 1991), 35.

13. Czeslaw Milosz, *Nobel Lecture* (New York: Farrar, Straus, Giroux, 1980), 16.

14. Henryk Grynberg, "Appropriating the Holocaust," *Commentary* 74, no. 5 (May 1982): 55.

15. "Polish Nobel Winners Slam Government Over Crosses," *Jewish News Weekly of Northern California*, October 9, 1998.

16. Michael C. Steinlauf, "Teaching About the Holocaust in Poland," in *Contested Memories: Poles and Jews during the Holocaust and Its Aftermath*, ed. Joshua D. Zimmerman (New Brunswick, N.J.: Rutgers University Press, 2003), 266.

17. Elaine Kahn, "First Polish Translation of Torah Since Shoah," *New Jersey Jewish Standard*, January 12, 2006.

18. Stanislaw Baranczak, "*Czeslaw Milosz laureatem literackiej nagrody Nobla*," *W drodze* 10, no. 6 (June 1980), quoted in Aleksander Fiut, *The Eternal Moment: The Poetry of Czeslaw Milosz* (Berkeley: University of California Press, 1990), 100.

19. See Theodor Adorno, "Cultural Criticism and Society," in *Prisms*, trans. Shierry Weber Nicholsen and Samuel Weber (Cambridge, MA: MIT Press, 1983). Milosz refers to Adorno's admonition in his essay "Anus Mundi" in *To Begin Where I Am: Selected Essays*, ed. and trans. Bogdana Carpenter and Madeline G. Levine (New York: Farrar, Straus, Giroux, 2001) and comments: "I wrote idyllic verses, 'The World' and a number of others, in the very center of what was taking place in the *anus mundi*, and not by any means out of ignorance. Do I deserve to be condemned for this? Possibly, it would be just as good to write either a bill of accusation or a defense" (371).

20. Terrence Des Pres, "Czeslaw Milosz: The Poetry of Aftermath," *The Nation*, Dec. 30, 1978, 741, 743.

21. R. Clifton Spargo, *The Ethics of Mourning: Grief and Responsibility in Elegiac Literature* (Baltimore: Johns Hopkins University Press, 2005), 225–226.

22. Jahan Ramazani, *Poetry of Mourning: The Modern Elegy from Hardy to Heaney* (Chicago: University of Chicago Press, 1994), 70, 8.

23. Susan Gubar, *Poetry after Auschwitz: Remembering What One Never Knew* (Bloomington: Indiana University Press, 2003), 210. In subsequent references, referred to as *Poetry*.

24. Aleksander Fiut, *The Eternal Moment: The Poetry of Czeslaw Milosz* (Berkeley: University of California Press, 1990), 101. In subsequent references, referred to as *Eternal*.

25. Czeslaw Milosz, *The Land of Ulro*, trans. Louis Iribarne (New York: Farrar, Straus, Giroux, 1984), 273. In subsequent references, referred to as *LU*.

26. Kazimierz Wyka, "Somnambulist Gardens and Pastoral Gardens," *Twórczość* [*Creative Writing*], May 1946.

27. Czeslaw Milosz, "A Semi-Private Letter About Poetry," in *To Begin Where I Am: Selected Essays*, 347–348. In subsequent references, referred to as "Semi-Private."

28. Czeslaw Milosz, *New and Collected Poems 1931–2001* (New York: Ecco, 2003), 170. In subsequent references, referred to as *NCP*.

29. Czeslaw Milosz, *The Issa Valley*, trans. Louis Iribarne (New York: Farrar, Straus, and Giroux, 1981), 7.

30. Zdzislaw Krasnodebski, *Democracy at the Periphery*, last modified 2003, www.ruf.rice.edu/~sarmatia/404/242kras.html.

31. For a bystander's account of the massacres at Ponary, see Kazimierz Sakowicz, *Ponary Diary 1941–1943: A Bystander's Account of a Mass Murder* (New Haven: Yale University Press, 2005). The diary was first published in Poland only

in 1999, after editor Rachel Margolis painstakingly tracked down the manuscripts in Lithuania. See also *The Good Old Days: The Holocaust as Seen By Its Perpetrators and Bystanders*, ed. Ernst Klee, Willi Dressen, and Volker Riess (New York: Free Press, 1991).

32. See Donna Coffey, "Blood and Soil in Anne Michaels' *Fugitive Pieces*," *Modern Fiction Studies* 53(10): 27–49.

33. Stanislaw Baranczak, "Milosz' Poetic Language," *Language and Style* 18 (1985): 321.

34. Shoshana Felman, "The Return of the Voice: Claude Lanzmann's *Shoah*," in *Testimony: Crises of Witnessing in Literature, Psychoanalysis and History*, ed. Shoshana Felman and Dori Laub (New York: Routledge, 1992), 232. In subsequent references, referred to as "Return."

35. Czeslaw Milosz, *A Treatise on Poetry*, trans. Robert Hass and Czeslaw Milosz (New York: Ecco Press, 2001), 35. In subsequent references, referred to as *Treatise.*

36. Stephen Castle and Dan Bilefsky, "At Talks on Europe's Charter, a Crisis Averted, for Now," *New York Times*, June 23, 2007. In subsequent references, referred to as "At Talks."

37.

38. "Jaroslaw Kaczynski: Poland Stronger After EU Summit Despite Trouble at Home," *Polish News Bulletin*, June 28, 2007.

39. "Controversial Catholic Radio Boss Slams Polish President over Jews," *Agence France Presse: English*, July 9, 2007.

40. Harry De Quetteville and Hannah Cleaver, "Ghosts of Past Haunt Merkel in Poland: German War Refugees' Demands Threaten to Reopen," *Ottawa Citizen*, March 16, 2007, A13.

41. Ray Lilley, "World Heritage Committee Renames Auschwitz Death Camp," *Associated Press Worldstream*, June 28, 2007.

42. "Auschwitz Death Camps Renamed at Poland's Request," *CBC News*, June 28, 2007.

43. Melissa Block, Anchor, and Emily Harris, Reporter, "Poland Appeals to Label Auschwitz 'German,'" National Public Radio, *All Things Considered*, June 22, 2007.

44. Vanessa Gera, "Poland's New Jewish Museum to Mark Community's Thousand-Year History," *Associated Press Worldstream*, June 24, 2007.

45. "Polish Museum Draws Scant Protest," *The Jewish Daily Forward*, June 29, 2007, A5.

BIBLIOGRAPHY

Adorno, Theodor. "Cultural Criticism and Society."In *Prisms*, translated by Shierry Weber Nicholsen and Samuel Weber. Cambridge, MA: MIT Press, 1983.

Baranczak, Stanislaw. *"Czeslaw Milosz laureatem literackiej nagrody Nobla."W drodze* 10, no. 6 (June 1980).

———. "Milosz' Poetic Language." *Language and Style* 18 (1985): 319–333.

Blonski, Jan. "The Poor Poles Look at the Ghetto." In *My Brother's Keeper?: Recent Polish Debates on the Holocaust*, edited by Antony Polonsky, 34–52. New York: Routledge, 1990.

Cavanagh, Clare. "Chaplain of Shades: The Ending of Czeslaw Milosz." *Poetry* 185, no. 5 (May 2005): 378–387.

Coffey, Donna. "Blood and Soil in Anne Michaels' *Fugitive Pieces*: The Pastoral in Holocaust Literature." *Modern Fiction Studies* 53, no. 1 (January 2007): 27–49.

Czarnecka, Eva and Aleksander Fiut. *Conversations with Czeslaw Milosz*. Translated by Richard Lourie. New York: Harcourt Brace Jovanovich, 1987.

Des Pres, Terrence. "Czeslaw Milosz: The Poetry of Aftermath." *The Nation*, Dec. 30, 1978, 741–743.

Felman, Shoshana. "The Return of the Voice: Claude Lanzmann's *Shoah*." In *Testimony: Crises of Witnessing in Literature, Psychoanalysis and History*, edited by Shoshana Felman and Dori Laub, 204–283. New York: Routledge, 1992.

Fiut, Aleksander. *The Eternal Moment: The Poetry of Czeslaw Milosz*. Berkeley: University of California Press, 1990.

Gross, Jan. *Neighbors: The Destruction of the Jewish Community in Jedwabne, Poland*. Princeton: Princeton University Press, 2001.

Grynberg, Henryk. "Appropriating the Holocaust." *Commentary* 74, no. 5 (May 1982): 54–57.

Gubar, Susan. *Poetry after Auschwitz: Remembering What One Never Knew*. Bloomington: Indiana University Press, 2003.

Iribarne, Louis. "Lost in the 'Earth-Garden': The Exile of Czeslaw Milosz." *World Literature Today* 73, no. 4 (April 1999): 637–643.

Kitlinski, Tomasz, Pawel Leszkowicz and Joe Lockard. "Poland's Transition: From Communism to Fundamentalist Hetero-Sex." *Bad Subjects* 72 (2005). http://bad.eserver.org/issues/2005/72/kitlinskileszkowiczlockard.html.

Klee, Ernst, Willi Dressen, and Volker Riess, ed. *The Good Old Days: The Holocaust as Seen by Its Perpetrators and Bystanders*. New York: Free Press, 1991.

Krasnodebski, Zdzislaw. *Democracy at the Periphery*. 2003. Accessed via www.ruf.rice.edu/~sarmatia/404/242kras.html.

Michaels, Anne. *Fugitive Pieces*. New York: Vintage Books, 1996.

Michnik, Adam. "A Farewell to Czeslaw Milosz." 2004. www.newschool.edu/tcds/Milosz1.

———. "Milosz Has Gone." *Common Knowledge* 11, no. 2 (February 2005): 175–184.

Milosz, Czeslaw. "Anus Mundi." In *To Begin Where I Am: Selected Essays*, edited and translated by Bogdana Carpenter and Madeline G. Levine. New York: Farrar, Straus, Giroux, 2001.

———. "Dialogue about Wilno with Tomas Venclova." In *Beginning with My Streets: Essays and Recollections*, translated by Madeline G. Levine, 23–57. New York: Farrar, Straus, Giroux, 1991.

———. *The Issa Valley*. Translated by Louis Iribarne. New York: Farrar, Straus, Giroux, 1981.

———. *The Land of Ulro*. Translated by Louis Iribarne. New York: Farrar, Straus, Giroux, 1984.

————. *Native Realm*. Translated by Catherine S. Leach. London: Sidgwick and Jackson, 1981.

————. *New and Collected Poems 1931–2001*. New York: Ecco, 2003.

————. *Nobel Lecture*. New York: Farrar, Straus, Giroux, 1980.

————. "A Semi-Private Letter About Poetry." In *To Begin Where I Am: Selected Essays*, edited and translated by Bogdana Carpenter and Madeline G. Levine. New York: Farrar, Straus, Giroux, 2001.

————. *A Treatise on Poetry*. Translated by Robert Hass and Czeslaw Milosz. New York: Ecco Press, 2001.

Polonsky, Antony. "Introduction." In *My Brother's Keeper?: Recent Polish Debates on the Holocaust*, edited by Antony Polonsky, 1–33. New York: Routledge, 1990.

Polonsky, Antony and Joanna B. Michlic. *The Neighbors Respond: The Controversy over the Jedwabne Massacre in Poland*. Princeton: Princeton University Press, 2004.

Ramazani, Jahan. *Poetry of Mourning: The Modern Elegy from Hardy to Heaney*. Chicago: University of Chicago Press, 1994.

Sakowicz, Kazimierz. *Ponary Diary 1941–1943: A Bystander's Account of a Mass Murder*. New Haven: Yale University Press, 2005.

Spargo, R. Clifton. *The Ethics of Mourning: Grief and Responsibility in Elegiac Literature*. Baltimore: Johns Hopkins University Press, 2005.

Steinlauf, Michael C. "Teaching about the Holocaust in Poland." In *Contested Memories: Poles and Jews During the Holocaust and Its Aftermath*, edited by Joshua D. Zimmerman. New Brunswick, N.J.: Rutgers University Press, 2003.

Wyka, Kazimierz. "Somnambulist Gardens and Pastoral Gardens," *Twórczość* [*Creative Writing*], May 1946.

Chapter Six

Disgrace and Torment

The Holocaust in
Zofia Nałkowska's Medallions

Zofia Lesinska

To the memory of a Jewish tailor who always cracked a good joke when
he visited my grandmother's home before the war. His name lived beyond
his death in my mother's fond childhood memories. The last time that
she saw him, she was thirteen. She looked out of the window, and he was
among the Jews herded on the streets of Lublin on their way to Majdanek.
After her death, over ten years ago, I cannot remember his name any more.

INTRODUCTION

In 1946, the Polish writer Zofia Nałkowska published *Medallions*, a forty-
page collection of documentary nonfiction in which she honored the victims
of the Holocaust, captured the voices of survivors, confronted the problematic position of Polish bystanders, and offered her own testimony both as a
private and a public person. Although *Medallions* was faithful neither to the
dictates of Socialist realism nor to the Stalinist party line, upon its publication
in 1946, the collection became part of the literary canon. It has been required
reading in Polish secondary schools for nearly six decades.

Thirty years ago, when I was a teenager in the People's Republic of Poland,
Medallions challenged my sense of national identity and my assumptions
about Polish history. It remained relevant during the political and intellectual
upheavals of the 1980s and 1990s, when Jews and Poles started a painful
dialogue about the Holocaust.[1] My friends' children in twenty-first century
democratic Poland will need to review *Medallions* before their secondary
school exit exams. In other words, this book is familiar to three generations
of educated Poles, and it continues to be relevant and disquieting.

Belatedly, in 2001, thanks to the efforts of the translator and scholar Diana Kuprel, *Medallions* was published in English with Kuprel's excellent introduction. Nałkowska's work is a valuable addition to the body of Holocaust representations available in English. In the context of American culture, the thought-provoking edge of *Medallions* consists in the book's ability to expose the incompatibility of Holocaust survivors' experiences with the optimism of conventional survival narratives.

Nałkowska (1885–1954) was already a prominent author during the interwar period, when she published several novels that positioned her as a social critic and a feminist. Secularism and left-wing leanings were part of her family tradition. Both before and after World War II, she enjoyed celebrity status at functions attended by dignitaries and artists, which for some proves Nałkowska's vanity, and for others confirms her charisma.[2] Nałkowska's commitment to progressive politics, her interest in the mechanics of power, and her graciousness as a self-effacing listener won her more friends than enemies. Interested in psychology in her prewar work, she probed the complexity of human motivations and emotions. To the extent that any analogy is ever accurate, Zofia Nałkowska was as important for twentieth-century Polish literature as Virginia Woolf was for twentieth-century literature in English.

Despite Nałkowska's literary credentials, the subjective position from which she wrote about the Holocaust might be seen as problematic.[3] Nałkowska was not Jewish and she did not experience Nazi prisons or camps. Like most ordinary Poles, she was a bystander, an onlooker, a witness. Her personal wartime experiences and the perspective that she brought to *Medallions* belong to the ambiguous territory between perpetrator and victim. At least since the 1980s, when Claude Lanzmann's film *Shoah* became a classic, Holocaust scholars have been preoccupied with exploring the complicity of collaborators, witnesses and bystanders.[4] In this context, Nałkowska's *Medallions* is an important source that captures an early testimony of a witness aware of her and her compatriots' problematic position vis-à-vis the suffering of the Jews during the Second World War.

Nałkowska spent the five years of Nazi occupation in Poland mostly in Warsaw. The writer's wartime diary records her everyday struggles for basic necessities amidst poverty, evictions from apartments, and the litany of deaths among friends, family, and acquaintances. *Dzienniki 1939–1944* (*Diaries*) also captures the author's despair and emotional disintegration during the Warsaw Ghetto Uprising in 1943. In the entry dated April 29, 1943, the tenth day of the uprising, Nałkowska wrote:

> That I am alive beside this, and I can live! But I am doing really badly; I am
> changing into someone else. How can I be forced to be part of this, to consent to
> this by being alive? And it is a disgrace, not only torment. It is a horrible shame,

not only sympathy. All efforts to stand this—not to go mad, not to lose oneself in this horror—feel like guilt.[5]

The guilt, shame, and perplexity that Nałkowska experienced during the war cracked the boundaries of her ethical self. Witnessing Nazi rule in Poland, particularly the murder of Jews, defied her prewar understanding of culture and human nature. She turned sixty in 1945 and felt ashamed to be alive after millions had perished.

The author's fractured self found its parallel in the fragmented form of *Medallions*. The eight texts in this small collection are brief: they range from three to seven pages. All of them approach history from different perspectives. *Medallions* juxtaposes dry journalistic reports and interviews with survivor testimonies recorded with little commentary. Two bystanders' accounts in the collection display characteristics of short fiction: though one is an autobiographical text, the other reads like a story shared by an acquaintance during the war. Finally, the panoramic summation at the end of the collection invokes the discourse of political history and exposes its limitations.

In an interview, Nałkowska stated that her method in the writing of *Medallions* was not the result of a conscious decision. Rather, it was the subject matter, "so difficult to comprehend, so emotionally unbearable," that dictated the shape of her responses to the Holocaust.[6] In other words, in *Medallions* the author felt that the theme of Nazi genocide exceeded the frameworks of familiar literary and historical narrative forms.

Nałkowska realized that the discourse of testimony is particularly appropriate for communicating and assessing Holocaust trauma. In *Medallions* the author's own voice seldom resonates powerfully. Nałkowska's writing is driven instead by an impulse to capture stories that she heard either in private conversations or during her service on the Commission for the Investigation of Nazi War Crimes, which was formed in 1945 by the Soviet-backed Polish government. As a member of the commission, Nałkowska visited numerous extermination sites and interviewed witnesses and survivors.[7]

Although six out of eight texts in *Medallions* are about the ordeals of Jews during the Second World War, the collection is not dedicated exclusively to the Jewish Holocaust. Notably, *Medallions* is framed by two pieces that invoke the official historical discourse on the Second World War promoted by the postwar Polish government. For decades after the war, in the Soviet-controlled countries, official Socialist ideology internationalized the Holocaust and submerged the unique fate of Jews in the larger context of Nazi war crimes against humanity.[8] The first text in *Medallions*, entitled "Professor Spanner," mourns victims of unknown nationality and German political prisoners. The phraseology of official history also resonates in a few paragraphs in "The Adults and Children of Auschwitz," the panoramic summation at

the end of *Medallions*. Inevitably, Nałkowska's work reflects the historical
context in which it was created. On the one hand, the author might have been
influenced by omnipresent party-line messages. On the other hand, ever politically savvy, Nałkowska probably knew that to have *Medallions* published,
she needed to acknowledge the authorized interpretation of World War II.

Despite the framework of the state-imposed ideology, *Medallions* offers
ample evidence that Nałkowska regarded the murder of European Jewry as
the gravest crime committed during the war, the crime that resulted in Europe's ethical bankruptcy. In *Medallions*, she mourns the lonely suffering of
Jews in three survivor testimonies. She also confronts the complicity of Polish bystanders in two intensely personal short stories. As a non-Jewish Pole,
she accepts her share of guilt as well. Obscuring the ethnic identity of victims
and bystanders was not part of Nałkowska's agenda in *Medallions*.

While Nałkowska didn't shy away from foregrounding her Polish compatriots' complicity in the suffering of the Jews during the Holocaust, she
also deemed it necessary to move beyond attributing national guilt and on
to prompting her readers to examine their own capacity for evil, not only
as Poles but also as human beings. "People brought this fate upon people,"
reads the epigraph on the front page of *Medallions*, raising disturbing questions about human nature and human coexistence. Nałkowska used national
labels sparingly. She was wary of them both as a citizen of ethnically diverse
but increasingly nationalist interwar Poland and as a daughter of an ethnically mixed couple: her father was Polish and her mother was Slovak. Jewish
victims in *Medallions* are represented first of all as Jews, but also as Poles or
Europeans, and above all as fellow human beings. Morally dubious bystanders in *Medallions* are recognizably Polish, but they are also colonized Nazi
subjects, and ordinary people confronting extreme circumstances. Germans
appear only on the margins of the text, most often in survivors' stories.[9]

BYSTANDERS

In the first section of this essay, I contextualize *Medallions* by drawing on
my personal recollections of reading the book in a Polish high school in the
late 1970s. The class discussion that I describe below was a transformative
experience for me, and perhaps for a few of my classmates. In my recollection, I emphasize both our teacher's affective investment in the history of
the Holocaust, and political constraints limiting Holocaust education in the
People's Republic of Poland.

At the very center of *Medallions*, in the middle of the book, Nałkowska
confronts her readers with the legacy of shame and guilt with which Poland

emerged from the Second World War as a nation of bystanders. While in all other texts the controlling narrative consciousness is associated with a post-liberation vantage point, in two stories the author reexperiences her own wartime fear, guilt, despair and perplexity in a world where Nazi rule inverted prewar ethical standards.[10]

Both texts challenge the favorite Polish self-image of a nation of heroic freedom fighters. Instead of describing brave resisters ready to shed blood for the oppressed, these two stories show Poles as frightened, confused, and morally degraded characters. For Poles who desire a positive cultural self-identification, Nałkowska's *Medallions* stories are as disquieting as Czesław Milosz's poems "*Campo dei Fiori*, 1943," and "The Poor Christian Looks at the Ghetto, 1943," both of which are about the Warsaw Ghetto Uprising. Milosz's well-known poems are dramatic and explicit. Nałkowska's narratives are morally challenging in a quiet way.

After nearly thirty years, I still remember a heated discussion about the *Medallions* story "By the Railway Track" that took place in my Polish literature class in a Warsaw public high school. If anyone is represented as a heroic figure in the story, it is a Jewish woman who takes the risk of escaping from a death camp transport. She is shot and wounded, while two other fugitives succeed in reaching the nearby forest. The wounded woman collapses by the railway track. At dawn, passersby appear, and they come and go as the day unfolds: "[N]o one would intercede by removing her before nightfall, or by calling a doctor, or by taking her to the station so she could get to a hospital."[11] Why? This kind of behavior would have been criminal in times of peace. Nałkowska's prose exposes the inversion of prewar ethical standards: "The day was white. The space open onto everything as far as the eye could see. People had already learned of the incident. It was a time of terror. Those who offered assistance or shelter were marked for death" (25).

For many critics, teachers, and students in Poland, this argument suffices to conclude conversations about the text. But the story is not only about the German terror that defeated a sense of solidarity, community, and moral courage in so many Poles—a complex and painful topic in its own right. Clearly, people feared that other Poles could inform on them to local German authorities.[12] The story confronts deeper layers of degradation.

The plot is complex. At dusk, a young, "small-town guy" consents to the wounded woman's pleas to kill her. He borrows a gun from a Polish policeman who cannot bring himself to do anything. The anonymous narrator who shares the story with Nałkowska comments, "Why he shot her isn't clear. Maybe he felt sorry for her . . ." (27). During our class discussion in 1976, as a group of teenagers, we embraced the narrator's statement without noticing its dark irony within the context of the entire story.

A peculiar kind of sympathy, indeed, I say as an adult. Earlier in the text, the killer refuses to buy pain medication for the wounded woman, but he brings her vodka and cigarettes. Later in the text, at night, two people emerge from the forest to save the woman, but they leave when they find out that she is dead. Impatient with what she took to be our insensitivity and sloppy reading, our literature teacher called us monsters or dumb Fascists—I can't remember which epithet she chose. Whatever the insult was, it worked as an effective pedagogical strategy because—as adults—my friends and I periodically remember that discussion with embarrassment.

And yet, so many other questions should have come up in that classroom. Is it anti-Semitism that prompts the young man to shoot the wounded woman? Or does he take this opportunity to kill a defenseless human being simply because he knows that he will not be punished? Could we imagine a similar story with a Soviet prisoner of war or a Polish resister as the wounded fugitive? Would they have been shot if they had asked for it?

To engage with our national legacy and with our capacity for evil as individuals, as part of our education, we should have struggled with further dilemmas. Is "mercy" killing an ethical option for a Christian? Is social class significant in the story? And finally, who were the two people who emerged from the forest at night to get the wounded woman? Were they the two survivors who had run from the train with her? In the forest, could they count on the help of the Polish Underground?[13]

These questions did not come up in our classroom in 1976. At that time, the state apparatus was still powerful enough to eliminate from public education topics that challenged government-sanctioned ideology. Because the Soviet bloc supported the Arab countries in the Arab-Israeli conflict, official anti-Zionism precluded open and honest discussions of anti-Semitism in public schools. Also, it would have been unacceptable to challenge insensitive youths' ethical sense by invoking religion. While probably 80 percent of my classmates were practicing Catholics, moral issues were not discussed in religious terms in our secular school. Oddly, even social class was a delicate topic in the People's Republic of Poland. Any attempt to juxtapose the degradation of the Polish masses with the Polish intelligentsia's efforts to resist it would have gone against the official ideology of the Workers' and Peasants' State. Our teacher internalized these constraints. As students, we respected her intellect and liked her passion, but we didn't trust her political judgments. And so, at that time, our understanding of the Polish society's response to the Holocaust remained superficial despite reading Nałkowska's classic.

"By the Railway Track" speaks volumes about the moral degradation of ordinary Poles during the "time of contempt," as the German Occupation is called in Polish historiography. From an ethical standpoint, everybody in the story—including the bystanders who turned in disgust when the young, small-town volunteer pulled the trigger, and the anonymous narrator who shared the story with Nałkowska—participated in the act of killing, and therefore all of them were guilty. From a political perspective, the act was a murder encouraged by Nazi laws and therefore an act of collaboration. I wish our teacher had helped us understand at least that much. Raised on popular Polish television programs about World War II, at sixteen we knew that collaborators were the villains, and that anti-Nazi resisters were the heroes.

Our history textbooks didn't help us much to contextualize Nałkowska's stories.[14] They discussed Nazi racism and mentioned the annihilation of millions of Jews, but they did not articulate clearly the principal difference between Nazi politics regarding Jews and Poles. Jews were systematically murdered for being Jews. Poles were permitted to live as slaves, and were killed if they resisted or sometimes as a random cautionary measure. To our teacher's credit, her emotional reaction to our refusal to read carefully and to think independently prompted at least a few of us to become critical students of Holocaust history. The times were changing, and in the 1980s, the nascent democracy in Poland brought with it the beginning of a public debate about Polish society and the Holocaust.[15]

Stories of human degradation are not easy to read, and are not easy to tell, but Nałkowska considered them important and personal. Her wartime diary documents the author's own struggle to withstand physical and spiritual decline. In 1939, she chose to stay in Poland with her sister and mother, rather than escape to the West with her handsome, dashing, young secretary. This decision condemned her to witnessing both the Holocaust and the degradation of her defeated compatriots. Between 1939 and 1945, on Polish territory, the conquerors had time to execute their plans to turn Poles into the enslaved *Untermenschen* (subhumans). Both the extermination of the elites and the moral and physical degradation of the populace progressed swiftly. Food was scarce, but the consumption of vodka was encouraged. Anti-Semitic propaganda filled Nazi newspapers for Poles and flowed through public loudspeakers in the streets. Alternative points of view were not available to the faint of heart: owning radios and reading underground publications were political crimes for which people were sent to concentration camps. In those years of terror and humiliation, many succumbed, internalizing oppression, and losing their humanity.

Nałkowska confronts this bitter truth again in the story "Cemetery Woman."[16] Cemetery women are familiar figures in Poland. For a small fee, they sweep cemetery paths and take care of tombstones. The title character is based on a person mentioned in Nałkowska's diaries. In 1942, Nałkowska's mother died, and the writer frequently visited the Powązki cemetery in Warsaw, which during the war shared a wall with the Ghetto, where she met this woman. In this story, Nałkowska testifies directly against those ordinary Poles who appeased their guilty conscience by blaming victims. In an oblique fashion, though, the author also confesses her own fears and guilt.

Set in the spring of 1943, during the Ghetto Uprising, the story juxtaposes the peaceful green Powązki cemetery with the struggle across the Ghetto wall. The sky reverberates with the grumble of airplanes as the writer walks along a cemetery path. In a sentence that echoes *Dzienniki 1939–1944*, Nałkowska reflects, "Ordinary, private death, next to the immensity of collective death, seems rather improper. Yet to live is an even greater impropriety" (17). Here, once again, the writer admits that she feels ashamed to be alive while others are dying. At the same time, indirectly, using the controlling narrative voice, the author reveals her own fear of death: "Nothing of the past world is real. Nothing has remained. People are made to survive what seems to lie beyond their capability. Fear ultimately divides them—fear that the other may cause their death" (17).

In the new world, the ruler's law sanctions the murder of innocent Jews. Ethical acts of human solidarity are punished by death. Poles are afraid that helping Jewish fugitives will bring the Gestapo to their homes and that other Poles might turn them in. People like Nałkowska do not live up to their own ethical standards, and feel ashamed to be alive.

The cemetery woman is distraught as well. Yet, despite her emotional distress over the suffering of people across the wall, in a conversation with the narrator, the cemetery woman reveals her own delusional anti-Semitism:

> "They are human beings after all, so you have to feel sorry for them," she explained. "But they despise us more than they do the Germans." She seemed offended by my naïve words. "What do you mean, 'Who told you that?'"

> "No one had to tell me anything. I know very well myself. And anyone who knows them will tell you the same thing . . . . If the Germans lose the war, the Jews will kill us all. You don't believe me? Listen, even the Germans say so . . . ." (20, tm)[17]

The cemetery woman uses Nazi propaganda to alleviate the guilt that she feels as a powerless witness who has no courage to risk her family's life to save neighbors across the wall. Nałkowska shows how identification with the oppressor's point of view and moral degradation under duress led some from unbearable empathy to the irrational fear of the victimized other. In a twist of historical irony, the Holocaust turns the cemetery woman into a paranoid anti-Semite. And we know that she was not alone. It is a realistic story, and it invites generalization.[18]

"People brought this fate upon people," reads the epigraph on the first page of *Medallions*, prompting readers to confront the abject, twisted aspect of humanity that is part of our psychological and historical constitution. Because the reality of mass murder is an abyss that cannot be represented directly, Nałkowska "struggles to gather it up, arrest it, and understand it" by listening to the stories of witnesses (18). And inevitably, these stories reveal more about the storytellers than about the reality of the Holocaust. Ultimately, the book is about witnesses and survivors.

SURVIVORS

While Nałkowska's stories about bystanders challenge her Polish readers to confront the bequest of moral ambiguity or outright moral bankruptcy left by five years of Nazi rule and terror, her stories about Holocaust survivors call into question the compatibility of conventional survival narratives with Holocaust survivor experiences. My reading of the survivor stories captured in *Medallions* is informed by Lawrence Langer's work on Holocaust testimonies and Holocaust narratives. One of Langer's important insights is that American culture creates expectations that survival narratives should be uplifting. These expectations engender the popularity of what Langer calls "deflective" Holocaust texts that conceal losses and emphasize the triumph of the human spirit over evil. Not only do such texts obscure the fate of the vast majority of victims who were murdered, but they also minimize the psychological and physical devastation that the Holocaust wrought on survivors.

In Poland, cultural memory precludes any notion of triumph or optimism in reference to the Second World War. Even today, the evasive phrase "the end of the war" is used to describe the Allied victory. With the loss of 20 percent of its population, including almost all Polish Jews, who numbered 3 million people in 1939, and between 2 and 3 million non-Jewish Poles, Poland had nothing to celebrate in 1945.

The conventional narrative patterns of survival stories are couched in terms of resilience, heroism, and triumph. As a survivor of the Nazi Occupation of Poland, Nałkowska was aware that the Holocaust disrupted narrative codes that had served humanity for centuries, and she chose the discourse of testimony as particularly appropriate for capturing the Holocaust trauma. Apart from a few introductory sentences, the author's own voice is rarely audible in the survivor stories captured in *Medallions*. She invites the survivors to speak for themselves. Not unlike documentary filmmakers or creators of visual archives of survivor testimonies, the author positions herself as a listener, recorder and editor.

The stories "The Bottom" and "Dwojra Zielona" present the testimonies of two women that Nałkowska ran into by chance in postwar Warsaw.[19] One is an unnamed, gray-haired, Polish survivor of the women's camp in Ravensbrück; the other, Dwojra Zielona, is a thirty-five-year-old Jewish survivor of Majdanek.[20] The texts "Visa" and "The Man is Strong" capture the stories of two people that Nałkowska met as a member of the Commission for the Investigation of Nazi War Crimes.

Without Nałkowska's encouragement and assistance, the survivors interviewed in *Medallions* were not likely to share their written testimonies with the general reading public.[21] The patterns of speech reproduced in *Medallions*, as well as entries in the author's *Dzienniki 1945–1954* indicate that these survivors had limited educational backgrounds, which would have prevented them from publishing their testimonials independently. To Nałkowska's credit, she didn't appropriate the voices of her witnesses by concealing her own mediation. Because in 1945 she didn't have access to modern audio and visual technology, her stories are presented as recollections of conversations. In *Medallions*, the recreated statements of survivors appear in quotation marks. The author's voice as an unobtrusive listener and the editor of the presented material is revealed in brief introductory comments and occasional succinct references to silences, gestures, facial expressions, and other forms of nonverbal communication.

Medallions is a book about grieving, not about new beginnings. The four survivors interviewed have lost all of their family members. All three women have been disfigured by torture and gratuitous brutality. One needs a glass eye, another a hip operation. Michał P., in the ironically titled text "The Man is Strong," may impress with his athletic physique, but he will always be burdened by the memories of how his family and his entire community perished in gas vans.

In "The Man is Strong," Michał P.'s memory emerges as "humiliated memory," a term introduced by Lawrence Langer to describe recurring characteristics of Holocaust testimonies. The Nazi perversion of values turned Michał P.'s strength into the cause of his suffering. Because he was capable of hard physical labor, the SS forced Michał P. to dig mass graves. When the bodies of his wife and children arrived to be buried, he lay down on them and begged to be shot. The guards refused, although they routinely shot slow laborers: "One German said 'The man is strong. He can still work hard.' And he beat me with a cudgel until I got up" (43). Despite his strength, and despite the power of his love, Michał P. was deprived of control over the fate and unity of his family. To invoke Langer's discussion of humiliated memory, Michał P.'s "[m]emory functions here to discredit the idea of family unity and to confirm an order of being or disorder of being that appears to the witness to be a unique creation of the Holocaust."[22] Michał P.'s testimony doesn't help him overcome his trauma. However, it helps his listeners realize the fragility of our civilization's commitment to respecting human life and dignity.

Nałkowska's brief introductory comments to the chapter emphasize Michał P.'s dignity. He speaks quietly and calmly about Nazi extermination operations in Chełmno. His testimony sounds like a solemn prayer; his silences indicate the unspeakable anguish of reexperiencing the past. With all his qualities, Michał P. is an archetypal noble hero. The Holocaust damaged the heroic ideal that he represents and, by extension, one of the foundational narratives of civilization.

Another story in *Medallions* captures the quiet dignity and personal grace of Dwojra Zielona, a small Jewish woman whom Nałkowska met at an optometrist's office. Dwojra Zielona punctuates her matter-of-fact, slightly auto-ironic testimony with smiles and sighs. Before the war, she lived in Warsaw. Her husband owned a cobbler shop. In 1939, bombs destroyed everything they owned. Later, her husband was taken to a concentration camp and killed.

Resettled to a *Judenstadt* (Jewish town) in Eastern Poland, Dwojra Zielona managed to avoid several Nazi roundups for transports to the Treblinka death camp. She tells the narrator that once during an attempt to escape, she was shot:

> "When they shot me, I thought, 'Maybe I am still alive'." She lowered her voice and said confidentially, "I'll tell you: I wanted to live. I don't know why. Because I didn't have a husband or family, no one, and I wanted to live. I was missing an eye, I was hungry and cold, and I wanted to live. Why? I'll tell you why to tell everything just like I'm telling you now. To let the world know what they did. . . . I thought, 'I'm the only one who's going to survive.' I thought, 'There won't be a single Jew left on the face on this earth.'" (32)

In simple words, this survivor's testimony affirms the value of life in defiance of the Nazi exaltation of death. The combination of Dwojra Zielona's fragility and fortitude inspires admiration. Her desire to serve as a witness implies her faith that humanity will eventually condemn Nazi crimes and prevent atrocities in the future.

Yet, Dwojra Zielona's premonition that the Jewish community will be destroyed undercuts this faint glimpse of hope in her story. She realizes that the Jews face their ordeals alone, and that nobody is likely to help: "When they transported the last of Jews, I stopped hiding. I followed the others to Majdanek myself. . . . Did we help each another? I don't know. A bit, yes. Not a lot. Ach, you know, everyone has his own troubles. What can you do? Every two weeks there was a selection. What could you do?" (32–33).

Dwojra Zielona's decision to die with others is a tribute to human solidarity. At the same time, however, her story demonstrates the limits of that solidarity under extreme circumstances.

The chasm between the world of Nazi atrocity and the world of established values is exposed in the text "The Bottom." The unnamed Polish survivor of Ravensbrück doubts that anyone would believe her story. She has trouble even beginning her story, not knowing where to start. Nałkowska shows how the survivor slowly moves from the post-liberation perspective—associated with the layer of the story where the conversation between the author and the survivor takes place—to the deep memory of camp experience that transcends the limits of accepted ethical and cognitive frames.[23] The interviewer/author comments, "It's obvious she passed over much in silence" (12). As the survivor moves deeper into the memory of her camp experience and away from ordinary life, she reaches the limits of culture and language when she obliquely reveals that hunger and systematic dehumanization drove some women to cannibalism and psychotic breakdowns.

Lawrence Langer's work on Holocaust testimonies sheds light on why, in *Medallions*, Nałkowska commented only minimally on her conversations with survivors. Langer insists that reducing the cognitive gap between survivors and the general public is important for preventing genocide in the future. Interviewers and the general public rely on a vocabulary of hope, "chronology and conjunction," notes Langer, while survivors use "a lexicon of disruption, absence, and irreversible loss."[24] When approaching Holocaust testimonies, listeners/readers must be aware that ordinary language and conventional assumptions impede their ability to understand "our age of atrocity," and by extension, our ability to dismantle its destructive power.

The disjunctive testimony of the young Auschwitz survivor recorded in the story "Visa" confirms Lawrence Langer's insight that, unlike official historical discourse, testimonies "are a principal source for transmitting the disorders of time, place, and language that accompanied the Holocaust experience."[25] The survivor keeps talking about regular selections for gas chambers:

> She speaks always of them, never of herself. So it isn't clear whether she was in there with them, or whether she looked on from the outside. . . . They were chased out all week. Until the selection. "One day, it was cold, too, but the sun came out in the afternoon. Then they shifted toward where the trees didn't hide the sun. They shifted, not like people, but like animals. Or like in one single mass . . . "That day the Greeks sang a national hymn. Not in Greek. They sang a Jewish hymn in Hebrew. In the sunshine they sang, beautiful, loud, and strong, as though they were healthy. It wasn't physical strength, because, of course, they were the weakest. It was the strength of yearning and desire. "Next day, there was a selection. I came on the visa and the visa was empty." (37–38, tm)

In the survivor's memory of the camp experience, the distinction between the living, the dying, and the dead is blurred. In Auschwitz, she felt closely bonded with those who were about to perish. After the liberation, as her conversation with Nałkowska indicates, she continues to consider the story of her own survival to be less important than the story of other women's deaths. Clearly, for this young woman, the Holocaust experience was so damaging that she is unable to transition to the post-liberation reality.[26] A story of fortitude in death (not of fortitude and survival) is the only memory that she wants to share.

MOURNING THE DEAD

Medallions is a dirge for the murdered millions. The story "Cemetery Woman" foregrounds the representation of Poland as a giant burial ground: the metaphor that casts a shadow over both Nałkowska's wartime diary *Dzienniki* and *Medallions*. Carved in stone, medallions commemorate the dead in the Warsaw graveyard described in "Cemetery Woman;" the literary collection *Medallions* mourns those who were never honored "in accordance with the funeral rite" and who were humiliated and dehumanized before they died (3). The desecration of the dead emerges as a theme in the first story in *Medallions*. The title, "Professor Spanner," refers to the director of the Institute of Anatomy at the University of Danzig (now Gdańsk) that Nałkowska visited in 1945 as a member of the Commission for Investigating Nazi War Crimes. The text contrasts the banal and the horrifying. Two conventionally dressed professors accompany the commission members to a modest building that turns out to be a place of excess: "The university's Anatomy Institute required the supply of fourteen cadavers; there were three hundred and fifty here" (4). The narrative gaze mourns the dead by focusing on the expressions of their facial features when they are visible.

Most bodies are heaped on top of each other, cut up to pieces, skinned, or boiled in giant cauldrons. Further investigation reveals a utilitarian purpose behind this profanation:

> We saw a chest with layers of thin pieces of prepared human skin, stripped of its fat, some vials of caustic soda on a shelf, a cauldron with a brew mounted on the wall, and a huge stove for burning scraps and bones. Finally, pieces of rough, white soap and a pair of metal molds stained with dried soap lay on a high table. (5)

Professor Spanner—a university teacher, scientist, Nazi Party member and volunteer SS doctor—conducted an experiment on practical uses of the cadavers obtained from prisons, camps and psychiatric institutions. Spanner's young employee, brought before the commission from prison, comments with admiration, "In Germany, you can say, people know how to make something out of nothing . . ." (9). He speaks in broken Polish with a German accent, another colonized subject in awe of his oppressors. His father was sent to a concentration camp at the beginning of the war, probably for being an ethnic Pole or a Polish civil servant in the ever-disputed city of Gdańsk (Danzig).[27]

The *Medallions* stories are usually built around such shocking statements, which reveal the human degradation brought on by National Socialism. In 1945, only Spanner's respectable-looking colleagues from the Danzig medical school are available to offer testimonies because Spanner himself is on the run in the West. One professor explains Spanner's motivation by characterizing him as an obedient Nazi Party member. The other professor describes Spanner as a conscientious citizen who tried to help Germany cope with the wartime shortage of fats (10). The perplexity, grief, and guilt that permeate Nałkowska's collection are palpably absent from the testimonies captured in this story. Perhaps the professors are apprehensive because Gdańsk is full of Soviet soldiers. Diana Kuprel in her introduction to *Medallions* argues that the story is an indictment of the German intelligentsia (xvii). I would argue that the story is also a critique of any social order that does not prioritize the value of human dignity in life and death over political and economic interests.

In "The Adults and Children of Auschwitz," the panoramic summation that ends *Medallions*, Nałkowska presents a sustained argument about the twofold—political and economic—purpose behind Nazi war crimes in general, and the extermination of Jews in particular. Filled with a sense of menace and perplexity, and punctuated with images of heaps of "woolen clothing, shoes, precious articles, personal items" that the author saw in Auschwitz, the last text in *Medallions* sounds at times like a documentary soundtrack recorded in Stalinist Poland.[28] On the first two pages of the text, the voice of Nałkowska as a member of the official Commission for the Investigation of Nazi War Crimes resonates more prominently than the voices of numerous witnesses that are incorporated into the author's own commentary.

Ultimately, despite a few rhetorical gestures to placate the Stalinist guardians of the authorized version of truth, in this coda to *Medallions*, witnesses and survivors eventually take center stage to complement and counterbalance official history. As Primo Levi recognized in *The Drowned and the Saved*, the gravest of Nazi crimes might have been implicating the victims in their own torment and in the anguish of fellow sufferers.[29] As in the entire text of *Medallions*, in the coda, the theme of the psychological devastation that mass murder wrought on its survivors emerges as the most emotionally charged issue in the book.

Auschwitz prisoners were forced to run the camp that was designed to destroy them. In Nałkowska's words, they were the spectacle's "executors and victims" (47). In "The Adults and Children of Auschwitz," Nałkowska introduces numerous survivors that filed before the commission: "Among them were scientists, politicians, doctors, professors—the pride of their respective nations. Each was the sole survivor in his family. Each had learned of the death of his parents, wife, or children. Each has been saved without having really counted on it" (47). Nałkowska emphasizes the sacrifices that some of these survivors, particularly physicians, made to save others. And camp physicians had the most chilling stories to share about the fate of children in Auschwitz. Because they had no economic value as laborers, children were the first candidates for gas chambers. At the same time, they had a frightening capacity to adapt quickly to their environment.

Nałkowska ends *Medallions* with the darkest image and quote in the entire collection. Recounting a witness's story, she writes:

Doctor Epstein, a professor from Prague, was crossing the street between the barracks in Auschwitz on a pleasant summer day when he noticed two young children, still alive. They were sitting in the sand and poking at something with a stick. He stopped and asked, "What are you doing here children?" He received in reply: "We are playing at burning Jews." (49, tm)

These are the last words in *Medallions*, the words that arrive to the writer and her audience from the realm of the dead. Nałkowska leaves her readers in silence: unconsoled, crushed, dejected. The text approaches the abyss where language fails and where evil is triumphant.

Reflecting on the incompatibility of the Holocaust with the narrative of hope, Lawrence Langer writes:

If Germany had won the war, systematic mass murder would have been added to the normal pursuits of everyday existence, and the idea of *civilization* would have been permanently redefined. Superior military force rather than moral idealism implicit in the universe forestalled this loathsome scenario, but it came close enough to realization to raise disturbing issues about human nature that still need to be examined. And we would be deluding ourselves to believe that the Holocaust marked the end rather than a fresh beginning for parallel loathsome scenarios.[30]

In *Medallions*, the recollection of children playing executioners and victims before they are themselves murdered reveals a glimpse of the world redesigned by victorious Nazis.

CONCLUSION

"People brought this fate upon people": this epigraph to *Medallions* sets forth the overarching theme for the collection and indicates that, like Langer, in the aftermath of the Holocaust, Nałkowska saw the exploration of the human capacity for evil as a pressing ethical enterprise. The undercurrent of cruelty in interpersonal relationships was an important theme in her interwar prose, but her earlier work and life, including the experience of the First World War, left Nałkowska unprepared for the gratuitous spectacle of murder and abuse that she witnessed during the Second World War.

A sense that the Holocaust is the caesura that divides history into the pre-catastrophe era and the post-catastrophe era permeates both *Medallions* and *Dzienniki*. Like many writers of her generation, she believed that the legacy of the Second World War threw European civilization into a major ethical and intellectual crisis. After Auschwitz, the notion of humanity acquired disturbing new connotations: we have no doubt that human communities are capable of devising and accepting legal codes and inverted value systems that justify and encourage murder, torture, expropriation, and humiliation of innocent men, women, and children. To understand why and how this happens is a prerequisite for protecting people from the lethal and corrupt potential within human nature and culture.

As for World War II's legacy of torment and disgrace in Poland, Poles have both lived it and repressed it for over sixty years. Nałkowska was among the first who challenged her compatriots to recognize their problematic roles as bystanders, victims, and victimizers. As her dark vision of human nature and culture indicates, Nałkowska knew that the capacity for evil and degradation was not unique to Poles, but her critical goal was to prompt her Polish readers to confront their complicity and to accept their share of guilt.[31]

NOTES

1. For a comprehensive account of the development of the Jewish-Polish dialogue on the Holocaust, see Joshua D. Zimmerman, ed., *Contested Memories: Poles and Jews during the Holocaust and its Aftermath* (New Brunswick: Rutgers University Press, 2003), 1–16. The 1980s public debate in Poland on the vexed question of the Polish response to the mass murder of the Jews is captured in the collection *My Brother's Keeper* edited by Antony Polonsky (London: Routledge, 1990).

2. The Polish critic Marian Stępień, in "*Nie musiatum sig przetamywac: Zofia Nałkowska po 194 roku*" in *Tworczosc* LVII, no. 11.672 (2001), 58–75, argues that Nałkowska tended to drift toward the world of government dignitaries regardless of their political orientation primarily because she was interested in the mechanism of

power. He documents his article with references to the reminiscences of a number of prominent Polish (and Polish-Jewish) left-wing intellectuals including Jan Kott. Gustaw Herling-Grudziński, a conservative Christian writer, ridiculed Nałkowska's vanity and her indiscriminate passion for diplomatic receptions in "*Nekrofiliacje Sanacyjne*," in *Wyjście z milczenia* (*Leaving Silence*) (Warsaw: Biblioteka Więzi, 1993), 39–50.

3. Grudziński, himself a survivor of the Soviet Gulag, criticized *Medallions* as a secondhand narrative with intellectual pretensions ("*Medaliony Nałkowskiej*," in *Wyjście z milczenia* [*Leaving Silence*], 79–80).

4. Among the most often cited contributions to this field are: Michael R. Marrus and Robert O. Paxton, *Vichy France and the Jews* (New York: Schocken, 1981), Henry Rousso, *The Vichy Syndrome: History and Memory in France since 1944*, trans. Arthur Goldhammer (Cambridge: Harvard University Press, 1991), Raul Hilberg, *Perpetrators, Victims, Bystanders: The Jewish Catastrophe, 1933–1945* (New York: Harper Collins, 1992), and Daniel Goldhagen, *Hitler's Willing Executioners: Ordinary Germans and the Holocaust* (New York: Knopf, 1996).

5. My translation from the Polish. Zofia Nałkowska, *Dzienniki 1939–1944*, ed. Hanna Kirchner (Warsaw: Czytelnik, 1996).

6. Zofia Nałkowska, "*Pisarze wobec dziesięciolia*" [Writers Vis-à-Vis the First Decade] *Nowa Kultua* 2 (1954).

7. Nałkowska's work for the commission is well documented by the editor of the author's diaries, Hanna Kirchner.

8. See James Young's discussion of Holocaust memorials in the Soviet bloc countries, particularly in Poland, *Writing and Rewriting the Holocaust: Narratives and the Consequences of Interpretation* (Bloomington: Indiana University Press, 1990), 175–80.

9. Nałkowska didn't focus on German perpetrators for several reasons. First of all, she didn't have much contact with Germans either during or after the war. Moreover, as a writer, she was interested in prompting Poles to accept their share of guilt rather than in helping her compatriots to project all of their guilty feelings on the absent and distant German other. In this respect, she was an oppositional intellectual challenging mainstream Polish culture. For a provocative discussion of how Poles project their wartime guilt on Germans, and how Germans project their historic anti-Semitism on contemporary Poles, see Joanna K. Stimmel's article on post-memory in Polish and German contemporary literatures, "Holocaust Memory Between Cosmopolitanism and Nation-Specificity: Monika Maron's *Pawels Briefe* and Jaroslaw Rymkiewicz's *Umschlagplatz*," *The German Quarterly* 78, no. 2 (Spring 2005): 151–71.

10. Because the two "bystander" stories are told from the wartime perspective, and because they echo the tone of Nałkowska's personal diaries (*Dzienniki 1939–1944*), I see them as Nałkowska's own effort to move into the deep layers of her memories of the Occupation. I am borrowing the concept of "deep memory" from Lawrence Langer's discussion of the Auschwitz survivor Charlotte Delbo's commentary on her camp experience. Delbo distinguishes deep memory from common memory. Common or reflective memory recalls and assesses the traumatic past from the vantage point defined by standards governing everyday life in times of peace. Deep memory is sensory and emotional, and it causes the witnesses to reexperience past traumas in the

reality where common standards of conduct simply don't have much meaning. These two kinds of memory are often in conflict. See Langer's *Holocaust Testimonies: The Ruins of Memory* (New Haven: Yale University Press, 1991), 1–38.

11. Zofia Nałkowska, *Medallions* (Evanston, IL: Northwestern University Press, 2000), 25.

12. Helena Zaworska's well-researched book on *Medallions* is a good example of interpreting "By the Railway Track" as a story about German terror. Published for the audience of high school teachers and students, the study offers a sophisticated analysis of Nałkowska's formal achievements and draws on archival materials documenting Nazi crimes. Zaworska discusses Nazi genocide with no emphasis on the uniqueness of the fate of the Jews, and "By the Railway Track" with no consideration of anti-Semitism in *Medaliony Zofii Nałkowskiej* (Warsaw: Państwowe Zaklady Wydawnictw Szkolnych, 1969).

13. For two different perspectives on the Polish Underground's response to the Holocaust, see Stefon Korbonski, *The Jews and the Poles in World War II* (New York: Hippocrene Books, 1989); and Shmuel Krakowski, "The Attitude of the Polish Underground to the Jewish Question during the Second World War," in Zimmerman, *Contested Memories*, 97–106.

14. Two Polish historians, Tomasz Kranz and Krysztof Ruchniewicz, analyze Polish history textbooks in Chapter Four of Hanns Fred Rathenow and Norbert H. Weber's study published in German, *Nationalsozialismus und Holocaust. Historisch-politisches Lerner in der Lehrerbildung* [*National Socialism and the Holocaust: Historical-Political Education in Teachers' Training*] (Hamburg: Krämer, 2005). My statements are based on personal recollections rather than on Kranz's and Ruchniewicz's analyses.

15. See Zimmerman, *Contested Memories*, and Polonsky, *My Brother's Keeper*.

16. Diana Kuprel translates the title of the story that I call "Cemetery Woman" as "Cemetery Lady."

17. Here and elsewhere, the abbreviation "tm"—"translation modified"—indicates my alterations to the English translation.

18. In his recent book *Fear: Anti-Semitism in Poland After Auschwitz, An Essay in Historical Interpretation* (New York: Random House, 2006), Jan T. Gross argues that several postwar pogroms that occurred in Poland between 1945 and 1946 were motivated by paranoid fear fueled by reverse guilt. Nałkowska's insights in "Cemetery Woman" confirm the value of Gross's take on the social psychology of postwar anti-Semitism in Poland.

19. Diana Kuprel translates the title of the story that I call "The Bottom" as "The Whole."

20. The Ravensbrück survivor worked as a charwoman in a hotel for members of the Parliament, see Zofia Nałkowska, *Dzienniki VI: 1945–1954* [*Diaries 1945–1964*], ed. Hanna Kirchner (Warsaw: Zytelnik, 2000), October 5, 1945 entry.

21. Dori Laub—a psychoanalyst and a co-founder of the Fortunoff Video Archive for Holocaust Testimonies at Yale—argues that the presence of an unobtrusive yet engaged listener is an essential component of working through trauma and a reexternalization of evil that "affected and contaminated the trauma victim." See "Becoming

Witness, or Vicissitudes of Listening," in *Testimony: Crisis of Witnessing in Literature, Psychoanalysis and History*, ed. Shoshana Felman and Dori Laub (New York: Routledge, 1992), 57–74.

22. Langer, *Holocaust Testimonies*, 112.

23. Maciej Podgórski, "*Główne problemy analizy* Medalionów *Zofii Nałkowskiej*," *Roczniki humanistyczne* 13, no. 1 (1965), 151–80, presents an in-depth analysis of the multilayered construction of *Medallions*.

24. Langer, *Holocaust Testimonies*, xi.

25. Ibid.

26. The editor of Nałkowska's diaries, Hanna Kirchner, tracks in a note the post-war story of the narrator in "Visa," Maria Michałowicz. She entered the University of Warsaw in 1949, became a psychiatrist, and worked in Warsaw until 1957. Kirchner was unable to trace Maria Michałowicz's later biography. She might have emigrated from Poland. See *Dzienniki VI: 1945–1954*, 71.

27. The testimony of the historical employee of the Danzing Anatomical Institute, Sigmund Mazur, is recorded in *Nuremberg Trial Proceeding* 7: 596. It is available online via the Avalon Project at Yale Law School: http://www.yale.edu/lawweb/avalon/imt/proc/02-19-46.htm.

28. Nałkowska, *Medallions*, 46.

29. Primo Levi, *The Drowned and the Saved* (New York: Vintage, 1989).

30. Lawrence L. Langer, *Using and Abusing the Holocaust* (Bloomington, Indiana, 2006), 121–22.

31. Naomi Mandel argues that, by confronting the complicity of the previous generation and assuming our own, we can further our understanding of the culture of atrocity and acquire means to dismantle its power. The assumption that the Holocaust exceeds language shouldn't stop scholars from making an effort to articulate and thus understand the Holocaust in the interest of disempowering the genocidal impulse in human nature and culture. See "Rethinking 'After Auschwitz': Against a Rhetoric of the Unspeakable in Holocaust Writing," *boundary 2* 28, no. 2 (2001): 203–28.

BIBLIOGRAPHY

Auschwitz: Inside the Nazi State. DVD. Directed by Laurence Rees. Burbank, CA: Warner Home Video, 2005.

Delbo, Charlotte. *Days and Memory*. Marlboro, VT: Marlboro, 1990.

Felman, Shoshana and Dori Laub, ed. *Testimony: Crises of Witnessing in Literature, Psychoanalysis and History*. New York: Routledge, 1992.

Goldhagen, Daniel. *Hitler's Willing Executioners: Ordinary Germans and the Holocaust*. New York: Knopf, 1996.

Gross, Jan. T. *Fear: Anti-Semitism in Poland After Auschwitz, An Essay in Historical Interpretation*. New York: Random House, 2006.

Herling-Grudziński, Gustaw. "Medaliony *Nałkowskiej*." In *Wyjście z milczenia* (*Leaving Silence*), 79–80. Warsaw: Biblioteka Więzi, 1993.

————. "*Nekrofiliacje Sanacyjne.*" In *Wyjście z milczenia* (*Leaving Silence*), 139–50. Warsaw: Biblioteka Więzi, 1993.

Hilberg, Raul. *Perpetrators, Victims, Bystanders: The Jewish Catastrophe 1933–1945*. New York: Harper Collins, 1992.

Korbonski, Stefan. *The Jews and the Poles in World War II*. New York: Hippocrene Books, 1989.

Krakowski, Shmuel. "The Attitude of the Polish Underground to the Jewish Question during the Second World War." In *Contested Memories: Poles and Jews during the Holocaust and its Aftermath*, edited by Joshua D. Zimmerman, 97–106. New Brunswick: Rutgers University Press, 2003.

Kuprel, Diana. Introduction to *Medallions*, by Zofia Nałkowska, translated by Diana Kuprel, xi–xxi. Evanston, IL: Northwestern University Press, 2000.

Langer, Lawrence L. *Holocaust Testimonies: The Ruins of Memory*. New Haven: Yale University Press, 1991.

————. *Using and Abusing the Holocaust*. Bloomington: Indiana University Press, 2006.

Laub, Dori. "Bearing Witness, or Vicissitudes of Listening." In *Testimony: Crisis of Witnessing in Literature, Psychoanalysis and History*, edited by Shoshana Felman and Dori Laub, 57–74. New York: Routledge, 1992.

Mandel, Naomi. "Rethinking 'After Auschwitz': Against a Rhetoric of the Unspeakable in Holocaust Writing." *boundary 2* 28, no. 2 (2001): 203–28.

Milosz, Czeslaw. *Selected Poems: 1931-2004*. New York: Harper Collins, 2005.

Marrus, Michael R., and Robert O. Paxton. *Vichy France and the Jews*. New York: Schocken, 1981.

Nałkowska, Zofia. "*Pisarze wobec dziesięciolecia*" (*Writers Vis-à-Vis the First Decade*). *Nowa Kultura* 2 (1954).

————. *Dzienniki V: 1939–1944* (*Diaries 1939–1944*). Edited by Hanna Kirchner. Warsaw: Czytelnik, 1996.

————. *Dzienniki VI: 1945–1954* (*Diaries 1945–1954*). Edited by Hanna Kirchner. Warsaw: Czytelnik, 2000.

————. *Medallions*. Translated by Diana Kuprel. Evanston, IL: Northwestern University Press, 2000.

"Nuremberg Trial Proceedings." Vol. 7. Sixty-Second Day, February 19, 1946. The Avalon Project at Yale Law School. Accessed August 28, 2006, http://www.yale.edu/lawweb/avalon/imt/proc/02-19-46.htm.

Podgórski, Maciej. "*Główne problemy analizy* Medalionów *Zofii Nałkowskiej.*" *Roczniki humanistyczne* 13, no. 1 (1965): 151–80.

Polonsky, Antony, ed. *My Brother's Keeper: Recent Polish Debates on the Holocaust*. London: Routledge, 1990.

Rathenow, Hanns Fred, and Norbert H. Weber, eds. *Nationalsozialismus und Holocaust. Historisch-politisches Lernen in der Lehrerbildung* (*National Socialism and the Holocaust: Historical-Political Education in Teachers' Training*). Hamburg: Krämer, 2005.

Rousso, Henry. *The Vichy Syndrome: History and Memory in France since 1944.* Translated by Arthur Goldhammer. Cambridge, MA: Harvard University Press, 1991.

Shoah. VHS. Directed by Claude Lanzmann. New York: New Yorker Films, 1985.

Stępień, Marian. "'*Nie musiałam się przełamywać*': *Zofia Nałkowska po 1945 roku*" (I Didn't Need to Force Myself: Zofia Nałkowska After 1945). *Twórczość* LVII, no. 11.672 (2001): 58–75.

Stimmel, Joanna K. "Holocaust Memory between Cosmopolitanism and Nation-Specificity: Monika Maron's *Pawels Briefe* and Jaroslaw Rymkiewicz's *Umschlagplatz.*" *The German Quarterly* 78, no. 2 (Spring 2005): 151–71.

Young, James E. *Writing and Rewriting the Holocaust: Narrative and the Consequences of Interpretation.* Bloomington: Indiana University Press, 1990.

Zaworska, Helena. *Medaliony Zofii Nałkowskiej.* Warsaw: Państwowe Zakłady Wydawnictw Szkolnych, 1969.

Zimmerman, Joshua D., ed. *Contested Memories: Poles and Jews during the Holocaust and Its Aftermath.* New Brunswick: Rutgers University Press, 2003.

Part II

THE UNITED STATES AND ISRAEL: LIVING WITH THE PAST IN NEW LANDS

Chapter Seven

Vulnerability in Spielberg's America

Schindler's List *and the Ethic of Commerce*

Sarah Hagelin

During the *Schindler's List* press junket in December 1993, director Steven Spielberg told an oft-repeated anecdote about the film's production. Spielberg and the film's cast and crew celebrated Passover in Krakow during filming, and the presence of German actors, cast as Nazis in the film, sitting alongside Israeli actors at the Seder triggered what Spielberg described as an emotional breakthrough: "Some kind of closure happened that day. I—I wept."[1] Spielberg narrated this as a moment of personal awareness, of his own acknowledgment of the repressed rage he felt toward the German actors. This slippage between actor and role, spectacle and history, recurs constantly in the press surrounding the film, and I argue that the emotional work it registers can help us understand the film's project as a national product. *Schindler's List*, which opened on November 30, 1993 to wide critical acclaim and deep scholarly suspicion, attracts a great deal of criticism for its attempts toward making a totalizing statement about the Holocaust. But the film's affective dynamics write the history of the *Shoah*, and of the American memory of it, onto a far more intimate stage. If we ask, as does Miriam Bratu Hansen, about the place of affect in the Holocaust's challenge to the limits of representation, we are able to see in the film's intimacy the cultural stakes of the story Spielberg tells about the connections between art, personal narrative, and national history.[2] In Americanizing Schindler—from lighting him as a film noir antihero to adorning him with the mantle of Christian savior—Spielberg reimagines the Holocaust as a space of triumph for American commerce but also as a space of American moral education. And here the emotional tone of Spielberg's confession to the Foreign Press Association has historical implications. If America came of age, morally, during WWII, as Spielberg's oeuvre as a director has continued to suggest,[3] *Schindler's List* takes a further affective step. The film suggests that in the early 1990s, America—like

Spielberg with his German actors—had emotional work left to do with a newly reunified Germany, a formerly Communist East Germany beginning the process of adopting the commerce that *Schindler's List* insists is a precursor to moral awakening.

This national project is unstated—dependent, I argue, on the emotional dynamics of commerce and vulnerability Spielberg so carefully establishes. The film's more explicit national narrative involves an American Jewish search for meaning in history that Yosefa Loshitzky argues "is expressed by the transformation of the Holocaust into a new locus of identity."[4] The public desire for a "*summa* of the Holocaust film genre" (evidenced by *Schindler's List*'s unprecedented commercial and critical success) can be traced, in this view, to a desire on the part of second-generation American Jews to affirm a religious and ethnic identity. James Young similarly argues: "There are a couple of gigantic institutions now, Spielberg being one and the U.S. Holocaust Memorial Museum being another, which are defining a kind of public consciousness of the Holocaust."[5] Certainly this public goal is one of the film's challenges to the problem of realism and what Saul Friedlander dubbed the Holocaust's challenge to "the limits of representation."[6] Scholars focused on the ethics of representation often compare *Schindler's List* unfavorably to the more elliptical, allusive *Night and Fog* (Alain Resnais, 1956) or *Shoah* (Claude Lanzmann, 1985).[7] While some scholars defend Spielberg's attempts at realism,[8] most members of a 1994 *Village Voice* roundtable on the controversy including film scholars Getrud Koch and Annette Insdorf as well as Art Spiegelman and James Young, among others, agreed with *Village Voice* reporter Richard Goldstein: "I think that most works of popular history, maybe most works of popular art, if they are reality-based at all, have an authoritarian aspect that is inherent in the process of taking dramatic forms that are very accessible, almost so that they are transparent, and applying them to situations that are inevitably more complicated than the forms."[8]

But if Spielberg's goal was the consolidation of an American Jewish identity around the historical memory of the Holocaust, why does his narrative focus so intently on the figure of the German Christian Schindler and the emotional dynamics of his moral growth? The answer, I believe, is in Spielberg's affective—not visual—challenge to the Holocaust's limits of representation. Indeed, *Schindler's List* largely avoids the visual representation of bodily vulnerability, excepting a few very key scenes, which work on a capitalist use-value structure that renders cash as payment for protection. Though the historical Oskar Schindler—like the character played by Liam Neeson—is German and a member of the Nazi party, the film establishes him as an outsider in that world. He charms Nazi officials with his easygoing American-coded jocularity, just as he courts his Jewish accountant Itzhak

Stern (Ben Kingsley) with bourbon-drinking offers of friendship, which Stern resists with European-style propriety. Spielberg encourages his audience to identify with Schindler, who introduces himself to Nazi power brokers in the film's opening nightclub scenes at the same time that we are introduced to them, then codes Schindler as American through two key images: Schindler as capitalist and Schindler as lover. Art Spiegelman suggests in the round-table discussion that this address to the audience overshadows the film's other narrative: "The film is not about Jews or, arguably, even the Holocaust. Jews make people uncomfortable. It's a movie about Clinton. It's about the benign aspects of capitalism—Capitalism With a Human Face."[9] The comparison between Schindler, played by Neeson as a good-natured, sensual con artist with a wandering eye and a soft heart, and President Clinton, elected a year prior to the film's release, is apt on an affective if not conscious level. This valence is deepened and complicated by the film's continual focus on Schindler as lover, not just to the endless string of young women he employs as secretaries but also to Itzhak Stern and Amon Goeth (Ralph Fiennes), the brutal, charismatic commandant of the Plaszow camp. The intimacy of Schindler's interaction with these characters helps to establish what Richard Goldstein sees as the film's actual address to its American Jewish audience:

> And then there is the question of the righteous Christian in the movie, the superman figure, who flies in and saves Lois Lane, the Jew. You have to remember 50 percent of American Jews marry non-Jews. I am living with a Christian, and that is my most intimate relationship. It corresponds on a primal level to my expectations of what this person would do for me, and I see my own lover as a Schindler.[10]

Intimacy here functions as the ultimate fantasy of protection, with Schindler as both American and lover. Central to this effect is the way Spielberg treats Schindler's Nazi party membership. It is a costume, necessary to the tense drama of infiltrating Nazi prisoner supply lines by way of Nazi affections. The swastika pin Schindler places on his lapel in the film's opening scenes is never, for the audience, more than a fiction—yet another instance of Spielberg's fascination with acting as an ethical enterprise.[11]

Spielberg mounts this intimate protection fantasy most vividly in two scenes that explicitly display the female body. Both scenes replace masculine physical action in protection of women with a commercial language of use that reduces women's (and Jewish males') value to commodities to be traded for their own salvation. This seems counterintuitive—traditionally, it is to teach less ethical men that women are not commodities to be bought and sold that the on-screen hero uses his masculine power—but the effect of the two scenes is crucial to the film's redemption narrative, focused on Schindler himself.[12] Far from dehumanizing Schindler or his Jewish factory workers, Spielberg frames Schindler's movement toward empathy, ethical engagement, and sexual monogamy as a product of his growing ability to see people as commodities that can be bought and sold.

The film sets up Schindler and the benign capitalism he represents against the repressive apparatus of Nazi state power. This places the blame for Jewish suffering on that power, exempting capitalism from complicity in Nazi atrocities, even as Schindler makes money from Jewish labor. In this vision, commerce *protects* the workers' bodies. Economic "use" might not mean anything to Goeth, who executes camp prisoners indiscriminately, but its deployment by Schindler has nearly magical power. The film constantly figures Schindler's economic power through his ability to create the illusion of intimacy with the Nazi officials he manipulates. This works to focus audience attention away from global concerns and toward intimate ones—to replace state conflict with individual moral development. Schindler's influence exists outside the realm of state-conferred power and state-sanctioned violence. His power is economic but also emotional; the bribes he pays Nazi officials in exchange for their silence appear in the film to be less important than the gifts he sends for their wives' and children's birthdays. Spielberg is aware of how precarious this kind of power is, how vulnerable it is to the whims of those with state-sanctioned power; when Schindler's kiss with a Jewish woman lands him in jail, only his intimacy with Goeth can win his release.

But where does intimacy with Jewish bodies fit into this scenario? Here, Spielberg strikes an uneasy balance, asking his audience to care about Schindler's Jews as part of a collective—because they are, as the dialogue keeps insisting, "his." But Spielberg's competing interest in memorializing asserts itself again and again in scenes of the *Schindlerjuden* lining up, giving their names, and accessing the privilege of being on Schindler's saving list. The film demands our attention to their names because their specificity matters,[13] but Spielberg's camera nearly always represents their suffering collectively. The tense mix of intimacy and distance with which Spielberg's camera registers the Jewish body is central to the film's most controversial scene, where the camera enters the gas chamber. Narratively, this scene provides a charged turning point; Jews from the Plaszow camp—who Schindler had offered protective employment in his factory—have been threatened with removal to Auschwitz and the gas chambers. After Schindler has paid Nazi officials to send "his" Jews to his factory in Czechoslovakia instead, the female *Schindlerjuden* are mistakenly sent to Auschwitz. The camera begins positioned behind the naked women huddled together as the door to the shower/gas chamber opens in front of them. This door opening is shown from the perspective of the women themselves, as if the spectator is among them, handheld camera work cementing the sense of the victims' perspective. The camera cuts from a handheld shot of women clinging to each other in fear to a long shot of the open door with the last of the women shoved inside. The doors close, and the shot closes in toward the porthole-style window. We look through the window at the women trapped inside, then cut to a shot above them, inside the room. After several close-ups of the women's increasing panic, the camera again adopts the perspective of the trapped women, glancing up at the shower heads, waiting for either water or gas. As the water begins to fall, Spielberg cuts to an artful shot of water spraying down on the women, reflecting the traces of light in the dark room as the musical track swells.

The camera's multiple address in this scene serves to ratchet up tension—the audience comes to the film with the knowledge of what those "showers" usually meant—and to place the audience in the position of both victim and perpetrator. The tension-breaking relief the audience is encouraged to feel by the shots of relieved faces awash in light and water cements both our sense of Schindler's protective power (though this reprieve is technically unconnected to Schindler's list) and our concern for these specific women. Geoff Eley and Atina Grossmann call this "a reworking of the standard trope: the list and selection as life, not as condemnation to death; the sealed trains as transport to safety, not destruction; and (most problematically) the shower scene, in which water and not gas descends." Eley and Grossmann treat this disruption of expectations with skepticism, even as they argue that it "works repeatedly against the benign relief of the viewer for those who are saved."[14] Their generous reading of the audience dynamic this creates fails, in my view, to account for how unabashedly the narrative *does* ask for our partiality toward those people Schindler has designated as "his." The scene of display—naked bodies herded into the chambers—cuts immediately to Schindler's meeting with Nazi officials, where he rails against the mix-up. When the bureaucrat offers to reroute a different trainload of Jewish women bound for Auschwitz to Schindler's factory instead, he angrily insists, "I want *mine*." Spielberg treats this as an emotionally rousing call for the specificity of each life, that one Jewish woman is not interchangeable with any other. But it is also the substitution of a named person for a faceless one, who will die at Auschwitz. Our relief at seeing the women we recognize loaded onto trains heading for Schindler's factory hides the reality that the other train, with the non-Schindler women, will now take its place on the track to Auschwitz. Schindler's anger at the Nazi official will not save more people, but the audience is encouraged to take pleasure in it because it saves *his* people. This dynamic matters because Spielberg uses it to subvert the paradigm of intimacy in the way the Holocaust is represented.

The shower scene itself, often criticized for its voyeurism, illustrates the politics of watching that are central to Spielberg's insistence on intimacy and its dependence on the language of use. Tracing the way this trope works in subsequent scenes of the Jewish body on display reveals the ethical bait-and-switch of this strategy. Spielberg's camera conflates watching and per-petrating, which ought to implicate his audience in the horror documented on-screen. But, through the continued replacement of vulnerable Jewish bodies with the language of commerce, Spielberg implies that the perpetra-tors, too, are victims of the Holocaust. This is, of course, an ethically fraught enterprise, dependent on the intimacy between Schindler and Goeth and on Spielberg's fascination with the emotional dynamics of Goeth's violence.

Actor Ralph Fiennes describes performing the following scene, where Goeth beats Helen Hirsch (Embeth Davidtz), his Jewish maid, as a moment of delayed affect. Initially pleased with the "presence" of the illusion, "after-wards I felt I had raped her."[15] This is a revealing locution, rape being the one form of physical violence his character will *not* inflict on Helen, as Goeth's paranoia generates from his illicit sexual desire for the Jewish female body. Fiennes's choice of that word speaks to the ethics of exploitation audiences and actors attribute to this kind of scene, which Spielberg's camera frames as a moment of both intimacy and danger. "You really are a wonderful cook and a well-trained servant. I mean it," Goeth murmurs softly as he circles Helen. Her clothes cling to her wet body in a way that many critics of this sequence see as gratuitously sexual,[16] but it increases the audience's awareness of her vulnerability and helps to establish the tension between the scene's threaten-ing visuals and its nearly tender dialogue. Goeth offers to write Helen a refer-ence letter after the war, a bizarre conflation of her actual relation to him—a slave in his house—with what he imagines that relation to be—servant and employer. The narrative implies that he needs the comforting fictions of a use-value relationship, and movement outside the bounds of that relationship causes the growing sense of danger.

Helen trembles in fear and Goeth works himself into an anti-Semitic and misogynistic frenzy at the intimacy created by his proximity to her body. Goeth's increasing estrangement from his usual emotional control disrupts the film's visual formulation of Nazi violence as cold, institutional, and col-lective. Seconds after murmuring "I feel for you, Helen," Goeth snaps and beats her—a swift, brutal scene that is jarringly crosscut with the wedding scene of a Jewish couple in the barracks of the camp. Goeth's attack on Helen is the most intimate and extended sequence of violence and bodily vulnerabil-ity in the film, and its placement after the tense scene of thwarted sympathy that proceeds it frames male desire for women as danger. Spielberg increas-ingly figures the Holocaust as an intimate drama; this scene of violence fades into a scene of Schindler kissing a Jewish woman at his birthday party, which leads to his brief imprisonment and the attendant audience fear of his rescue efforts being derailed. Violence against the vulnerable female body is coded as an act of individual male aggression, prompted by male anxiety about sexual desire. This appears at cross-purposes with the Holocaust genre's focus on state-sanctioned genocide, until we remember Spielberg's interest in the language of use and the saving power of that language. Helen Hirsch, and her value as an object of exchange between Goeth and Schindler, is a microcosm of the film's larger argument about the saving power of commerce.

Spielberg establishes this trope of human slavery long before Schindler and Goeth's climactic final scene of exchange over Helen. The film documents Schindler's plot-level movement from indifferent capitalist to humanitarian, but the development of the Schindler/Goeth dynamic shows how Schindler's moral awakening depends on the maturation of his capitalist drive. Use-value provides Schindler a way out of the problem posed by his own conscience and Spielberg an explanation for the sympathy his film offers Goeth. Throughout the narrative, as Schindler makes the Nazi contacts necessary to his procurement of Jewish labor for his factory and sets up the system of bribes that will protect his workers from murder, the language of conscience and the language of commerce become increasingly intertwined. In the film's first hour, Schindler becomes visibly upset when Jewish workers in his factory or those outside his protection seeking aid call him a "good" man. The elaborate façade of the industrialist who uses Jewish labor solely for financial gain serves as both a personal and a social fiction. The language of use and commerce remains separate from the language of morality; Schindler is comfortable with the former but not the latter. After Nazi soldiers murder a one-armed machinist from Schindler's factory, his failure to protect the man registers as a failure to adequately convince the Nazis of the man's "use." He was "quite skilled," Schindler insists, too late. Spielberg continues to train his audience to see the language of use as a code for the vulnerability of Jewish bodies. After the machinist's death, Schindler becomes more skilled in this code. Soon he convinces Nazi officials that he needs his workers' children because their fingers are small enough to clean the inside of shell casings and that he needs "his" Jews instead of others because it saves money to use workers he has already trained. The film's intimate protection narrative depends on use-value, never more evidently than in the final scene between Schindler and Goeth, as they haggle over Helen's fate while Plaszow is being emptied and its victims sent to Auschwitz.

Schindler meets with Goeth to "purchase" his workers and thus spare them from the implementation of the Nazi "final solution." Schindler has left a space open on his list for Helen's name. Goeth refers to this as a "clerical error," opening the language of commerce that will serve as their code in talking about Goeth's emotional entanglement with Helen. In this scene between two Nazis, absent any of the Jewish people who are technically the focus on Spielberg's protection fantasy, the film's dynamics of protection and vulnerability are given their most explicit expression. It is worth examining this scene's structure, since it collapses the language of protection onto the language of use. Schindler proposes a card game to settle Helen's fate; if he wins, Helen goes on his list. Goeth insists that he "can't wager Helen in a card game," as it "wouldn't be right." Schindler points out that she's only going to be sent to Auschwitz anyway, if she stays. The scene plays as a gamble to see which man will break the elaborately constructed language of commerce their relationship has depended upon. Goeth's control begins to unravel, and he spirals into a stream of consciousness monologue of self-delusion, meant to convince himself that he means to protect the vulnerable Jewish body he has terrorized: "She's not going to Auschwitz. I'd never do that to her. No, I want her to, um, come back to Vienna with me. I want her to come, um, to work for me there. I want to grow old with her." Goeth's façade, and the language of commerce that supports it, cracks when Goeth cannot stand to barter over Helen as if she is property. "Are you mad?" Schindler asks, almost kindly. "You can't take her to Vienna." Goeth clarifies that this is what he would *like* to do. If he was "any sort of a man," he would take her into the woods and shoot her, this being the next most merciful thing. Manhood having been predicated on the ability to protect or kill women, both men gratefully let the saving artifice of commerce again cloak their conversation.

Schindler wordlessly picks up the cards and Goeth asks, "What is it you said? For a natural twenty-one, was it fourteen-thousand eight hundred?" This return to the blackjack game that will seal Helen's fate is a retreat to the language of commerce, favored by Schindler even when Goeth's scruples reject it. Actor Ben Kingsley, who plays Itzhak Stern in the film, specifically addressed the jarring effect of the Schindler/Goeth relationship in response to a question about how he imagined Germans would receive the film:

> I think that this film will address itself to those millions who are saying there is grief here and there is shock at what—at what happened to us because Ralph's character is a victim of the Holocaust. He's a victim of the Holocaust, Amon Goeth. His spirit was broken on the back—on the rack of that terrible machine just as millions of other spirits were broken. That child was mangled by it just as all the other children were and that I think is what this film says when it says "witness this," it says witness everything.[17]

The "everything" that Kingsley wants witnessed includes the emotional trauma the film projects onto Goeth, who here represents the German public, imagined by Spielberg and Kingsley to be ready to come to terms with the consequences of history.[18]

Helen herself, the vulnerable Jewish subject, is secondary to this account. The next time we see Helen, she is at the end of a line of *Schindlerjuden* giving their names, which are the human catalog of the trade in money and people between Schindler and Goeth. We never see the outcome of the card game, never explicitly see Goeth sell Helen to Schindler. The details of the transaction are less important than Spielberg's fascination with the emotional dynamics of this fraught language of commerce. Schindler gets what he wants—Helen—because he is a more successful actor than Goeth. He embraces the ethic of commerce in a way that Goeth does not, perhaps cannot. Goeth's reluctance to treat Helen as property to be won in a card game would, in reality, condemn her to Auschwitz. The new masculine protection fantasy this film advocates replaces male honor with the ethic of commerce, as both a shield and an actual method of exchange. Goeth's uneasiness with the language of commerce in the business of intimacy registers as indignation that Schindler would treat Helen as an object to be bartered. But here the language of morality is the language of delusion.

The film constantly ties the language of commerce to the ethical impulse to protect Jewish bodies. When explaining the rules of his factory to the Nazi overseers, Schindler demands "nothing will interfere with production," when he means that nobody is to be killed. As it becomes increasingly clear that the factory exists to protect workers, not generate capital, Schindler's redemption narrative escalates. He pledges fidelity to his wife and gives openly sentimental speeches. But when the language of commerce starts to recede, the film loses some of its tense power. It was not Schindler's sentiment but his industrialist's ease with the language of commerce, that has moved the Holocaust onto an intimate stage. But even in the film's sentimental ending, Spielberg does not abandon commerce; he mourns the lack of its full deployment. Schindler's emotional breakdown after the Allied victory comes at the realization that the trappings of wealth he still retains—his gold pin, his car—could have had a different, and better, use-value if he'd spent the money to buy more people instead: "If I'd made more money. I threw away so much money . . . if I had just . . ." If he had just been an even better capitalist, more lives might have been saved. Stern's absolution, "You did so much," is then also Spielberg's attempt to absolve America, and American capitalism, from its lack of protective power during the Holocaust.

When Schindler chokes, "I could have got more," Stern soothes him: "Oskar, there are 1,100 people who are alive because of you. Look at them." Stern directs him to look at the actual product of his factory—the *Schindlerjuden* themselves. Here, Stern's directive that Schindler "look" at the survivors finally collapses the language of commerce onto the language of morality, and of sentiment. Schindler's reserve breaks, and the emotional relationship between him and Stern (and the rest of the *Schindlerjuden*) comes out from behind the façade of employer/employee that had heretofore been strenuously maintained. Schindler collapses in sobs, and "his" Jews surround him, holding him, protecting him. The scores of critics who defend the film but balk at this turn to sentimentalism miss that this scene—heavy-handed as it is—represents the logical conclusion of Spielberg's attempt to see the violence of the Holocaust as intimate rather than global. *Schindler's List* takes a history of institutionalized violence and institutional failure and makes it a drama of individual morality. Thus Schindler's keening is not the indictment of American inaction that it might be, since it dramatizes an emotional breakthrough in a film that, in its narrative strategies and its press campaign, labels emotional catharsis the sign of true witness.

But *Schindler's List* does not end in Europe and with Schindler. It ends in modern-day Israel, with a fourth wall-breaking montage of the Schindler Jews and their descendants laying rocks on Oskar Schindler's grave in Jerusalem, accompanied by the actors who portrayed them in the film. This conscious movement from memory to history, and the embrace of the second-generation descendents of Holocaust victims implied in the film's final address to the viewer ("There are more than six thousand descendants of the Schindler Jews"—more than the four thousand Jews alive in Poland today) includes a modern-day Jewish audience in the film's circle of witness. Spielberg says of his decision to film this sequence:

> Just before I finished the movie in Poland, in the last five weeks of shooting, I was sitting up in bed one night thinking what I really need to do is to—wouldn't it be wonderful if I could get survivors to come from all over the world and meet me in Jerusalem and pay a final regard to Oskar Schindler and so it was an idea that was never in the script.[19]

In order to clarify the ethical stakes of this approach to "witness," we must examine what *is* in Steven Zaillian's script as a final image. The screenplay describes images set to run under the end credits:

> Moving slowly over the road of fractured gravestones winding through Plaszow. Tufts of grass and weeds between the spaces. A pick pries at one of the stones, and—Thousands of mismatched fragments of unearthed stones on the ground like pieces of a jigsaw puzzle. A workman's hands place two together that fit, and—A wall under construction, a memorial made entirely of the recovered gravestones. Moving across them, two letters of a name are all that remain of one, four letters of another, then a full name, then half a name, three letters of another, two, and, finally, only a Jewish star.[20]

While the presence of the Jewish survivors appears at first to privilege their story, the camera's final image of Schindler's grave shows the rocks arranged on his gravestone, the negative space forming a cross. This replacement of a "Jewish star" with a cross as the film's closing symbol is a jarring retreat from the embrace of diasporic Jewish identity that breaching the fourth wall had implied. The participation of the actors in *Schindler's List*'s final sequence brings the film explicitly back to the questions of acting and catharsis, and includes filmmaking in the film's affective embrace.

The filmmaker who has admitted that he "wasn't always proud to be a Jew,"[21] and that coming of age as a member of the baby boom generation meant hearing about the Holocaust in "candid expression[s] of rage . . . never [sadness]for the Jews" has produced a film that looks on America and even Germany more in sadness than in anger. In the final estimation, Spielberg offers us not just Schindler as America, but Schindler as Hollywood, and ultimately, as Spielberg himself.

NOTES

1. From a transcript of Spielberg's Dec. 9, 1993 press conference with the Hollywood Foreign Press Association, housed in the Argentina Brunetti Papers of the Margaret Herrick Library of the Academy of Motion Picture Arts and Sciences. I would like to thank the staff of the Herrick Library for allowing me to examine these transcripts and the unpublished *Schindler's List* shooting script.

2. Miriam Bratu Hansen, "*Schindler's List* Is Not *Shoah*: The Second Commandment, Popular Modernism, and Public Memory," *Critical Inquiry* 2 (Winter 1996), 303. Hansen argues "if we understand the Shoah's challenge to representation to be as much one of affect as one of epistemology, the specific sensory means of engaging this challenge cannot be ignored."

3. Spielberg's 1998 film *Saving Private Ryan* views WWII as a crucible of American national identity. As early as *Raiders of the Lost Ark* (1981), Spielberg's films have figured an American hero's triumph over Nazi enemies.

4. *Schindler's List* (1993) "merges[s] and Americanize[s] these European cinematic traditions into a single film conceived and designed as the *summa* of the Holocaust film drama" (Yosefa Loshitzky, ed., *Spielberg's Holocaust: Critical Perspective on "Schindler's List"* [Bloomington: Indiana University Press, 1997], 4). J. Hoberman adds, "If nothing else, Oscar night demonstrated that the existence of *Schindler's List* justifies Hollywood to Hollywood" (Roundtable discussion "Schindler's List: Myth, Movie, and Memory," *The Village Voice*, March 29, 1994, 24). Loshitzky on the influence of the 1978 NBC miniseries *Holocaust*: "*Holocaust*, as the television counterpart to *Roots*, cultivated the idea (which since then has become pervasive in American Jewish discourse) that being Jewish is primarily an ethnic rather than a religious category and that Jewish identity can be affirmed through the Holocaust," *Spielberg's Holocaust*, 7.

5. James Young, "Schindler's List: Myth, Movie and Memory," 24.

6. See Saul Friedlander, ed., *Probing the Limits of Representation: Nazism and the "Final Solution"* (Cambridge: Harvard University Press, 1992). For useful summaries of the debate over the ethics of Holocaust representation, see Joshua Hirsch, *Afterimage: Film, Trauma, and the Holocaust* (Philadelphia: Temple University Press, 2003), 1–27, and Judith E. Doneson, *The Holocaust in American Film* (Syracuse: Syracuse University Press), 143–96. An influential strain of scholarship on Holocaust representation prefers memory films such as *The Pawnbroker* (Sidney Lumet, 1965) and *Sophie's Choice* (Alan J. Pakula, 1982) to films that set their action during the Holocaust itself, because they see a memory structure as an acknowledgment that the "true" story of the Holocaust is always personal, contingent, and incomplete. Annette Insdorf argues, "Films that depict a character's memory of a horrific past—and that character's enslavement by it—can have more consistency and integrity than a movie that purports to show *the* past in an objective way. A fictional reconstruction of a concentration camp is not quite as 'truthful' as one person's subjective memory of it, for the latter acknowledges the partiality of the recollection," *Indelible Shadows: Film and the Holocaust* (Cambridge: Cambridge University Press, 2003), 23. See also Hirsch on vicarious trauma in *Afterimage*, 17 and Alison Landsberg on the theory of "prosthetic memory" in Holocaust representation in "America, the Holocaust, and the Mass Culture of Memory: Toward a Radical Politics of Empathy," *New German Critique* 71 (Spring/Summer 1997): 63–86.

7. Michael Bernard-Donals and Richard Glejzer argue, for example, that Lanzmann's and Resnais's focus on memory and witness "constructs a space that we would call a traumatic kernel, a space that is an effect of the same tension between the horror's presence in the present and its emanation back to the origin of its memory"; Bernard-Donals and Glejzer, ed., *Witnessing the Disaster: Representation and the Holocaust* (Madison: University of Wisconsin Press, 2003), 112.

8. Though Miriam Bratu Hansen does not wholeheartedly embrace the film, she calls *Schindler's List* "a more sophisticated, elliptical, and self-conscious film than its critics acknowledge"; Roundtable discussion "Schindler's List: Myth, Movie, and Memory," *The Village Voice*, March 29, 1994. Hansen, "*Schindler's List*," argues that "the lack of attention to the film's material and textual specificity is itself a symptom of the impasse produced by the intellectual critique, an impasse I find epitomized in the binary opposition of *Schindler's List* and *Shoah*" (306). Though writing before the release of Spielberg's film, Ilan Avisar acknowledges the ethical problems with Holocaust representation, but argues that critics' "final conclusions are unacceptable. For if indeed art is inadequate to deal with the Holocaust in any meaningful manner—intellectually stimulating or ethically constructive—then we face a colossal cultural scandal"; Avisar, *Screening the Holocaust: Cinema's Images of the Unimaginable* (Indianapolis: Indiana University Press, 1988), viii.

8. See citation of the transcript of the roundtable discussion "Schindler's List: Myth, Movie, and Memory," published in the *Village Voice*.

9. Art Spiegelman, "Schindler's List: Myth, Movie, and Memory," 30.

10. Richard Goldstein, "Schindler's List: Myth, Movie, and Memory," 27.

11. As Annette Insdorf argues in the roundtable discussion: "Oskar Schindler himself was a larger-than-life figure, who did indeed save over 1100 Jews. How? By manipulation. By a showmanship (not unlike Spielberg's) that knows—and plays—its audience, but in service of a deeper cause"; see Insdorf, "Schindler's List: Myth, Movie, and Memory," 28.

12. See, for example, Art Spiegelman, who argues in the roundtable discussion: "*Schindler's List* refracts the Holocaust through the central image of a righteous gentile in a world of Jewish bit players and extras. The Jews function as an occasion for Christian redemption," "Schindler's List: Myth, Movie, and Memory," 26–27. See also Landsberg, "America, the Holocaust, and the Mass Culture of Memory": "Out of that cipher of a con man/grifter/gambler develops an "authentic" person, an integrated and intelligible character, a morally responsible agent" (310). See Eley and Grossmann on the characterization of Schindler: "He's the liberal capitalist, the paternalist, the good plantation-owner, the benevolent potentate who looks after his Jews;' he's the Christian who restores Judaism; he's the great white father, the protector of 'his' people, who leads the Jews to safety ('Who are you,' Goeth asks sarcastically, 'Moses?')" Geoff Eley and Atina Grossmann, "Watching *Schindler's List*: Not the Last Word," *New German Critique* (1997), 51–52.

13. The obsessive focus of Spielberg's camera on names recalls the memorializing projects of both Maya Lin's Vietnam Veterans Memorial on the National Mall and the walls of photographs memorializing Holocaust victims at the U.S. Holocaust Memorial Museum.

14. Eley and Grossman, "Watching *Schindler's List*," 49.

15. Spielberg, press conference with Hollywood Foreign Press Association, Dec. 9, 1993, transcript, Argentina Brunetti Papers, Margaret Herrick Library, 2.

16. Hansen, for example, labels the staging of this scene "sadistic-voyeuristic fascination with the female body" (Hansen, "*Schindler's List*," 298).

17. Ben Kingsley, press conference with Hollywood Foreign Press Association, Dec. 10, 1993, transcript, Brunetti Papers, Herrick Library, 12.

18. Eley and Grossmann read Schindler himself in this context: "In a cynical reading of the film's reception, the man of conscience (and better still an industrialist), who sacrificed his fortune to save the Jews, is a godsend to German conservatives, who are always on the lookout for some new alibi for Nazism, a new way to get the German nation off the hook" ("Watching *Schindler's List*," 51). I argue instead that Spielberg separates the categories of industrialist and German (partly through the doubling of Schindler and Goeth), and that the inclusion of Germany in the film's embrace proceeds more problematically through Goeth himself.

19. Spielberg, press conference with Hollywood Foreign Press Association, Dec. 9, 1993, transcript, Brunetti Papers, Herrick Library, 12.

20. From Steven Zaillian, *Schindler's List* shooting script, Script Collections, Margaret Herrick Library.

21. Spielberg, press conference with Hollywood Foreign Press Association, Dec. 9, 1993, transcript, Brunetti Papers, Herrick Library, 4.

BIBLIOGRAPHY

Avisar, Ilan. *Screening the Holocaust: Cinema's Images of the Unimaginable.* Bloomington: Indiana University Press, 1988.

Bernard-Donals, Michael and Richard Glejzer. *Between Witness and Testimony: The Holocaust and the Limits of Representation.* Albany: State University of New York Press, 2001.

Doneson, Judith E. *The Holocaust in American Film,* 2nd edition. Syracuse: Syracuse University Press, 2002.

Eley, Geoff and Atina Grossmann. "Watching *Schindler's List*: Not the Last Word." *New German Critique* 71: Memories of Germany (Spring/Summer 1997), 41–62.

Friedlander, Saul. *Probing the Limits of Representation: Nazism and the "Final Solution."* Cambridge: Harvard University Press, 1992.

Gelley, Ora. "Narration and the Embodiment of Power in *Schindler's List.*" In *The Films of Steven Spielberg: Critical Essays,* edited by Charles L. P. Silet, 215–236. Lanham, MD: Scarecrow Press, 2002.

Hansen, Miriam Bratu. "*Schindler's List* Is Not *Shoah*: The Second Commandment, Popular Modernism, and Public Memory." *Critical Inquiry* 22 (Winter 1996), 292–312.

Hirsch, Joshua. *Afterimage: Film, Trauma, and the Holocaust.* Philadelphia: Temple University Press, 2004.

Insdorf, Annette. *Indelible Shadows: Film and the Holocaust.* New York: Random House, 1983.

Keneally, Thomas. *Schindler's List.* New York: Scribner, 1982.

Kingsley, Ben and Ralph Fiennes. Press conference with the Hollywood Foreign Press Association, December 10, 1993. Argentina Brunetti Papers, Margaret Herrick Library, Academy of Motion Picture Arts and Sciences, Beverly Hills, CA.

Landsberg, Alison. "America, the Holocaust, and the Mass Culture of Memory: Toward a Radical Politics of Empathy." *New German Critique* 71: Memories of Germany (Spring/Summer 1997) 63–86.

Loshitzky, Yosefa, ed. *Spielberg's Holocaust: Critical Perspectives on "Schindler's List."* Bloomington: Indiana University Press, 1997.

"Schindler's List: Myth, Movie, and Memory," roundtable. *Village Voice,* March 29, 1994, 24–30.

Spielberg, Steven. Press conference with the Hollywood Foreign Press Association, December 9, 1993. Argentina Brunetti Papers, Margaret Herrick Library, Academy of Motion Picture Arts and Sciences, Beverly Hills, CA.

Weissman, Gary. *Fantasies of Witnessing: Postwar Efforts to Experience the Holocaust.* Ithaca, NY: Cornell University Press, 2004.

Zaillian, Steven. *Schindler's List.* Script Collections, Margaret Herrick Library, Academy of Motion Picture Arts and Sciences, Beverly Hills, CA.

Chapter Eight

The Erotics of Auschwitz

An American Tale

Phyllis Lassner

Among all the artistic risks represented by American Holocaust fiction, Philip Roth's creation of an adult Anne Frank in his novel *The Ghost Writer* is exemplary. Not only does Roth challenge Anne Frank's iconic and perhaps reified status in collective Holocaust memory, but he blatantly eroticizes the figure that has come to represent the quintessential innocence of Holocaust victims.[1] In a similar vein, one of the strongest criticisms of Steven Spielberg's film *Schindler's List* is that its scenes of Amon Goeth's brutal lust for Helen Hirsch come too close for comfort to anti-Semitic tropes of Jewish women's lethal sexual allure and therefore risk titillating the audience.[2] Because these scenes recall the Nazi construction of the Jewish woman as a sexual temptress, sexually titillating the audience could invite identification with the perpetrator, the victim, or even the trauma of the Holocaust itself.[3] Another facet of this problem in representation is informed by feminist scholarship—the dominion of the male gaze controlling the self-determination of the historically determined female character.

These representational problems are complicated even further by the testimonial record: women's Holocaust narratives of their own sexual experiences have taken decades of documented research to be accepted as historically authentic.[4] What is striking about all of the above criticism is that it singles out depictions of women's experiences as trivializing or even fragmenting Holocaust history.[5] Critics are concerned that to distinguish women's Holocaust experiences denies the fact that the Nazis' plan was to exterminate all Jews—men, women, and children. But such criticism represents a problem in itself because the anger with which it is expressed betrays an unstable or lack of critical distance.[6] Rather than dismiss it, however, we must consider that since this criticism appears primarily in

143

American periodicals, it represents a significant perspective on American representations of and responses to the Holocaust.

One of the major criticisms of Spielberg's film is that it represents an exceptional case: of rescuing Jews and of a Nazi's moral transformation, and therefore can be seen to offer a particularly American perspective on the Holocaust by satisfying audiences' desire for an uplifting message that transforms ashes into hope.[7] Paradoxically, the film bridges and yet widens the audience's distance from the Holocaust by offering an emotional safety valve in its insistence on the possibility of physical and moral rescue from the atrocities. Even though rescue is trumped by history in both Roth's novel and Spielberg's film, they each reinscribe an American cultural myth: the nation of new frontiers and immigrants inspires infinite possibilities for imagining rescue, for imagining new lives that leave privation and oppression behind or for creating a second chance that forgives past mistakes.[8] As an American creation, Sherri Szeman's 1994 novel *The Kommandant's Mistress* offers both a representational and critical response to these concerns. Sherri Szeman's novel plots America's identification with and distance from the Holocaust as a double-sided myth and as a critical dilemma as it imagines an erotically violent relationship between a Jewish woman prisoner and an S.S. perpetrator as it is born in Auschwitz and ends in the United States. In Szeman's America, however, there is no escape or rescue, no new life, no moral regeneration, and no resolution or closure for the Holocaust survivor.

Though critically acclaimed, *The Kommandant's Mistress* remains controversial for its graphic depiction of a sexual relationship that in its intensity and brutality resembles Spielberg's depiction of Amon Goeth's brutal sexual passion for his Jewish prisoner, Helen Hirsch. There is a crucial difference, however. Szeman portrays the Jewish woman as a sex slave with agency and desires of her own. Shortly after the novel's publication, when I was considering teaching it, a woman scholar I consulted responded with great passion as follows: "I wouldn't touch that book with a ten-foot pole!" Such a reaction reflects a sense of danger that, despite years of study, the subject of the Holocaust and women's sexuality defies critical detachment. We can certainly understand how survivors would feel reticent about revealing behavior that violated the social codes that gave their prewar lives coherence and meaning, whether that behavior was forced, coerced, or chosen. Such reticence would also help explain the paucity of testimony about sexual experiences in the camps.[9] Furthermore, a fictional representation of sexual complicity could very well seem to elide the actual suffering and helplessness of victims and survivors. Integral to the issue of women's representations is the danger of trivializing the Holocaust by transforming a woman's bodily pain into an object of pleasure, capitalizing on brutally extenuating circumstances to exploit the suffering female subject as an object of voyeurism. Compounding such a representation and reception would be to characterize the woman's consciousness as a willing or complicit partner with both her corporeal experience and the desires of her sexual abuser and thus foreclose the closeness between victim and perpetrator. The combination of these elements could produce what is arguably a grotesque pornographic denial of the Nazis' control, of the decimated bodies of the prisoners, and of the manifold forms of the prisoners' resistance. If we are to take such concerns seriously, we must ask: does this subject risk offending not only readers and critics but women survivors who would rather not draw attention to the horrors committed on their bodies that may never heal?

Sherri Szeman's novel compounds this controversy not only with its subject matter, but with its structure. Divided into the Kommandant's narrative and the Jewish woman's, the novel enters debates about who is authorized to narrate the Holocaust and what and who should be its subjects. Situating sexual obsession at the core of both narratives, Szeman also creates herself as a subject of debate, taking the risk as a non-Holocaust survivor that her narrative won't be treated with the respect we feel for those of victims and survivors. Her novel is shaped as an artifact, however, not as testimony; not only is it not a historical document, it also begs the question of the viability of writing purely imagined Holocaust fiction. As I argue, however, the battle for the woman's body becomes the logical site for representing and indicting Nazi racialist ideologies as a desperate struggle for masculinist power and authority. In turn, as we discover that the enslaved mistress is also a writer, the novel endows her with both the consciousness and corporeality to construct a female resistance to her embattled state. By extension, the novel resists the view that Holocaust fictions are deviant and detract from historical evidence. I contend that Szeman's sexualized Holocaust narrative is substantiated by the claim of many women Holocaust memoirists that when women authorize what is normative or deviant about what they choose to do with their own bodies, we learn necessary truths about the Holocaust.[10]

Instead of condemning Maximilian von Walther, the fictional Kommandant of Auschwitz, as an evil monster, offering him his own narrative has the effect of humanizing him. Unlike Spielberg's portrait of Amon Goeth, which substantiates testimony and documentation of the perpetrator's increasingly deranged but always conscious brutality, Szeman's Kommandant is both consciously brutal and compelled by his passion for his Jewish mistress, seemingly beyond his control. Both von Walther's narrative and that of Rachel Levi, his Jewish mistress, also problematize the status and survival strategies of the woman as victim and survivor. Read in tandem, their narratives suggest a kind of mirroring or reflexive effect that blurs and transgresses important ethical, psychological, and historical differences between perpetrator and victim/survivor.[11] While this effect can be seen as ethically compromised, I maintain that Szeman's representation of an inextricably entangled sexual relationship between perpetrator and victim/survivor offers new insights into themes that inform and emerge from American literary criticism on and theories about the Holocaust. For example, Holocaust suffering and victimization have inspired the use of the term survivor to explore trauma as it originates in the experience of sexual abuse. We see this inspiration in Szeman's statements about writing the novel. While the novel's exploration of the sexualized brutality of Holocaust perpetrators is based on extensive research and interviews with survivors, the reader identification it may inspire also derives from Szeman's personal experience. As she wrote to Karin Doerr, she was raised in a postwar "abusive and violent family, [. . .] identified with the fate of the Jewish Holocaust victims and considered the brutal Nazi camps the epitome of power abuse and violation of people, specifically women. [. . .] All my life I had nightmares about being in the concentration camps."[12] Of course, this personal identification with sexual abuse represents problems of diffusing and misapplying the historically and ideologically specific targeting of Jewish women.

In her critique of recent American Holocaust trauma theories, Debarati Sanyal questions claims that history "occurs *as* trauma, as something that resists immediate knowing and representation" and that "is not available to immediate and conscious understanding. Instead, the event (or history) is belatedly and repetitively recorded by the psyche in complex and indirect forms that entangle knowing with unknowing."[13] A consequence of this entanglement is "the impulse toward identification" that enables readers to "posit" themselves "as survivor-witness" or to analogize the Holocaust with other brutally traumatizing events. The problem is both historical and ethical because the "extension of shame, guilt, and trauma, of responses to the affective and bodily experiences occurring in the extreme conditions of the camps to 'us' and 'now' disregards the irreducible particularity of the gray zone" (Sanyal, 8). The gray zone on which Sanyal builds her essay is that morally ambiguous terrain witnessed and dissected by Primo Levi, "a zone of violence and ambiguity in which victim, perpetrator, accomplice, and witness were 'bound together by the foul link of imposed complicity'" (Sanyal, 1). When Levi's meaning is extended "to include 'us' in a general condition of traumatic culpability [. . .] it also, paradoxically, proposes an infinitely elastic notion of victimhood" (Sanyal, 9).[14] Despite her own identification with Holocaust trauma and victimization, Sherri Szeman examines "the complex web of complicity between victims and executioners" in Auschwitz and the problems of transforming it "into the allegory for a recurrent, unlocatable and transhistorical violence, one contaminating the civilian world of even a liberal democracy and its daily rituals [. . .]" (Sanyal, 6). *The Kommandant's Mistress* weaves its own "complex web of complicity" between a perpetrator and a prisoner while granting both protagonists subjectivity and individuality in their self-portraits. Likewise, as the novel moves from the violent despotism of Auschwitz to the "liberal democracy" of the United States, it offers a critical gloss on assumptions on which trauma theory is based in relation to American myths of the innocent victim, the second chance, rescue, and reparation.

Concerning the characterization of the perpetrator, the novel beckons readers to understand the Kommandant by presenting his voice as the focalizing consciousness of his narrative; at the same time, however, we are stalled in the process. Even as his narrative draws us in with its fictional proposition that the perpetrator's character is multifaceted and dynamic, we do not witness any kind of moral epiphany or transformation that might result from his feelings of intimacy and attachment to the woman whose Jewish identity and fate, despite his efforts, can neither be ignored nor rationalized. While Maximilian von Walther is not the sadistically deranged Amon Goeth, neither is he Oskar Schindler. Instead, his narrative consists of variations on a theme of self-justifying defenses while he starves Rachel and subjects her not only to his sexual assaults, but to those of his colleagues. Yet despite behavior and self-disclosures that would render his character one-dimensional and repellant to most readers, Szeman's carefully nuanced portrait provides a critical space for analyzing his character beyond the confines of denunciation.

For example, by having von Walther save Rachel's life and yet pursue her to the United States, always jeopardizing his own escape, the novel rejects the stereotype of S.S. inhuman indomitability. As Karin Doerr observes, survivors most often recall the perpetrators as "an anonymous threat, someone who instilled deadly fear and meted out death" ("Memories of History," 60). In much fiction, "the usually attractive male Nazi type often exudes pride, power, and sexual prowess" ("Memories of History," 61). Such a fictional prototype finds its nexus in conventional, indeed trite, assumptions about the essentially aggressive nature of male sexuality; yet rarely do scholars question the image of a ramrod black uniformed S.S. officer as an authentic representation of Nazi sexualized violence or as glamorizing the Holocaust. Szeman's novel questions this representation by opening von Walther's character to the possibility of moral rescue and to being viewed as the object of a self-inflicted trauma. This possibility is dramatized by developing his emotional dependency on the Jewish woman and his act of rescuing her. Yet unlike Oskar Schindler, the Kommandant is not saved by the Jew and his self-inflicted trauma has no outlet for expression except perhaps in his death and by proxy in his mistress's writing. But as this perpetrator/pilgrim wends his way to a confrontation with his victim, we find no progress. There is no righteousness, no redemption, and no reparation that emanate from his act of rescue. In fact, as we shall see, the American myth of heroic rescue is demolished by the fates of these enmeshed characters in the United States.

Since neither trope, the eroticized woman victim nor the sexually tormenting and tormented Nazi, can exist without the other, we can begin to unravel the theoretical issues attendant on them by examining Szeman's depiction of their relationship as it is informed by Auschwitz and then the United States. Given the dehumanizing conditions to which concentration camp victims were actually subjected—systematic starvation, filth, arbitrary beatings and shootings, gratuitously brutal and useless labor, and gassing—questions arise about identifying the nature of a relationship between perpetrator and victim. As Primo Levi suggests in "The Gray Zone," how does any extant critical, psychological, or ethical model of normativity apply when the motivations and behavior of both parties derive from dehumanizing ideologies and the conditions of genocide? The relationship does not simply result in trauma but is constituted in it—born of it. In turn, the very extremes of Holocaust conditions and relationships highlight the difficulty of identifying the ethical and psychological norms by which such a fictional relationship can be judged when it continues beyond the camps. If we cannot judge the moral and psychological behavior of Holocaust relationships, how do we assess their narrative representations, whether they are composed by victims or survivors or by non-survivor artists? Especially as time goes on and the proliferation of survivors' testimonies will end with their deaths, as more fictional accounts leap into the void, these ethical challenges become even more complicated and more urgent.

One of the problems of humanizing and therefore providing complexity to the character of the Nazi Kommandant in the novel is its correlate, interpreting Rachel's involvement with him as monstrous. While graphically painted scenes represent von Walther's intense attraction to Rachel as abusively realized and her responses as designed to evade and temper his attacks, instead of the spontaneous combustion we might expect from their sexual encounters, the novel takes us in another interpretive direction. We are asked to view Rachel's undoubtedly traumatic experience as at least partially self-inflicted and self-knowing. Like the experience and memory of actual trauma, the repetitions and rhythmic cadences of the narrative produce a sense of ritual that both expresses and contains Rachel's rage and hatred of the Kommandant. This is a performance that suggests an impassioned entanglement that she cannot be said to emotionally avoid. This narrative strategy applies to von Walther's continuous rapes of her, to their immediate aftermaths, and long afterward, when she is married, to her life as it is impelled by her obsession with his coming after her. Even after she immigrates to the United States and marries David, a sensitive and nurturing son of Holocaust survivors, she cannot let go of the past, with the Kommandant at its center. And while the inability to recover from a Holocaust past may typify the workings of traumatic memory, several features of her narrative indicate a willfulness that betrays choice. Going against the grain of the American dream, she chooses to deny herself the rewards of rescue; she repudiates the idea of a second chance or the possibility of a new life and *moving on*. Though her ability to conceive remains ambiguous, she rejects David's desire to adopt a child and thus rejects her role in the regeneration of the Jewish people, an axiom if not an imperative of American Jewish communities.[15] In itself a transgression of the respect we bear survivors, this representation also suggests that Rachel's decisive rejection of Jewish continuity affirms the Kommandant's power and therefore constitutes a Nazi victory. How the novel resolves this representational dilemma challenges definitions of trauma victimhood and of Holocaust resistance, and the availability of Holocaust knowing.

Rachel's trauma results not only from her experience as a sex slave but from recognition of her complicity in that experience, as we see in her writing. That Rachel's part in the entanglement defies her role as victim and questions how the production of Holocaust trauma can be applied elsewhere, to other kinds of suffering, is confirmed by the novel's different voices. As the narrator of her responses, she can be held responsible for designing their presentation, the result of which is an ambiguity that leads the women resisters to doubt her victimization: "'Oh, no, Kommandant,' Rachel said breathlessly, her hips pounding, 'Please don't torture me this way'" (*Kommandant's Mistress*, 154). This doubt guides us to become readers who resist oppositional categories of victim and resister while being alerted to their differences as we also doubt the validity of the resisters' taunts. Szeman's portrayal of Rachel's behavior and self-representation reflects what Sara Horowitz has referred to as "an ambivalence about certain gendered strategies for survival [and] about sexual atrocity."[16] As Horowitz explains, "While other forms of Holocaust atrocity seem unthinkable in the present world of the survivor, sexual violence continues, and may seem, in retrospect, more ordinary—merely shameful and hence, inexcusable" ("Martyrdom," 29). As suggested by the resisters' mockery of Rachel, an example of reading this shamefulness into the novel is ambivalence over whether "Rachel's narrative disrupts the erotic pleasure of the Kommandant's text" or contributes to it and therefore to the possibility of his victory as well ("Martyrdom," 31).

While the disruption affirms the novel's richness and complexity, we must also consider that, for some readers, the images of Rachel's resistance to the

Kommandant's embraces may very well be a source of sexual arousal. In turn, this arousal would erase the distance between text and reader. Implied in such arousal is the reader's identification with the Kommandant, a vicarious effect in which the reader joins the pleasures of yielding to, yet retaining victorious control of the woman as sexual object. Not simply defined as sexual experience, this textual/sexual relationship cannot be divorced from the woman's Jewish identity, and so acquiesces to what Gisela Bock calls "sexist racism." Bock's terms, "sexist racism" and "racist sexism" help explain how the Nazis determined women's fates according to intertwined racial and gender classifications. Racist sexism affected women who were deemed "socially or ethnically superior" and who were coerced into bearing children to regenerate the Reich. Women who were found to be deviant or inferior were prohibited from bearing children and therefore victims of "sexist racism." This prohibition was based not only on racial and genetic readings of women, "but on grounds of their real or supposed deviation, *as women, from social or ethnic standards for superior women*" (Bock's italics).[17] We see implications of this reading in the Kommandant's treatment of his wife and his mistress. Whereas his wife earns his respect for bearing two beautiful Aryan children but suffers his increasing emotional distance, the Kommandant's Jewish mistress is categorically, that is, racially placed to be the appropriately transgressive target of his uninhibited, unimpeded sexual passions.[18] In his reading of Rachel's responses, she deserves his sexual aggression because she deviates from the Nazis' prescribed definition of a "superior," much less, acceptable woman. To share such a reading would then be tantamount to acceding to "sexist racism" and, in another vicarious adventure, participating in the production of trauma.

   While it is easy to condemn such a response for constructing the text as a pornographic extension and object of the reader's desires, we must also recognize ethical issues concerning the production of trauma raised by alternative reading strategies. For example, various reader response theories avoid traditionally constraining moral judgments in order to validate the complex cultural and social spectrum of reading and interpretive communities and by extension, how they choose and assess the texts they read. While such literary theories have resulted in important reevaluations of canonical and noncanonical writers and texts, in doing so, they have also neutralized or simply ignored the ethical implications of readers' responses.[19] Instead, what is of interest is the impact of various interpretive practices on the status of the text. Where Holocaust fiction is concerned, between concerns about denial and distortion and the ongoing traumatic memories of survivors, there may be no neutral reading. In the case of *The Kommandant's Mistress*, neutralizing the sexually aroused reader normalizes his or her response and by implication, the character of the perpetrator with whom he or she identifies. Such a critical framework places both reader and character beyond the pale of being judged as complicit with sexual violence. As a result, the critical reader, as well as the aroused, are complicit with denying the trauma of sexual violence. In this sense, as literary critics, we are positioned to judge not only the Kommandant's behavior as human or as monstrous, but also the reader's response, including ours.

The question of whether the narrative design also challenges the categories of victim and perpetrator and their roles in the production of trauma becomes a focus when viewing the Kommandant's and Rachel's narrations in light of each other. Despite differences in the two narratives between her version of events and von Walther's, the contrapuntal balance those narratives achieve also suggests that the effects Rachel and the Kommandant have on each other humanize them by exposing their frailties; but these same effects also incite a passion for brutality in each of them. If this incitement merely confirms the view of the Kommandant as villainous, how does the text lead readers to judge Rachel? Nowhere is this dilemma more evident than in an oft cited incident where after forcing himself on her, von Walther shows Rachel a six-pointed Star of David he has drawn on his forearm. In her version, Rachel tells us that she makes the mark her own by taking his knife and cutting the star, but his version recounts the cut as self-inflicted. As Karin Doerr points out, despite their differences, the combination of the two versions "mocks" several aspects of Nazi blood brotherhood as well as Nazi racial hierarchies ("Verisimilitude," 157). For together, the two versions produce a metaphor of mixing superior Aryan and subhuman or poisonous Jewish blood. Despite insistent differences, there are many parallels that tease us with these characters' mutual erotic suggestiveness, as when both von Walther's and Rachel's narratives begin with almost the same line, and ones that announce the immediate and provocative effect of the perpetrator and his victim on each other: "Then I saw her" and "Then I saw him" (*Kommandant's Mistress* 3, 127). This mutuality is reinforced in the pivotal scene cited above; where in Rachel's account, she not only wishes to scar the Kommandant with the iconic Jewish sign, but the act arouses her sexually and therefore we can conclude that it marks her as an agent of violence. This is no passive victim.

Unlike those women who had no way of knowing what was being done to them when Dr. Mengele performed his ghastly experiments, Rachel's narrative shows her to be fully cognizant and active. While we can argue that Rachel's sexual movements are performative in that she pretends to be aroused so as to end von Walther's assault more quickly, the above scene indicates her actual and unplanned sexual response. If performance suggests not only disguise, but also the willed activation of a self one designs, the inclusion of

Rachel's spontaneous sexual arousal would seem to foreclose the possibility that she desires being rescued or remaking herself at any time or in any place, including the United States, where she is positioned in a new life. This foreclosure also provides a critical gloss on the idea that Rachel's relationship with the Kommandant is traumatizing.

The novel destabilizes American myths of repairing or remaking the self and of finding coherent meaning in these acts or in writing as a process of imagining them. With their jarring, fragmented movements from scene to scene, moment to moment, and constant dialogic interruptions, both the Kommandant's and Rachel's narratives cohere only to convey a conflicted mutuality of opposing passions. In the middle of an exchange between two characters, whether in Auschwitz or the United States, whether between perpetrators or victims, words or a line will be cut off only to be repeated as these words begin a dialogue from another scene, possibly between other characters, and often in another temporal and spatial setting. In this way, not only is the resolution of each scene persistently disrupted, but each blends into another, even when the blend is of perpetrator and victim or survivor. Especially as the plot moves to the United States, the presence of the perpetrator blurs the boundaries between victory and defeat and between vengeance and justice. This blurring, however, does not represent ambivalence, that is, the equally powerful desire of opposites, but rather an insistent opposition, and this opposition unsettles any sense that Szeman is aiming for a humanizing equivalency between the Kommandant and his mistress. If the characters can find no coherence to what is happening to them, for even the Kommandant's feelings for Rachel are beyond his control as is her obsession with him, the novel's ambiguous resolution would seem to respond to Elie Wiesel's pleas that for those of us who are only in a position to imagine the Holocaust, rather than supplying all too easy answers, we must continue to ask questions.[20]

The scenic and dialogic disruptions and ambiguities as well as the novel's appendix and afterword call attention to the questioning constructedness of both narratives. Designed to explain the *real* identities of Rachel Levi and Maximilian von Walther, the appendix and afterword are ironic, self-reflexive devices that exclaim the narrative's fictionality, especially since it is common knowledge that the Kommandant of Auschwitz was named Rudolf Höss. This novel is thus shaped self-consciously as an artifact, but in its very fictionality, it creates questions about slippages or relationships between the documentation of Holocaust memory, trauma, and representations of both. The novel's primary clue to these questions is the fact that Rachel is a writer of both fiction and memoir. We discover that Rachel's first book, *Bitter Herbs*, written in captivity, is interspersed with the Kommandant's words. This is not only an act of appropriation or plagiarism, for she incorporates his poetry without acknowledging that he wrote it, but also the fusion that results creates an intimate explosion of words and writing that in Rachel's narrative and his, as well as in Szeman's, represents their triangular and enmeshed relationship.

One scene in particular illustrates the conflation of this odd couple's sexual behavior and the urgent drive to write the Holocaust. Immediately following a scene where Rachel welcomes her husband's gentle sexual approach, her own narrative switches to her response to von Walther's kisses. Though this response may very well be designed to produce his prolonged sleep, Rachel narrates her performance as an act of sexual agency: "I had stroked his face and kissed him. I had put my tongue in his mouth. I had wrapped my legs around him and breathed his name against his throat. I had trembled and sighed, as if he had touched me" (*Kommandant's Mistress*, 252). Even if we accept Rachel's narration of the two sexual encounters as antithetical, they are deeply connected. What draws them together, including their proximity on the page, is a relationship between sexual agency, sexual manipulation, and writing as an act or process of manipulating the lives and words of others. When David, Rachel's husband, approaches her, she is in bed with two of her books: *The Dead Bodies That Line the Streets* and *Survivor: One Who Survives.* In order to move closer to him, she kicks the books out of the way, an act that metonymically suggests that a normative, mutually caring intimate relationship is not possible if the Holocaust past intrudes as a traumatic trace. And yet, at the same time, the presence of the books implies that even in its virtual form, that is, as a written representation, the Holocaust past must be as much a part of their relationship as it is of defining Rachel's sense of herself, her life, and her writing after Auschwitz, all occurring in the mythic safety of America. This presence of the past, however, even as it occurs in the land of second chances, does not affirm the possibility of reconciliation with the past or of another American myth, healing. Instead, the novel dramatizes the process of transfiguring the all too intimate horrors of Auschwitz into writing that will perpetuate the presence of a traumatic past.

Most startling is the demonstration that the writer's muse or inspiration is her Auschwitz experience. Instead of craving healing even if she cannot achieve it or using writing as a healing process,[21] this survivor fuels the flames of her trauma, keeping her wound open and the possibility of healing at bay. In a scene featuring Rachel and von Walther, immediately juxtaposed with the one cited above, as soon as the satiated Kommandant falls safely asleep, Rachel tells us: "I looked down at the papers in my lap. I lifted a corner of the first page. I tore off a small piece. I put it in my mouth. I swallowed. . . . I tore off another piece. I put his words in my mouth" (*Kommandant's Mistress*, 252–53). Here writing becomes a primal sexual act of fulfillment, like the impulses of infants who take objects into their mouths to explore their worlds and close the fearful distance between the unknown and the self. In this case, however, the fulfilling act must violently incorporate the fearful Other in order to declaw its danger. Having experienced the Holocaust as a sexually racialized object and subject, having been forced into a devolved condition of speechlessness and elementary need, Rachel transforms that condition into knowledge and a fully developed writing self by aggressively imbibing the words that captivity has denied her.

Yet, as we have been reminded so often, because the Holocaust may very well be beyond understanding, even when it is someone's own experience, such knowledge is not the same as understanding or a pathway to reconciliation with the past. With this in mind, we can consider that Szeman may very well have written the above scene to implicate her own writing, that is, to represent the act of imagining the Holocaust as one of violation and expropriation. And in order to do so, like the events it would recount, and like Rachel swallowing the Kommandant's words, Holocaust fiction must therefore incorporate the violence it represents even as it imaginatively transforms it. On the other hand, the multiple meanings suggested by Rachel's willful act do not all lead to the conclusion that in eating his words, she has accepted either him as human or the idea that his words make her and her writing monstrous. Instead, Rachel's act may be transformative in another way. If we assess Holocaust testimony as necessitating all the ugly truths we would rather not face, then Rachel's act suggests that to write the Holocaust, the presence of the perpetrator in the body and consciousness of the survivor cannot be denied.

And yet even as it proposes this incorporation, the novel questions its possibility. At the very end of Rachel's narrative and of the novel itself, when von Walther has found her and stands outside her door reading to her from her own book, *The Dead Bodies*, she recounts the scene as though his act of reading her words is his most violating. But if we remember how she tore into and devoured his writing, then perhaps we are being asked to see these acts as reciprocal:

> I knew the words that came out of his mouth. They were my words: they were spelled with my skin, my blood, my bones. I know those words he was giving to me. They were the Kommandant's words, but they were forged with my skin, my blood, my bones. The Kommandant opened his mouth and *The Dead Bodies* poured out of him. I readied the gun for firing. (*Kommandant's Mistress*, 254)

If we follow the narrative logic of this unlikely scenario, then we might conclude that writing the Holocaust is an act of vengeance. Having been cast as subhuman into what Primo Levi refers to in "The Gray Zone" as the upside down moral universe of the *Lager* (concentration camp), the survivor is forced into anti-human conditions that produce barbarous acts that we who weren't there cannot judge. Karin Doerr maintains that Rachel uses her writing "as a personal and political act against [the Kommandant and in] so doing *he* becomes the victim of *her* public voice" ("Memories," 61). If Rachel does shoot the Kommandant at the end, we have been given enough evidence to know what drove her to do so. But because the novel's last scene not only takes place but is written in the post-Holocaust *free world* of The United States, it raises the question of whether Primo Levi's plea applies to these circumstances.

Let's look again at the novel's self-questioning structure to help us decide. As my students ask, if Rachel did shoot the Kommandant, what did she do with the body? Wouldn't she have to face her husband's questions? What does it solve or teach us about the Holocaust and its American reception to bring the brutalizing Auschwitz relationship to the United States where Rachel's killing of the Kommandant ends the story but not necessarily the trauma? The novel addresses these questions by incorporating those about its status as an American Holocaust fiction. For example, in addition to the American myths discussed earlier, the novel embeds various conventions we find in popular American Holocaust films, including *The Boys from Brazil*, *The Marathon Man*, and most recently, the *X-Men* franchise. All of these films focus on the sinister presence and manipulation of economic or political power by disguised Nazi war criminals who escaped Germany and war crimes trials. Recalling as well American film noir, the appearance of von Walther, "out of the past" and in the United States is replete with his murder of a bystander/witness and the suspense of whether he will be caught. This suspense is heightened by the sense of danger he represents to American security and stability, especially as we now know that Nazi war criminals did find haven in the Americas. Instead of flattening his character, however, these stock elements ironically challenge the kinds of resolution and closure we find in popular Holocaust films.

This challenge is foreshadowed earlier in the novel when Rachel's husband brings home a child he has adopted. After months of separation, this son of Holocaust survivors makes a life-affirming decision that he foists on his resisting wife. Although Rachel never indicates that she accepts the child, her frenetic writing activity during their separation and her delight in a completed manuscript suggest a metaphoric birth. Having overcome a severe writer's block or difficult conception, she has recovered a will to live that will subvert any hint that Nazism triumphs in this novel. Since we know that Rachel is a Holocaust writer, but that in addition to recounting her own experience, she incorporates pieces of von Walther's writing into her own, is it possible that the novel positions her as the writer of both her own narrative and the Kommandant's? In other words, in the novel's metafictional strategy, the manuscript Rachel has completed during her separation from David is *The Kommandant's Mistress*. It is thus possible that the book could only be completed by imagining a resolution that purges the death-embracing presence of the Kommandant and the inspiration of her trauma but perpetuates them in her writing and readership. If we can accept this interpretation, then we might view the ending as a statement that in order to imagine the Holocaust, we must concede that there is no rescue from or reparation for its inhuman horrors. But instead of condemning the survivor for mimicking the violence of the perpetrator, the novel urges us to view Rachel's shooting the Kommandant as an act of escaping from barbarity by writing it.

NOTES

1. Roth's invented Anne Frank defies the controversial decision of Otto Frank to edit out of the original diary her reflections on her developing sexuality and her difficult relations with her mother, all of which have now been restored in a definitive edition; *The Ghost Writer* (New York: Farrar, Straus, and Giroux, 1979).

2. For discussion of the cultural history of this image, see Sander Gilman's chapter "The Jewish Nose" in his book *The Jew's Body* (New York: Routledge, 1991).

3. See the essays in Yosefa Loshitzky, ed. *Spielberg's Holocaust: Critical Perspectives on "Schindler's List"* (Bloomington: Indiana University Press, 1997).

4. A poignant example of how such concerns are internalized is Fanya Heller's memoir *Strange and Unexpected Love: A Teenage Girl's Holocaust Memoirs* (Hoboken, NJ: Ktav Publishing, 1993), which focuses on her teenage love affair with a young Ukrainian militia man who hid her family. After decades of secrecy and only after her husband died, against the wishes of her children, she published the book, only to be shunned by friends and synagogue co-congregants. Whether they were incensed over the fact that in order to survive, Fanya's parents encouraged the affair, that she really loved Jan, the perceived enemy, or that she never resolved her ambivalence about not marrying him, raises questions about the complex roles of women's sexuality in the formation of Holocaust memory and memorialization. Myrna Goldenberg argues that women's biology and roles as "caregivers" inspire memoirs that "are dominated by images and anecdotes of horrific violence related to sexuality" ("Women's Voices in Holocaust Literary Memoirs," *Shofar* 16:4 [Summer 1998], 79). She also cites several examples of rape in the ghettoes and camps, despite policies against *rassenschande* (interracial sex).

5. Sara Horowitz notes feminist complaints that Holocaust master narratives omit stories of women's sexual violation, but because she also reflects on both "the reluctance to open up [such] material to a prurient voyeurism" and how "the woman victim as erotic object has become a trope of Holocaust representations," she is moved to ask, "What are the ethics of representing sexual violation?" ("Mengele, the Gynecologist, and Other Stories of Women's Survival," in *Judaism Since Gender*, ed. Miriam Peskowitz and Laura Levitt [New York: Routledge, 1997], 202, 207, 208).

6. Debates about the subject of women and the Holocaust reached fever pitch with Gabriel Schoenberg's diatribe "Auschwitz and the Professors," *Commentary* (June 1998). Responses in the form of studies of women's experiences include Judith Tydor Baumel, *Double Jeopardy: Gender and the Holocaust* (London: Valentine Mitchell, 1998), and Marlene Heinemann, *Gender and Destiny: Women Writers of the Holocaust* (Westport, CT: Greenwood Press, 1986), as well as Deborah Lipstadt, Paula Hyman, Lenore Weitzman and Dalia Ofer, Marion Kaplan, and Lore Segal, "Women Scholars Speak Up," *Lilith* (Fall 1998), 10–13.

7. Though Spielberg clearly directed this project with great seriousness, his intention to reach and educate as wide an audience as possible produced creative choices that sentimentalize the complex characters and fates of Schindler and his Jews. For example, the film incorporates various motifs and perspectives that have marked Spielberg's career, such as the child's experience of danger perpetrated by morally and psychologically compromised adults. Like the iconic Anne Frank, Spielberg's child figures can never develop complexity and are despoiled only by the brutal world that ensnares them.

8. Roth's commitment to the American dream is apparent even in his most incisive critiques of American culture, as in his novels *American Pastoral* and *The Plot Against America*. In the latter novel, even the eruption of a powerful fascist movement in America is defeated ultimately by the steadfast and basic sense of fairness in American society. At the end, the charismatic fascist leader Charles Lindburgh, flies off into the stratosphere, never to be seen or heard from again, while America heals itself.

9. As testimonies show, even when women survivors have been victims of sexual abuse, as with Dr. Mengele's experiments, disclosure has been very painful. Some information is emerging regarding non-Jewish women prisoners from Ravensbrück who were forced into sexual labor in a total of ten concentration camps by false promises of being released. There is, however, little firsthand testimony since they were not asked and they feared humiliation. See Brigitte Halbmayr, "Sexualized Violence and Forced Prostitution in National Socialism," excerpted and translated from Halbmayr, *Sexualisierte Gewalt* (Vienna: Mandelbaum, 2004). In their introduction to their recent edited volume of essays, Sonja M. Hedgepeth and Rochelle G. Saidel show that the Nazis' "meticulous records [record] virtually no official Nazi documentation of rape and sexual abuse of Jewish women," but that "a solid core of testimonies and memoirs by victims and witnesses [. . .] serves as evidence [of] forced sexual contact"; *Sexual Violence against Jewish Women During the Holocaust* (Waltham, MA: Brandeis University Press, 2010), 2, 5. Wendy Sarti shows how German women guards participated in the sexual violence of women victims in *Women and Nazis: Perpetrators of Genocide and Other Crimes During Hitler's Regime, 1933-1945* (Bethesda: Academica Press, 2011).

10. See for example, the Auschwitz memoirs of Charlotte Delbo and Gisella Perl.

11. Karin Doerr interprets Rachel's character as being trapped by the Kommandant but also as participating actively in her sexually abusive relationship with him in "Verisimilitude and the Holocaust in Sherri Szeman's *The Kommandant's Mistress*," *Philological Papers* 44 (1998–1999): 154–61.

12. Sherri Szeman, letter to Karin Doerr, February 26, 1995, quoted in Doerr, "Memories of History: Women and the Holocaust," *Shofar* 18:3 (Spring 2000), 54.

13. Debarati Sanyal, "A Soccer Match in Auschwitz," *Representations* 79 (Summer 2002): 10.

14. The subjects of Sanyal's critique are writings by Giorgio Agamben, Shoshana Felman, and Cathy Caruth, whom she puts into dialogue with Primo Levi and Albert Camus.

15. The technicolor epilogue to Spielberg's film tells of the birth of 6,000 heirs to Schindler's Jews.

16. Sara Horowitz, "Martyrdom and Gender in Jewish American Holocaust Memory," in *Religious Perspectives in Modern Muslim and Jewish Literatures*, ed. Glenda Abramson and Hilary Kirkpatrick (New York: Routledge, 2006), 179–208.

17. Gisela Bock, "Racism and Sexism in Nazi Germany: Motherhood, Compulsory Sterilization, and the State," in *When Biology Became Destiny: Women in Weimar and Nazi Germany*, ed. Renate Bridenthal, Atina Grossman, and Marion Kaplan (New York: Monthly Review Press, 1984), 178.

18. Partially because of laws prohibiting sex between Germans and Jews and the constructed fear of poisonous Jewish women, there are few reported cases of camp guards raping Jewish women. There are accounts of Jewish women trading sexual favors to save the lives of sisters and mothers. Women confined to camp brothels were mostly Polish.

19. A telling example occurred on the *Oprah Winfrey Show* about Bernhard Schlink's novel *The Reader*, where readers found its depiction of a sexual relationship between a former concentration camp guard and a fifteen-year-old German boy obscene because the novel appeared to them to condone sexual abuse. With an open-armed gesture and incredulous look, Oprah then asked, "Have you people never heard of the Holocaust?"

20. See for example, Elie Wiesel's essay, "A Plea for the Dead," in *Art from the Ashes: A Holocaust Anthology*, ed. Lawrence Langer (New York: Oxford University Press, 1995), 138–52.

21. See for example, collections of Holocaust accounts that grow out of workshops designed to use writing as therapy, such as Anita Brostoff and Sheila Chamovitz's *Flares of Memory: Stories of Childhood During the Holocaust* (New York: Oxford University Press, 2001).

BIBLIOGRAPHY

Baumel, Judith Tydor. "'Can Two Walk Together if They Do Not Agree?': Reflections on Holocaust Studies and Gender Studies." *Women: A Cultural Review* 13:2 (Summer 2002): 195–206.

——. *Double Jeopardy: Gender and the Holocaust.* London: Valentine Mitchell, 1998.

Bock, Gisela. "Racism and Sexism in Nazi Germany: Motherhood, Compulsory Sterilization, and the State." In *When Biology Became Destiny: Women in Weimar and*

Nazi Germany, edited by Renate Bridenthal, Atina Grossman, and Marion Kaplan, 162–78. New York: Monthly Review Press, 1984.

Brostoff, Anita and Sheila Chamovitz. *Flares of Memory: Stories of Childhood During the Holocaust*. New York: Oxford University Press, 2001.

Delbo, Charlotte. *Auschwitz and After*. New Haven: Yale University Press, 1995.

Doerr, Karin. "Verisimilitude and the Holocaust in Sherri Szeman's *The Kommandant's Mistress*." *Philological Papers* 44 (1998–1999), 154–61.

———. "Memories of History: Women and the Holocaust." *Shofar* 18:3 (Spring 2000), 49–63.

Gilman, Sander. *The Jew's Body*. New York: Routledge, 1991.

Goldenberg, Myrna. "Women's Voices in Holocaust Literary Memoirs." *Shofar* 16:4 (Summer 1998), 75–89.

Halbmayr, Brigitte. "Sexualized Violence and Forced Prostitution in National Socialism." Excerpted and translated by the author from *Sexualisierte Gewalt*. Vienna: Mandelbaum, 2004.

Hedgepeth, Sonja M. and Rochelle G. Saidel, eds. *Sexual Violence against Jewish Women During the Holocaust*. Waltham, MA: Brandeis University Press, 2010.

Heinemann, Marlene. *Gender and Destiny: Women Writers of the Holocaust*. Westport, CT: Greenwood Press, 1986.

Heller, Fanya Gottesfeld. *Strange and Unexpected Love: A Teenage Girl's Holocaust Memoirs*. Hoboken, NJ: Ktav Publishing, 1993.

Horowitz, Sara. "Martyrdom and Gender in Jewish American Holocaust Memory." In *Religious Perspectives in Modern Muslim and Jewish Literatures*, edited by Glenda Abramson and Hilary Kirkpatrick, 179–208. New York: Routledge, 2006.

———. "Mengele the Gynecologist and Other Stories of Women's Survival." In *Judaism Since Gender*, edited by Miriam Peskowitz and Laura Levitt, 200–12. New York: Routledge, 1997.

Levi, Primo. "The Gray Zone." In *The Drowned and the Saved*. New York: Vintage, 1989, 36–69.

Lipstadt, Deborah H., Paula E. Hyman, Lenore J. Weitzman, Dalia Ofer, Marion Kaplan, and Lore Segal. "Women Scholars Speak Up." *Lilith* (Fall 1998), 10–13.

Loshitzky, Yosefa, ed. *Spielberg's Holocaust: Critical Perspectives on "Schindler's List."* Bloomington: Indiana University Press, 1997.

Perl, Gisella. *I Was a Doctor in Auschwitz*. N. Stratford, NH: Ayer Co. Publishers, 1948.

Roth, Philip. *The Ghost Writer*. New York: Farrar, Straus, and Giroux, 1979.

Sanyal, Debarati. "A Soccer Match in Auschwitz." *Representations* 79 (Summer 2002): 1–27.

Sarti, Wendy A. *Women and Nazis: Perpetrators of Genocide and Other Crimes During Hitler's Regime, 1933-1945*. Bethesda: Academica Press, 2011.

Schoenberg, Gabriel. "Auschwitz and the Professors." *Commentary* (June 1998).

Szeman, Sherri. *The Kommandant's Mistress*. New York: HarperPerennial, 1993.

Wiesel, Elie. "A Plea for the Dead." In *Art From the Ashes*, edited by Lawrence Langer, 138–52. New York: Oxford University Press, 1995.

Chapter Nine

Reading Holocaust Fiction at the End of the Twentieth Century

Jakob the Liar *and* Life Is Beautiful

Jennifer Taylor

At the end of the twentieth century, two mainstream narrative films, Peter Kassovitz's *Jakob the Liar* (1999) and Roberto Benigni's *Life Is Beautiful* (1998), stirred up a great deal of argument about representation of the Holocaust. On the surface, the debates appear very similar to earlier ones about Holocaust-themed texts by such writers as Elie Wiesel, Edgar Hilsenrath, and Art Spiegelman, focusing on realism, autobiographical authority, and of course, the use of humor. The debates about *Life* took place in the international arena and often pitted national narratives against one another. While American film critic David Denby describes *Life* as a completely unrealistic and unauthentic picture[1] of the Holocaust, Italianist Maurizio Viano makes an emotional defense of Benigni's tragicomic film as grounded in Italian cinematic tradition.[2] And American historian Sander Gilman expresses some concern about what he reads as devolution of the Holocaust film into a vehicle for the comic.[3]

Indeed, the international popularity of *Life*, even in the face of critique about its use of comedy, appears to signal a major shift between earlier, serious Holocaust texts and more recent comedic ones. Even the less popular *Jakob* relied on the comedic talents of Robin Williams. More important than the shift toward the comic, though, the two films reflect national myths that appeal to audiences in both the United States and Italy at the end of the last century. Specifically, they reflect, in *Jakob*, the American myth of universal suffering in the Holocaust (the Kassovitz film is an American-French co-production, despite the fact that it is based on a German novel from 1969, a matter I will take up later), and in *Life*, the Italian narrative in which anti-Semitism is understood to be a German import.

The national myths that inform both of these films derive some of their effectiveness from public memory and discourse in the United States and

Italy, of course, but they also reflect a qualitative shift in the way Western society reads the *Shoah* in the late twentieth century. Specifically, this shift is one of narrative perspective, reflecting the emergence of a younger group of artists and audience members, relatively unburdened by this event. As the older generation of writers and artists who actually experienced the Holocaust passes away, their perspective, too, recedes.

Kassovitz's 1999 *Jakob* is based loosely upon one of the older genera- tion's texts—Holocaust survivor Jurek Becker's 1969 East German novel, *Jacob the Liar*—and the two versions give us the opportunity to compare the interesting changes that have occurred during this time. How and why does Becker's novel, an Eastern European Holocaust story aimed at a specifically German-speaking audience, become the American Holocaust story about the universal nature of humanity as well as a vehicle for the actor Robin Williams? What narrative changes had to be made to Becker's original nar- rative to make it resonate in the United States (what is lost or gained)? The Robin Williams film asks us to empathize with the Jewish inhabitants of a German ghetto in Poland and to imagine their pain. Nevertheless, the deep engagement Becker's narrator has with the past, as well as his struggle to put into words what he has experienced, is lacking in Kassovitz's cinematic version of this text. Scholar Angel Loureiro has suggested that this engage- ment might be thought of as the "ethical" struggle with the "other," which he sees as central to autobiography.[4] Loureiro argues that autobiographical texts, specifically memoirs about Holocaust experiences, function ethically. That is, these memoirs acknowledge their own incompleteness and instead engage in discussions with the self, with the other, and with the reader. While Becker's novel is not an autobiography, of course (the author actually claimed to have no memories of the Holocaust because he was only six years old at the end of 1945) he is nonetheless a survivor-author, close to the event and deeply engaged in the project of working through the past.

The newer film texts, as non-autobiographical pieces and as texts far removed in time from the Holocaust itself, do not engage in this particular "ethical" discussion. Instead, both *Jakob the Liar* and *Life Is Beautiful* reflect a shift in narrative perspective that manifests itself in two closely connected ways. First, they both tend to universalize the Holocaust experience, focusing on the human tragedy of Guido and Jakob while de-emphasizing the protago- nists' Jewish identities and the historical specificity of the Holocaust. Na- tional myths at work in both Italy and the United States certainly contribute to the desire to see the Holocaust as a human tragedy more than as a historic genocidal event. Secondly, these popular mainstream texts have eliminated the very narrative structures that allow Becker's novel to function, not just as Holocaust fiction, but also as an ethical autobiographical discussion with the other, as Loureiro describes. That is to say, the kind of fictional internal discussions Becker's narrator has with the Nazis, with his parents, and, perhaps most importantly, with his German readers throughout *Jacob the Liar*, are missing in the cinematic texts. In *Life* and in Kassovitz's *Jakob*, both narrators—Guido's son as well as the disembodied voice of Jakob himself—are depicted as whole and almost at peace in a healed, unscathed post-Holocaust world, a world seemingly without trauma.

If the more recent film texts are not focused on engagement with the past and the role of the survivor, what do they accomplish? How should we read them? What kinds of new questions, if any, do these new narratives offer? The international celebration and debate surrounding the films mean that their new Holocaust narratives ring true for many audiences. This demands our attention, but, again, how do we read them? If, in the 1990s, ". . . the *Shoah* has begun to become history rather than memory," as Gilman contends,[5] then these films might be understood as a form of evolution of the Holocaust text, posing new, national, and universal questions for the post-Holocaust audience. On the other hand, if the Holocaust represents a qualitative break with history and defies historicization, as Saul Friedlander and others have argued, then these film texts would have to be understood as a devolution, an erasure of the national and historical specificity and complexity of this event.[6] Both readings of the films, it seems, prove true simultaneously at the end of the twentieth century.

Even as many of its survivors are now dying, the Holocaust remains the event that has defined our last century. Attempts to understand and to narrate this event abound. The Historians' Debate of the 1980s in Germany, the much publicized debate between Martin Broszat and Saul Friedlander about historicization,[7] as well as the appearance of such books as Peter Novick's *The Holocaust in American Life*, analyzing the history of the American reading of Holocaust, all speak to the continuing need for more narratives, and for newer explanations and stories about this event. In the following pages, I will examine the competing and, at times, conflicting narratives we find in the three texts—Becker's *Jacob the Liar*, Kassovitz's *Jakob the Liar* and Benigni's *Life Is Beautiful*. What do these texts offer us? To what degree do they represent national points of view? To what degree are they international? And what do the narratives of the more recent film texts offer to younger audiences? Can we move beyond labels such as evolution and devolution?

BECKER'S *JACOB THE LIAR*

Becker's *Jacob the Liar* first appeared in 1969, published by the Aufbau Verlag in Berlin (East) and has enjoyed great success in Germany, the United

States, and other countries. In 1996, a new English translation by Leila Vennewitz met with critical acclaim.[8] Two film versions of the book have also
appeared, one produced in 1975 in the former German Democratic Republic
by Frank Beyer, as well as the recent American-French co-production star-
ring Robin Williams, which was released in 1999. While the 1977 version has
some commonalities in structure and theme with Becker's novel (he wrote the
screenplay and based the book in part on the idea for the film), the 1999 film
version is strikingly different from the original.

The Becker novel opens with a first-person narrator, a Polish Jewish Holocaust survivor, telling the target audience, German readers, about his own
story in a style close to free association. He moves from talking about trees
to his first love, his wife's murder under a tree, and then to the ghetto itself,
a place where, he tells us, trees were forbidden. Only then does he turn to
the story of Jacob Heym, a fellow slave-laborer in the Polish ghetto. In the
story within the narrator's frame, we learn that Jacob is forced to go into the
dreaded police headquarters where he chances to hear a radio report about
nearby Russian troops. Wanting to share the news, but sure that no one will
believe him (everyone assumes all Jews would be executed for entering police
headquarters), Jacob claims to have a contraband radio. His position becomes
more and more uncomfortable as he must invent news of the approaching
Russian army, moving them back and forth to appease his news-hungry com-
panions. As the ghetto comes to depend on the radio for hope, Jacob starts
to hate his role, but he doesn't dare to expose his "lie" after the one friend
he tells kills himself. In the end, in spite of the hopes that his lie raised, the
Russians do not arrive to save the Jews and all of them are deported to death
camps where, the narrator tells us, Jacob dies. The narrator, who jumps into
the Jacob story every now and then with his own stories and asides, makes it
clear that he can tell the story because he is alive; Jacob cannot tell his own
story because he is dead.

The Becker text opens up questions about the survivor/narrator's relationship to the German pre- and post-Holocaust world. Only the survivor can
tell the story; and yet, he feels ambivalent about his role as storyteller. In the
face of history, he tells us he will fail to tell Jacob's story adequately. The
dilemmas faced by the fictional survivor/narrator of *Jacob* can be understood
in terms of Loureiro's ethical act of writing about the self in the face of ".
. . a spectacle of confusion, uncertainty, moral anarchy, chaos and terror."[9]
Becker's narrative is deeply engaged on all of these levels. Throughout the
novel, even as he tells the central story of Jacob and the radio, the narrator's
voice surfaces again and again to comment upon Jacob's plight, to bring us
back into the present, to his own postwar problems.

In keeping with Loureiro's description of the ethical narrative as consciously incomplete, Becker's narrator simultaneously reveals himself as both powerful (in charge of the story) and impotent in the face of real history. Playing with alternative endings, for instance, the narrator has all the deported Jews from the ghetto saved by the Russian troops in one potential ending, while in another, he allows them all to die. In the end, though, he insists that he cannot, through literature alone, save people who really died. This is a very important point; literature about the Holocaust is for survivors. Its function (or one of them) is to allow us, the living, to work through, to imagine, to come to terms with, or even to reject the past. In *Life*, and in the Kassovitz version of *Jakob*, the function of the narrative is to thwart disaster during the Holocaust itself as well as to give the reader a feeling of well-being and assurance that our humanity will prevail even in the worst circumstances.

Becker's novel resonates on several levels; the survivor/narrator's voice is responsible for remembering and thus creating the past, just as Jacob himself narrated and created the radio. For Becker's narrator, fiction serves as a space to work through what it means to survive, to write, and, very importantly, to be Jewish and German after the Holocaust. For the readers, too, fiction opens up questions about the nature of memory and the role of the audience (the narrator addresses the reader openly on several occasions). Fiction cannot, though, save people from real arbitrary murder any more than Jacob's invented radio can really make the Russians appear. As we will see, this is no longer the case in Kassovitz's *Jakob* and certainly not in Benigni's *Life Is Beautiful*. In Becker's fictional world, the role of art is to speak to the living, to attempt to make sense of murder.

KASSOVITZ'S *JAKOB THE LIAR*

Something very interesting happens when the Becker novel is translated onto the screen in the 1999 American-French production. When this complex narrative moves into the visual, very public sphere of mainstream cinema, the narrative shifts from a focus on the problems of remembering and creating the past to a celebration of the power of the human imagination. The concerns of (American) society at the end of this millennium, not those of the Polish-German survivor-author, are now reshaping the text. Of course, this is not the first time this has happened with a Holocaust text. Cynthia Ozick's critically charged *New Yorker* essay "Who Owns Anne Frank?"[10] served to reopen questions about writing, reading, and editing canonical Holocaust texts. In his 1999 book, Daniel R. Schwarz examines the debates surrounding Anne Frank's diaries, contending that Ozick, "reminds us of how the Holocaust was transformed and domesticated in Otto Frank's editing."[11] Both transformed and domesticated, Kassovitz's *Jakob the Liar* certainly represents American and Western society's desire to "interfere" in the stories of the Holocaust. Specifically, this film reflects a desire similar to the one Ozick describes, in which the Holocaust becomes, instead of a reflection on the issues of trauma and survival, a space to celebrate the triumph of the human spirit, as well as the inherent strength and worth of art and hope in the face of death and despair.

Kassovitz's *Jakob the Liar* stars Robin Williams and has not enjoyed the public adoration of Benigni's *Life Is Beautiful*. Based on Becker's novel, this film version fails to engage its audience, suffering from poor editing, a confusing narrative, and poor timing, coming out after *Life* was released, even though the Kassovitz film was completed by the time *Life* appeared. The 1999 version differs from the novel enormously both in theme as well as in structure. First, instead of despising and fearing his role as radio owner, Kassovitz's Jakob embraces his fate in the end and sacrifices himself for the common good. Gilman reads the added heroics as a kind of nod toward those who want to see heroics in the story of the Holocaust (and this does not refer solely to Americans, of course. Even in the 1960s, Becker's father, a Polish Jew, had always insisted that his son should write a heroic story about the Jews in the ghetto and not a story about an antihero like Becker's Jakob). In the 1999 version, too, Jakob is not a believing Jew (he's more a "human being" than a Jew, like Benigni's Jewish protagonist,[12] making the Holocaust a human, not a particularly Jewish, tragedy). And, as Gilman points out, Lina—the child who dies in the novel as well as in the 1975 film version—must be saved in the Kassovitz film because she is innocent, and post-Holocaust sensibilities, particularly American ones, dictate that innocent people cannot or should not die. Finally, of course, Jakob must sacrifice himself for others in the Robin Williams vehicle, a heroic event that takes place neither in the novel nor in Beyer's 1975 film version.

In his reading of the 1999 *Jakob* film, Gilman argues convincingly that the Holocaust is, in fact, fast becoming a historicized narrative that now can include both the comic and the heroic in its structure: ". . . The heroic, as in Spielberg's complex and contradictory image of Schindler, can now be an acceptable part of telling the *Shoah*'s history."[13] After an interim in which Holocaust survivors themselves were telling their stories—even such ironic and darkly satirical stories as Edgar Hilsenrath's *The Nazi and the Barber* and Becker's *Jakob*—the heroic, and especially comedic, emerge in the new century: ". . . the remake of *Jakob the Liar* . . . so transformed the first version's inner structure that it serves as a barometer of how the comic can be used in representing the *Shoah*."[14]

The inclusion of the comic is only a secondary change between the original novel and the Kassovitz film. The primary shift is in narrative structure. The humor of the work is made possible only by the huge change in structure. In Kassovitz's version, there is no frame outside of the story. Jakob himself is narrating the events, even after his death. This has enormous implications: in Becker's novel, Jakob couldn't tell his story because he was dead. His voice had been killed with him. In the Kassovitz film, there is no recognition that mass murder is a real hindrance to storytelling (and thus to the continuity of life itself); Jakob goes right on existing, narrating his own story. Furthermore, there is no inner dialogue; that ethical discussion that the real survivor has with the past and present is missing altogether in the piece. The problem is not comedy, but rather the lack of narrative reflexivity, an awareness of the impotence of art in the face of random murder.

This is not to dismiss the Kassovitz film, however. It represents an interesting refocusing of history, revealing what appear to be very American concerns about what the Holocaust means for the generations born after the Holocaust. For many people born long after the event, the concern is not the burden of memory facing Becker's protagonist in the postwar era, but rather the need to see the Holocaust as a universal event with moral lessons we can learn. Some of the very things that make the Kassovitz film "unengaged" when compared to Becker's novel speak to American audiences in the 1990s, and we learn a good deal about American Holocaust narratives by investigating them. The film's ending, for instance, with the comically absurd appearance of a 1940s American jazz band outside of a crowded freight train of doomed Jews, provides relief even as it exposes itself as pure fantasy. Seeing the smiling Lina watching in rapture from the train as Andrews Sisters look-alikes belt out a jazzy love song underlines the improbability of the happy ending even as it makes us happy to see everyone "rescued." Kassovitz's film, in depicting the *Shoah* as universal and humanistic, might in fact, be speaking to today's audience's changing understanding of the Holocaust as a teaching moment.[15]

LIFE IS BEAUTIFUL

Life Is Beautiful, although not based on a novel or even the author's own experiences, shares several of the same problematic issues that arise in the Kassovitz version of *Jakob*. *Life*, like *Jakob the Liar*, was one of the last highly successful fictional works about the Holocaust to be publicly celebrated and/or debated in twentieth-century America. Winner of the prestigious Jury Prize at Cannes in 1998, and of forty international awards, it went on to great success with the Academy of Motion Picture Arts and Sciences. Nominated for seven Oscars, a record for a foreign-language film, it received three, including those for the Best Foreign Film and the coveted Best Actor award for Benigni himself. *Life* won Oscars despite being up against such huge American blockbusters as *Saving Private Ryan* and *Shakespeare in Love.* Co-written and directed by Roberto Benigni, *Life* is the highest-grossing foreign film in U.S. history. Favorable reviews, word of mouth, and even the many unfavorable reviews sent audiences to it in crowds. Benigni has been known among "hip" younger Americans for years through his work with Jim Jarmusch in *Down by Law* (1986) and *Night on Earth* (1991), as well as for his role in Fellini's last film, *La Voce della luna* (1989), but in Italy, Benigni has long been as famous as Robin Williams or Woody Allen (or a combination of sorts).

The story opens with an unidentified adult man telling us in voice-over that he will be telling a "fairy tale," thus setting the mood for the somewhat whimsical and fantastic story that unravels. In the first half of the film, we follow Guido (Benigni) as he wanders across the countryside and woos and marries the beautiful Dora (Benigni's wife, Nicoletta Braschi). Guido is, we learn quite late in the film, Jewish, and he is also the ultimate storyteller, literally rewriting the world as he moves through it. His creativity turns a schoolteacher into a princess, allows him to mock the absurd Fascists, and lets him create an insulated world for his non-Jewish wife and young son, Giosue, (Giorgio Cantarini) in Fascist Italy. Ultimately, though, his power to control the world through language is thwarted as he and his son are deported to a concentration camp, followed by the grieving Dora.

The second half of the film depicts the life in the camp, which is as dark as the first half was light. Undaunted by the deportation, Guido persists in narrating the world, attempting to spare his son the reality of the camp. He translates a German guard's harsh orders into the rules for a wonderful game. Everyone will pretend to be fighting, Guido says, and the boy's job is to stay hidden and try to remain uncaptured. At the end of the game, the winner will receive a tank as a prize. Even as he is marched off to be shot, Guido keeps up the image of the game before his son (the boy does not suspect what is really happening at this point), sacrificing himself for the next generation. We realize, of course, that the game is not real because of several objective camera shots that reveal Guido's anguish, something I will later discuss at greater length. Within the framed story of the fairy tale, though, the boy's experience of the camp is mediated entirely through the creative linguistic genius of his father. In the end, we discover that the narrator is, in fact, the boy, who has grown up to understand and appreciate the "gift" his father gave him.

The depiction of Guido's completely assimilated Jewish Italian identity as an integral part of Italian prewar culture poses some intriguing questions for the scholarly community. Gilman argues, for instance, that the idyllic nature of the first half of the film is supposed to represent an Italy that was specifically not anti-Semitic before the German invasion. The film reflects what he reads as a deep-seated Italian national narrative in which the Germans bring anti-Semitism to the Italians, even to the Fascist Italians. This national story about an Italy in which anti-Semitism played a relatively unimportant role before the Germans arrived is, in fact, reflected in several scholarly texts, including Maurizio Viano's review of the film and Susan Zuccotti's history of the Holocaust in Italy.[16] Zuccotti writes in her introduction, for example, that while 15 percent of Jews in Italy during the war were murdered, this number is larger than one would expect in ". . . a country that, despite its nineteenth-century ghettos and the promptings of its Fascist rulers, had no significant anti-Semitic tradition. Jews had lived in Italy since before the Christian era. In 1943, they were proportionately few, thoroughly assimilated, and physically indistinguishable from their Christian countrymen."[17] In other words, Benigni's text upholds and reproduces the national myth that, before the war, the Italian Jews did not suffer from anti-Semitism as did the German Jews. Gilman continues: "Roberto Benigni's character is Jewish only within the Italian model of the 'hidden Jew' . . . The Italian model was that Jews were literally invisible within Italian culture and that only the bestiality of the Germans differentiated them from their non-Jewish neighbors."[18] Gilman's thesis that the Italian model posits an "invisible" Jew presents problems for some Italian Studies scholars, however.

In fact, Viano defends the film's lack of emphasis on Guido's Jewish identity, by arguing that the very "Italian model" that Gilman rejects is actually historically accurate. Viano writes:

> In fact, *La vita e bella* intentionally conceals Guido's Jewish-ness for about forty-five minutes and rids the film's first half of tragedy. Benigni's choice emphasizes an uncontested historical reality: the "Italian-ness" of the Jews, their participation in Italian history at all levels. . . . Until the late 1930s, Italian Jews lived, loved, and laughed like anyone else in Italy. . . . Anti-Semitism did not enter official Fascist ideology until the race laws went into effect in 1938. Mussolini himself had a Jewish mistress, Margherita Sarfatti, until 1936.[19]

While Mussolini's love affair with a Jewish woman reveals little or nothing about anti-Semitism in pre-1938 Italy, Viano's staunch insistence that the film reflects "uncontested historical reality" nevertheless reveals a great deal about how deeply entrenched this narrative is, which essentially moves the culpability for anti-Semitic mass murder to external, non-national sources.

As I mentioned above, international debates about *Life Is Beautiful* focused largely on its use of comedy, the realism of the work (or the lack thereof), and the autobiographical authority of Benigni. Nevertheless, the real challenge in this film (and in Kassovitz's *Jakob*) appears at first glance to be not so much its unrealistic portrait of the camps, but rather its unrealistic or simplistic portrait of the act of narration. In both films, narration itself is touted as a force that changes the real world. Within the framed flashback (the "fairy tale" narrated to us by the grown son), the message is quite literal and unambiguous; there is no doubt about how we are to understand the meaning of story. The boy never guesses that his father's "game" is not real. At no time does the narrative suggest that the boy sees through his father's ruse. At the very end, when we realize that the narrator's voice belongs to the adult son (who has, of course, realized that his father's "game" was fictional), we are asked to understand the entire "game" as his father's "gift" to him; we are asked to believe at face value that a story literally saved the boy's life. In Becker's fictional world, stories allow the living to engage with a past they cannot change and with a present society that must admit culpability and guilt; in the Benigni text, stories literally save lives and allow the living to continue to believe in the myth of total assimilation. In the words of Viano, Benigni wanted to show with his film that "laughter can save us."[20] The film's insistence on this seems to be exactly the problem.

And yet, when we include the grown son's narrative point of view in our reading of the film, several interesting ambiguities arise—the grown son, after all, knows that the game was not real. This narrative perspective of the adult son, represented by the objective camera shots in the two-pronged narration of the story (Guido's "fairy tale" itself is represented by the subjective shots) is present throughout the film even though we hear his voice only briefly at the beginning and at the end. In Guido's death scene, discussed above, for instance, the boy is watching the Nazi and Guido through a slit in a shed where he is hiding. The third-person, objective narrative perspective shows us Guido's worried face, exposing his fear that his son might be killed if he realizes the "game" is not real. The following segment is then shot from the child's subjective perspective through the slit. Here, we (and the child, who is laughing) see a grinning Guido marching conspiratorially in an overzealous goose step. In this case, then, the two-pronged narration forces us to confront the fact that Guido's game or fairy tale, while it may have saved lives, was never real.

The consequences, even after the "laughter has saved us," of a narrative that is not real are interesting. The son calls Guido's stories a gift at the very end of the film, but what does this gift look like and what does it offer generations after the Holocaust? Let us examine Guido's narrative carefully. First,

Guido asserts the idea that humanism and its long tradition in Italy will allow him to transcend history and bigotry. Guido constantly seeks to write his own life and succeeds in the beginning. His story is a celebration of humanism, specifically the humanism located in the Jewish voice (his Jewish identity ultimately is extremely important, of course). This explains much of the appeal of the film to American audiences as well, where the national myths of the melting pot and the humanistic tradition have long been popular. Benigni has had success in the United States with a similar character in Jarmusch's *Down by Law* (1986), in which he plays a foreigner dedicated to the (almost forgotten) humanistic tradition of America, carting around a volume of Robert Frost's poetry. Guido is, in fact, so unmarked in the first half of *Life Is Beautiful* that he is "mistaken" for both the Italian king as well as a Fascist speaker.

Furthermore, although he makes light fun of fascist Italian anti-Semitic rhetoric about Jewish bodies, Guido ultimately exposes the German language as the true source of dangerous anti-Semitic rhetoric. In fact, German is depicted as so dangerous that he must literally translate the Nazi guard's hostile words into a "harmless game" in Italian. In the film, then, Germany serves as a foil or as a counter-model to Italian society, where the Enlightenment has been successful, and ethnicity and religion are secondary to Italian cultural identity. The German Enlightenment, though, is exposed as a failure. Dr. Lessing (G. E. Lessing was the German Enlightenment author of *Nathan the Wise*), the elderly German hotel guest to whom Guido turns in vain for help, proves self-absorbed and cowardly. Lessing is interested only in abstract reasoning, not in moral questions.

This film raises a number of interesting issues. To a large degree, *Life* upholds and promotes the Italian national myth of what Gilman terms the "invisible" Jew. Guido's "gift" to his son—the next generation—is his story, the triumph of humanism, specifically Italian humanism, over barbarity. Postwar, post-Fascist Italy has been restored to its prewar wholeness. At the same time, however, the film is engaged in exposing that very Italian myth of wholeness as problematic, if not false. As I argued above, the two-pronged narrative structure and the son's voice-over allow us to see Guido's "gift" from the perspective both of the naïve child as well as from that of the adult narrator. Thus, we know, as does the adult son, that the "game" is not real.

Following this line of argument, Guido's translation of the German officer's orders might be read as a metaphor for the way the Italians have chosen to read their own relationship to Fascism and to anti-Semitism as mediated. Guido, the assimilated and martyred Jew, must make the translation to give authority to the myth that the Italians had a mediated relationship to Fascism. They, the boy, and others in his generation and later, never understood what Fascism was really about; it was a German concept and, even more important here, it was linguistically German. The Jew's death, but also his story, allows the next generation to live whole in an otherwise broken world. His son, who is not Jewish by Jewish law, is able to accept his "gift" and to go on in the world. (Gilman describes this world as a restored Catholic one in which the Jew has been eliminated and mother and son are reunited.) In this way, the film exposes the "gift" as a problematic and false belief in the transcendence of humanism and the power of the human spirit.

CONCLUSION

The Italian *Life Is Beautiful* and the German *Jacob the Liar* certainly represent very different national narratives about the Holocaust. In the Italian narrative, the Jew and the literary are connected; the film celebrates, even as it simultaneously calls into question, a gift that allows post-Holocaust Italians to live in a world that is relatively whole, even after such a catastrophic event. This is not the case in Becker's German-Jewish narrative. Whereas Becker's *Jacob the Liar* can be said to celebrate the creative powers of the Jews as writers and storytellers (Jacob is a "liar"), the text nevertheless reveals a deeply traumatized, post-Holocaust world in which Jewish assimilation into German culture is tenuous at best. Becker wrote the book in High German for German audiences, certainly, but the survivor/narrator consistently throws in definitions and explanations of Eastern European Jewish culture for his German audience. In the Italian narrative, Guido can still be celebrated as a symbol of the humanistic tradition and of assimilation, while figures such as Heinrich Heine or Lessing's Nathan the Wise have lost the pre-Holocaust promise of the Enlightenment in Germany.

Becker's *Jacob the Liar*, Kassovitz's *Jakob the Liar*, and Benigni's *Life Is Beautiful* represent complex and conflicting national narratives about the Holocaust, what it means, and who "owns" it. The two film texts also represent a shift or change in Holocaust representation away from an engagement with the past to a more heroic, sometimes comic mode. Narratively, both films also focus on how art allows us to survive rather than how art helps us to understand survival. And yet neither of these films can be understood to be merely a devolution of the Holocaust text. As we have seen, both films open up complex questions about their own national contexts, even as they also create narratives that appear to confirm their national stories.

Who does "own" the Holocaust? As the survivor/narrators die and time passes, the story of the Holocaust moves from the private to the very public sphere. More and more, mass culture and the global society own the story of the Holocaust. Both the recent film versions of *Jakob the Liar* and *Life Is*

Beautiful feed the post-survivor desire for comedy and a happy ending, but not just any happy ending. In fact, both of these narratives are informed by a need for the story of the Holocaust to be that people survived because of the "triumph of the human spirit." These mainstream films, for good or ill, thus represent a shift from Loureiro's vision of the autobiographical Holocaust text as an ethical working through of the past to a celebration of the heroic in the face of mass murder.

NOTES

1. David Denby, review of *Life Is Beautiful*, directed by Roberto Benigni, *The New Yorker,* November 23, 1998.

2. Maurizio Viano, *"Life Is Beautiful*: Reception, Allegory, and Holocaust Laughter," *Jewish Social Studies* 5:3 (1999), 4766.

3. Sander Gilman, "Is Life Beautiful? Can the *Shoah* Be Funny? Some Thoughts on Recent and Older Films," *Critical Inquiries* (Winter 2000): 268–308.

4. Angel Loureiro, *The Ethics of Autobiography: Replacing the Subject in Modern Spain* (Nashville: Vanderbilt University Press, 2000).

5. Gilman, "Is Life Beautiful?," 304.

6. Saul Friedlander, *Probing the Limits of Representation; Nazism and the "Final Solution"* (Cambridge: Harvard University Press, 1992).

7. For more on the German Historians' Debate, see Saul Friedlander's *Probing the Limits of Representation.*

8. Jurek Becker and Leila Vennewitz, *Jacob the Liar [Jakob der Luegner],* 1st U.S. ed. (New York: Little, Brown and Co., 1996).

9. Loureiro, *The Ethics of Autobiography*, 10.

10. Cynthia Ozick, "Who Owns Anne Frank?," *The New Yorker*, October 6, 1997.

11. Daniel R. Schwarz, *Imagining the Holocaust* (New York: St. Martins Press, 1999), 20.

12. I will go into this in greater detail below, but the question of how "Jewish" Guido is has been hotly debated. While Gilman reads Guido's relative lack of Jewish identity as highly problematic, Viano insists that the film downplays his Jewishness in order to underline how very assimilated the Italian Jews actually were.

13. Gilman, "Is Life Beautiful?," 305.

14. Ibid.

15. See Peter Novick, *The Holocaust in American Life* (New York: Houghton Mifflin, 2000), for an interesting and informative reading of how Americans, specifically Jewish Americans, have constructed the Holocaust over time in the United States. Novick argues that the Holocaust has been read in radically different ways by the American public, largely due to domestic political debates and the status of ethnicity.

16. Susan Zuccotti, *The Italians and the Holocaust: Persecution, Rescue and Survival* (Lincoln: University of Nebraska Press, 1996).

17. Ibid., p. xxvi.

18. Gilman, "Is Life Beautiful?," 302.
19. Viano, "*Life Is Beautiful*," 163.
20. Ibid.

BIBLIOGRAPHY

Becker, Jurek. *Jacob the Liar* [*Jakob der Luegner*], 1st ed. New York: Harcourt Brace Jovanovich, 1975.

Becker, Jurek and Leila Vennewitz. *Jacob the Liar* [*Jakob der Luegner*], 1st U.S. ed. New York: Little, Brown and Co., 1996.

Denby, David. Review of *Life is Beautiful*, directed by Roberto Benigni. *The New Yorker*, November 23, 1998.

Down by Law. Directed by Jim Jarmusch, Otto Grokenberger, Cary Brokaw, et al. New York: PolyGram Video, 1986.

Gilman, Sander. "Is Life Beautiful? Can the *Shoah* Be Funny? Some Thoughts on Recent and Older Films." *Critical Inquiries* (Winter 2000): 268–308.

Jakob Der Luegner. Directed by Vlastimil Brodskây, Armin Mueller-Stahl, Erwin Geschonneck, et al. Northampton, MA: Icestorm International, 1999.

Jakob the Liar. Directed by Peter Kassovitz. Culver City, CA: Columbia Tristar Home Video, 2000.

Life Is Beautiful. Directed by Roberto Benigni. Burbank, CA: Miramax Home Entertainment; Distributed by Buena Vista Home Entertainment, 1999.

Loureiro, Angel. *The Ethics of Autobiography: Replacing the Subject in Modern Spain*. Nashville, TN: Vanderbilt University Press, 2000.

Night on Earth. Directed by Jim Jarmusch. Turner Home Entertainment, 1991.

Novick, Peter. *The Holocaust in American Life*. New York: Houghton Mifflin, 2000.

Ozick, Cynthia. "Who Owns Anne Frank?" *The New Yorker*, October 6, 1997.

Schwarz, Daniel R. *Imagining the Holocaust*. New York: St. Martin's Press, 1999.

Viano, Maurizio. "*Life Is Beautiful*: Reception, Allegory and Holocaust Laughter." *Annali D'Italianistica* 17 (1999): 163.

Zuccotti, Susan. *The Italians and the Holocaust: Persecution, Rescue and Survival*. Lincoln: University of Nebraska Press, 1996.

Chapter Ten

Homecoming Deconstructed in Israeli Holocaust Literature

Iris Milner

HEGEMONIC NARRATIVE:
A NEW HOME IN AN ANCIENT HOMELAND

In the years immediately following the end of World War II and the liberation of Jewish survivors from the Nazi death camps, the Zionist settlement in Palestine, then at the peak of its nation-building era, enthusiastically offered itself as the proper historical answer to the Jewish genocide. An ethos of "Holocaust and revival" (in Hebrew: "*Shoah utkuma*") was instantaneously defined as the core *raison d'être* of the Jewish national movement. Although some studies argue that the declaration of a Jewish state, toward which Zionists had been progressing prior to the war, was actually delayed by the catastrophic events in Europe,[1] the formation of an independent Israeli state was indeed closely associated in the public consciousness both inside and outside of Israel with the annihilation of European Jewry. The aspiration to heroism, which had been a principal component of the Jewish national movement from its outset, was now reinforced. The inherent weakness of the Jews in the Diaspora, stemming from their position as a defenseless, often rejected minority, was conceived of as one of the principal sources of anti-Semitism and as a crucial factor in the successful implementation of the extermination. Vigor and courage, materialized in the "Zionist Body" and aiming at the establishment of a strong, activist, self-defending national entity, was proposed, then, as the ultimate solution to this inherent vulnerability.[2]

The practical consequence of the Zionist agenda was Israel's immediate absorption, in 1948, of Holocaust survivors who since the end of the war had been forced to stay in displaced persons camps in Europe. This was accompanied by turning the ethos of "Holocaust and revival" into a leading motif in

175

Israeli national rhetoric. In the years to come, critics of Israeli politics of the first decades after World War II claimed that, to some extent at least, theolo Holocaust had been exploited for political needs, particularly with regard to the new country's relations with neighboring Arab states.[3] Moreover, retrospectively examining the initial encounter between the survivors and Israeli society, critics claimed that the public discourse of redemption had not been translated into an empathetic attentiveness to the unique and unprecedented circumstances of the survivors, whose entire world had been destroyed and who were left unsupported in their struggle to return to normal life. This criticism was sometimes accompanied by a condemnation of the survivors for allegedly going "like sheep to slaughter."[4]

Historian Anita Shapira proposes that while the Holocaust constituted a crucial aspect of the public discourse in Israel in the 1940s and 1950s, and its public memory was cultivated through various formal memorial projects, the private memory of the events did not find adequate channels of expression. This lacuna stemmed partly from the dominant perception that the ultimate victimhood of the Jews in Nazi Europe posed a threat to Israeli self-identity, which was being constructed at the time.[5] Consequently, and also as a result of the tendency of the survivors themselves to suppress their extremely traumatic experiences in an effort to reserve their psychological resources, a period of a so-called "silencing" of the Holocaust took place.[6]

Whether or not Israeli society was indeed initially limited in its attentiveness to the survivors—an issue that is still vigorously debated—there is no doubt that its sensitivity to "the voice of the wound," to use Cathy Caruth's terminology regarding the articulation of trauma,[7] sharpened considerably from the 1960s onwards. For various reasons, some of which were related to changing identity politics in the Israeli arena in general, both the Israeli nation and Israeli individuals became more capable of accepting testimonies from the "heart of darkness." Saul Friedlander argues that Israeli society had grown mature enough in the late twentieth century to confront the destruction and desperation of the Holocaust without attempting to place it within a framework of heroism, as it had done in the first years after World War II.[8]

The voice of the survivors in Israel thus erupted forcefully and has since been heard through many channels, just as an unexpected outburst of universal Holocaust discourse appeared in a wide scope of mediums and genres. The national narrative of redemption has nevertheless persevered and even strengthened: a growing acquaintance with the details of the tragic fate of European Jewry continued to be openly utilized as a rationalization for the fortification of the Jewish state and as a justification for its sometimes noncompromising policies.

Within the context of such a nationally specific Holocaust discourse, the concept of a "homeland," materializing in the image of a concrete home in which the survivor is expected to settle down, has played a crucial role. "Holocaust and revival" involved not only the emergence of an independent, self-defending collective entity, but also a construction of domestic spaces in Israeli towns and villages. This, too, directly continued the traditional home-coming motif in Zionist ideology. Zionism had originally defined itself as a project of return to an ancient homeland and reconstruction of that ruined home, symbolized by the destructed temple in Jerusalem (in Hebrew: *Beit Hamikdash*, literally meaning "the Home of Sanctification"). Following the destruction of the Second Jewish Temple by the Romans in 70 AD, the modern Israeli state is indeed often referred to as "the third home."

The present essay explores an Israeli counter-narrative that gives voice to a reality that does not fully correspond with the "Holocaust and revival" ethos. One principal domain in which such an undercurrent is covertly—but nevertheless consistently—expressed is literature. Literature thus functions in this context as a subversive agent, and fulfills its traditional role of "estranging" from and critically reflecting upon cultural norms and conventions. On the basis of the understanding of the status of the home in the nationalist agenda, the essay discusses its representation in Israeli Holocaust literature. My contention is that, rather than supporting the ideology of redemption, the home functions in this literature as a site of a compulsive repetition of trauma. It is, thus, through this literary image, which in earlier times symbolized—and at the same time concretized—the project of re-establishing a Jewish homeland, that the fractures in the hegemonic narrative areo interestingly exposed.

The texts analyzed here include literary works that are commonly read as outstanding examples of Israeli Holocaust literature. Their authors are well-known Hebrew writers, some of whom are themselves Holocaust survivors or descendants of survivors. The discussion here is synchronic rather than dia-chronic; this is in line with my assumption that although literary tendencies have transformed over time, in association with changing public and private moods, subversive counter-narratives have in fact been present in Israeli Holocaust literature since its early stages.

The essay begins with a demonstration of the process of recovery and redemption as it is manifested in a literary text that *does* adhere to hegemonic impositions, and an exploration of the text's minute nuances. This is followed by a discussion of real and symbolic fractures as they are exposed in some exemplary critical literary pieces, of the insights those pieces provide toward a sincere understanding of the post-traumatic condition of the survivors, and of the ethical implications of such an understanding.

REAWAKENING *OF* TRAUMA, REAWAKENING *TO* TRAUMA

Israeli Holocaust literature seldom describes the historical events of the genocide; its subject matter is mainly "the war after," as British author Anne Karpf defines the survivors' struggle for life in the years after liberation.[9] This theme obviously includes the encounter between Holocaust survivors and Israeli society.[10] In the representation of this encounter, most literary works have never sided with paternalist attitudes that have sometimes been implied by the heroic national ideology. Rather, they have outwardly condemned any manifestations of a demeaning attitude toward the survivors and objected to attempts to distinguish the so-called "heroes" of the Holocaust—the ghetto fighters and the partisans—from the majority of the victims who had no ability or means to rebel.

An outstanding example of a novel that pays tremendous respect to the community of the newly arrived Holocaust survivors, acknowledges their sufferings and pays tribute to their human dignity is *Shesh Knafayim Le'echad* (*They Each Had Six Wings*), published in 1954 by the Israeli-born author Hanoch Bartov, whose family originated from Poland.[11] The plot, which focuses on the integration of a group of survivors into a new life in Jerusalem, is nevertheless told from the perspective of the absorbing Israeli society and reflects its agenda of redemption through home-building. The novel is in fact a condensed index of the basic terms of the national narrative. The protagonists start their journey of recovery from a totally passive position: they are led in a truck to an unknown destination "in the mountains."[12] Left behind in an abandoned neighborhood, they hesitantly launch a project of reconstruction that gradually leads to their metamorphosis into confident and proud owners of their own homes.

One of the central figures of the novel declares at its very outset, while gazing from the still-moving vehicle at various buildings along the road, that, "as for himself—he wants a house. He is sick and tired of wanderings."[13] In his dreams, his old house is "covered with ruins."[14] Apparently, it is the sight of the ruins that surround him in the present, as the truck approaches a recently conquered and evacuated Arab area, which stirs up these memories. However, in Bartov's novel, no haunting voices block the way toward a successful integration.

The renovation of the empty, partly destroyed Arab houses is a leading component of the plotline. The new inhabitants all have the necessary skills for performing the job, and among their dull belongings they almost miraculously carry the required tools. Anxious to form a secure barrier between the inside and their threatening surroundings, they begin by sealing off breached doors and windows and re-installing broken locks. Though the materials they work with are simple and the furniture is only temporary (wooden boxes serving as chairs and tables and sheets of carton as screens), the experience is of establishing a permanent hold: "everything I fix here I may not have to move any more," a woman survivor says to herself, finally resuming her long-desired, lost role as the housewife in her own house.[15] At the same time, the men's working bodies, fully invested in the physical mission of renewal, acquire the strength and vitality of the New Jews—to use the terminology of the Zionist revolution.[16]

Indeed, Bartov's style of descriptions echoes that of Hebrew literature written during the first decades of the renewed Jewish settlement in Palestine in the beginning of the twentieth century: mundane procedures are endowed with an aura of holiness and in fact sanctified. Thus, for example, fixing a blocked water pipe and the eruption from it of a stream of fresh water echoes mythological descriptions of the digging of water wells in the Land of Israel by its new Jewish settlers. "A genesis of sacredness" marks the first meals eaten in the restored kitchen[17] and a blessed harmony is achieved in the wide rooms, between the newly painted walls. The heavy Jerusalem stones of the solid buildings hold the sun's warmth during the days, then blend it gently with the cool evening winds. Relaxing on their balconies and hearing friendly noises from neighboring apartments, the new inhabitants develop a sense of solidarity and mutual responsibility, thus gradually recovering from the aggressive suspicion planted in them by the Nazi terror.

An Israeli-born young woman who assists the newcomers openly articulates the equation between the rehabilitation of the houses and the recuperation of the crushed souls: "In the neighborhood I see how wrecked streets come to life again, and this makes me think that maybe the people too, in whose hearts there are ruins, may not forever remain wrecked."[18] The road to this destination is of course full of obstructions and delays, as the past time and again poses unexpected hindrances, but rehabilitation ultimately takes place in a most impressively comforting and optimistic manner.

From the perspective of trauma discourse, this prognosis is superfluously optimistic and rather unrealistic. The theory of the effects of external trauma, which Freud initially published in response to the upheaval of World War I, centers on the phenomenon of a compulsion to repeat—namely the continuous return to and repetition of a threatening event.[19] Theorists such as Shoshana Felman and Cathy Caruth, who reconsidered and expanded upon the theory of trauma in the second half of the twentieth century, partially in response to the catastrophes of World War II, discuss this fixation as it is manifested in literature, taking into account the resistance of traumatic experience to representation. They focus on trauma's so-called unspeakability or ineffability, and the various artistic strategies toward overcoming its muteness and voicing its voids.[20]

In the closing paragraphs of his book *The Reawakening*, written eighteen years after his liberation from Auschwitz, Primo Levi poetically demonstrates the tragic repetitiveness of his catastrophic experiences in the *Lager* (concentration camp).[21] He relates a recurrent dream, "varied in details, one in substance,"[22] in which the reality of his regained life, which materialized in his return to his home, family and friends, time and again turns out to be an illusion, as it abruptly disappears and gives way to the reality of the death camp. Everything around him, "the scenery, the walls, the people," collapses, and he is there once more, "alone in the center of a grey and turbid nothing," awakened by the Auschwitz morning call: "get up, '*Wstawàch.*'"[23] The "reawakening" of the book's title, which refers to a return to life, is obviously replaced in these closing lines by a different "reawakening"—a reawakening to the persistent hold of trauma. "Reawakening" is therefore a "traumatic awakening," to use Cathy Caruth's terms: "awakening," Caruth asserts, following Lacan, "[. . .] *is itself a site of trauma* [. . .]."[24]

This is precisely the essence of the experience of "reawakening," which, unlike the novel discussed above, many of the Israeli literary works that describe the post-Holocaust era indeed portray. These works often ironically subvert the hegemonic narrative of redemption by presenting a persistently compulsive, post-traumatic existence in its stead. A reawakening to life, particularly through the establishment of a new home, here too turns out to be a reawakening to a reality of "a grey and turbid nothing."

These works consistently deal with the physical setting in general and the figure of the home in particular, although such physicality does not necessarily function as the central dramatic factor in their plotlines, as it does in Bartov's novel. In fact, it is through these themes that the texts openly express their rejection of the hegemonic narrative: their portrayal of domestic sites defies the very concept of a home, and a devastating sense of unhomeliness, of *unheimlich*, to use Freud's terminology, arises from them.

There are varying degrees of directness and bluntness in the literary representations of the uncanny experience of reawakening. In the most straightforward instances, it is mediated through a concrete, threatening presence of chaos and death in what is supposed to be the homely haven of the Holocaust survivor. Other works deviate from the hegemonic conceptualization of the Israeli home in more subtle manners. Nevertheless, in all of these texts alike, a deconstruction of the home-building model is a major tool for questioning the "happy ending" narrative that the national agenda propagates.[25]

A most condensed representation of an un-homely being is offered in a novel by Yehudit Hendel, a distinguished Hebrew writer who was born in Warsaw in 1926 and brought to Palestine as a young child in the early 1930s. Hendel started her writing career at a very young age. Although she was close to the milieu of the labor party, Mapai, in government from the founding of Israel until 1968, and worked as a journalist in its daily newspaper, all her literary works daringly challenged political and cultural conventions. In 1969, she published a novel titled *Hachatser Shel Momo Hagdola* (*Big Momo's Courtyard*),[26] in which she radically subverted the "Holocaust and revival" ethos by meticulously undermining the very possibility of the victims' resettling in a new home.

The novel follows the short-lived love affair of a male Holocaust survivor with his married neighbor, as well as his hopeless attempts to form other meaningful personal ties in his alienated environment. The setting in which this takes place is a neglected urban neighborhood by the seashore, in the northern seaport town of Haifa. The textual energy of the plotline is kindled by the temporarily awakened erotic desire of the protagonist, whose name, Saul (in Hebrew: *Shaul*) echoes the Hebrew word for hell, *Sheol*. Nevertheless, the dynamics of the events are principally dictated by his continuous passive roaming from one rented room to another, with none of these rooms providing him with any sense of peace and the restfulness for which he yearns. He is a lonely nomad, frequently expelled from his places of residence and constantly moving among temporary stations, in an endless wandering journey of an eternally wandering Jew.

Big Momo is a Jewish woman of Eastern origin who owns a few rooms in a building with an inner courtyard. She spends much of her time sitting under a dying cypress tree (a tree associated in Israeli culture with a graveyard) in the filthy, neglected yard. Her pathetic figure, dressed in an old, ripped purple dress, is an ironic parody of the biblical redemptive prophecy that Zionism aspired to fulfill: "But they shall sit every man under his vine and under his fig-tree; and none shall make them afraid" (Micah 4:4). Having been asked to leave his recent station, the protagonist sublets a basement room in a tiny apartment from a couple of German Holocaust survivors, Big Momo's neighbors, in the same building complex.

Death is indeed all over the place, both literally and metaphorically. The neighborhood—a realistic representation of the oldest section of Haifa—is built around an old Jewish cemetery. The physical elements that Saul frequently comes across while roaming its streets, some of which belong to the close-by seaport, are readily associated with the concentration camp-like universe: train tracks, barbed wires, black coal heaps, a children's swing that looks to him like a hanging apparatus. Stinking odors, filthiness, crowdedness, disorder, a constant sense of vulnerability, horrifying sights projecting through the gaping doors of neighboring apartments, cracked walls, rusty grates of cage-like balconies, unbearable heat and sandy, red winds all create a hellish atmosphere. The eccentricities of the neighbors—

mostly newcomers who similarly attempt to find peace of mind—add a flavor of craziness to this chaotic setting.

This is particularly true regarding the sublet room in which the protagonist spends a few burning hot summer months. Having been occupied by an old woman who died in it a short while before the commencement of the plot, this room is obviously a site of recurrent trauma. A sign that had been posted on its door, "closed due to death," is quoted in the very first paragraph of the novel, and is repeated throughout as its refrain.[27] Saul keeps this sign in a table drawer as a constant reminder of the dead. He is also surrounded by other morbid metonymical objects: the iron bed in which the dead woman had lain for three days before her body was discovered, a line of her shoes underneath, to which he adds his own, and a suitcase that contains his childhood diary, written in his mother tongue, Polish, which he is no longer able to read. Emptiness and chaos gradually close down on him.

The association between this deadly physical setup and his tragic fate during the Holocaust is openly declared; at various points, the physical conditions are directly linked to a chain of past terrors. Thus, sights and sounds of black bats and crows that penetrate the room through its bare window are superimposed, in Saul's mind, on similar sights and sounds in his childhood home in Poland. As a young boy, black bats and crows were horrifying to him in themselves, but they also forecasted the approaching cataclysm.

Late in the novel, some hints about his most devastating memory are finally revealed. Unsurprisingly, they are indeed connected to his old family house: returning from school one afternoon he found it deadly silent and empty, and thus discovered that his family members had been deported, along with the entire community. It is exactly this terrible moment of "traumatic awakening"—a child's awakening to the truth of the catastrophic, abrupt destruction of his world—which the present emptiness of the haunted room continuously repeats.

"I was once covered with ruins, when I was brought out I was almost dead," Saul relates to his lover on a rare occasion when memories are allowed to emerge.[28] The belated experience of permanent homelessness retroactively gives voice to the inconceivable impact of these traumatic moments, which are by definition ineffable. Indeed, sitting in the small, stifling, death-infected room not far from the Haifa seaport, which in the national narrative represented the almost mythological redemptive destination of Holocaust survivors' "homecoming," he reflects upon his endless wanderings and tragically recognizes "that [for him] nothing will ever change and that his search for some rest is in vain."[29]

In various other literary works, different aspects of this homelessness are further explored and articulated. The fundamental dynamics in these cases, however, are all the same: the inherently compulsive repetitiveness of trauma, to which these texts are finely attuned, overpowers ideological agendas and collective narratives.

The literary oeuvre of Aharon Appelfeld, who survived the Holocaust as a child in Transnistria, begins with a collection of short stories that portray the very first period after the end of World War II. In one of these stories, titled "*Aviv Meuchar*" (A Late Springtime),[30] a small group of survivors misses the news of the end of the war and remains crowdedly packed in a bunker—a hole in the ground in which they have been hiding—until the melting snow floods it and forces them out. Their abrupt exposure to a liberated existence is another case of "traumatic awakening": thrown into an unrecognizably empty world, they are drawn back to their wartime hiding place, only to find it, too, incapable of protecting them any further.

Many of Appelfeld's short stories indirectly—and possibly unknowingly—reconstruct this liminal position, in between the inside and the outside of the bunker.[31] Different versions of the drama of lifting its cover and immediately pulling it back and withdrawing to the bunker's depth are acted out in them. Small basement apartments or tiny rooms with closed windows covered by heavy curtains replicate the bunker's boundaries. The survivors are always symbolically situated on the threshold of these rooms: they yearn to step out into the bright daylight and to assimilate into the dynamic movement of the city, but end up shutting themselves in again.[32] Critics have described the closed territory in which Appelfeld's protagonists live to be constructed in accordance with a "closed camp model."[33] This implies that the survivors never actually cease to experience themselves as locked in the concentrationary universe. I suggest that it is the concrete moment of a failed attempt to climb out of the bunker that is in fact reenacted in this permanent closure.

The constant temptation to withdraw into the shelter also reconstructs the status of the Jews in Nazi Europe as chased animals. The survivors conceive of their residences as moles' dens. Sometimes they are indeed as blind as moles: such is the case of blind Brundeh, one of Appelfeld's best-known and typical protagonists, who dies in her basement apartment while the celebrations of the Israeli Independence Day are taking place in the nearby city center, with choruses on high stages singing about a "Heavenly Jerusalem."[34]

Unsurprisingly, what awaits the survivors in their closed rooms is malady and death: Brundeh is not the only one who crawls into her den for her final sleep. While still living, the survivors, similarly to Brundeh, are markedly detached from their Israeli surroundings. One clear symptom of this detachment is the almost permanent winter that surrounds them. The aggressive heat-waves characteristic of Israeli weather—such as those that turn the life of the survivor in Hendel's novel into a burning hell—are replaced by a grayish, cloudy and cold atmosphere. Entrenching themselves in their narrow rooms, the survivors in Appelfeld's stories indeed constantly try to warm themselves by bundling with their fellow "inmates" as they did back in their frozen hiding places in Europe. This, too, is a reenactment of a dreadful moment, a shutting of a bunker's cover.

A different kind of architecture, but one that is similarly designated to create a thick barrier between an enclosed inner space and its surrounding landscape, characterizes a central building in another Israeli Holocaust novel. Adam Stein, the protagonist of Yoram Kaniuk's 1968 novel *Adam Ben Kelev* (*Adam the Son of a Dog*, or, *Adam Resurrected*),[35] is an inmate of a psychiatric institution for Holocaust survivors that is situated in a fancy, air-conditioned structure with thickly glazed windows and heavily carpeted floors. Kaniuk's novel is a grotesquely bizarre and carnivalesque representation of post-Holocaust Israel—the home of many Holocaust survivors—as a nuthouse.[36] The unique design of the psychiatric institution is one of its principal means of conveying the understanding that assembling living-dead refugees of the Nazi persecutions may create nothing but a storm of madness. The intended detachment of the building from the local scenery encapsulates the idea that the life of Holocaust survivors as psychiatric patients is led in total indifference to any local context.

At the same time, madness is far from being confined to the boundaries of this isolated, obscure building that is symbolically planted in the desert terrain of southern Israel, by the Dead Sea. When temporarily released from it, Adam Stein stays in a boardinghouse in Tel Aviv, run by a Jewish German woman as a replica of a bourgeois Jewish house in Berlin in the pre-World War II era. Obsessively vicariously experiencing his paradoxical sense of belonging to his lost home in the country that expelled him and destined his family and people to genocide, he lives as an outcast, a temporary guest, a tragicomic crazy alien. Only at nights can he detect signs from his fellow homeless detainees, whose common daily life obscures their maddening desperation: the screams they scream in their recurrent nightmares.

Israeli second-generation literature offers a different kind of visit to the residences of Holocaust survivors. A wide corpus of novels and short stories, written by sons and daughters of survivors and by Israeli-born writers who define themselves as "second generation by adoption," describes in great detail the experience of growing up as descendants of ruined families, who are expected to function as living tombstones and as memorial candles to the dead.[37]

The house is commonly portrayed in these works as a haunted fortress. Trauma is acted out in various rituals of further fortification: a compulsive locking of doors and windows, obsessive cleaning, hoarding of food, hiding of valuables. Children experience this environment as a threatening, secret crypt, where forbidden knowledge of mysterious atrocities—as well as treasured but undisclosed memories—are hidden. Cellars, attics, closets, drawers, suitcases, pockets, even fissures in walls, all contain unattainable and undecipherable ghostly objects or documents, which the parents anxiously guard out of their children's (and often their own) reach. In their attempt to find relief, the children, born in Israel and growing up in a native Israeli milieu, often prefer their own peer group and treat their parents as strangers. Cultural alienation, from which the domestic sphere is supposed to provide a safe haven, thus penetrates the survivors' most intimate spaces. This is obviously an uncanny setting at its most dramatic manifestation: the intimate and homely is experienced as threatening, unfamiliar strangeness. The *unheimlich* cannot be more closely connected with the land of death.

CONCLUSION

The objection of the literary body discussed here to hegemonic impositions that propagate an equation between national and personal revival is obviously drastic. However, it fundamentally differs from the critical public Israeli discourse of the turn of the twentieth century, which focused on Israeli society's reaction to Holocaust survivors and has quite harshly blamed it for abusive treatment. The literary works raise different and more profound questions. They point not only at the unrealistic and unfair expectations of the Israeli hegemony that the survivors adhere to its agenda, but also to the hegemony's possibly cynical exploitation of the survivors' misery for the reinforcement of its image as the ultimate cure of the "Jewish problem." The primary interest of these works is the life of the survivors in their hermetically closed and obviously ruined territories, both geographical and mental. In fact, these works of fiction do not even thoroughly explore the conduct of the absorbing society toward the survivors. In many cases, no representatives of this society are present in the texts at all.

Accordingly, the ethical and political implications of the deconstruction of the "Holocaust and revival" ethos extend beyond the Israeli arena and are quite radical. The stories suggest the utter irrelevance of collective narratives of any sort to the experience of individual suffering. Ideological remedies, according to this almost anarchistic proposition, may turn out to be blind and deaf to the well-being of the individual and thus inherently flawed or even false. The works thus recommend a suspicious position vis-à-vis any grand ideological agendas. Such a suspicious alertness toward any grand narratives and their rhetoric, Israeli Holocaust literature thus seems to suggest, is a universal lesson—the only significant lesson—that may be drawn from the Holocaust, as a warning sign against a possible recurrence of a similar man-made cataclysm.

NOTES

1. See a summary of these studies in Dan Michman, *Holocaust Historiography: A Jewish Perspective* (Portland, OR: Vallentine-Mitchell & Company, 2003).

2. The term "Zionist body" is offered by Michael Gluzman as a condensed articulation of the physical aspect of the "New Jew," constructed by Zionists in opposition to the allegedly weak, feminine and sick Diasporic body. See Michael Gluzman, *Haguf Hatsioni: Leumiut, Migdar Uminiyut Basifrut Haivrit Hahadasha* (*The Zionist Body: Nationalism, Gender and Sexuality in Modern Hebrew Literature*) (Tel Aviv: Hakibbutz Hameuchad, 2007).

3. One prominent advocate of this perception is historian Moshe Zuckermann, who writes about it in his book *Shoah Bacheder Haatum* (*Holocaust in the Sealed Room*) (Tel Aviv: M. Tsukerman Publication, 1993).

4. On the use of this phrase in the context of the victims of the Holocaust see Yael Feldman, *Glory and Agony: Isaac's Sacrifice and National Narrative* (Stanford, CA: Stanford University Press, 2010), 75–85.

5. Anita Shapira, "*Hashoah: Zikaron Prati, Zikaron Tsiburi*" (The Holocaust: Private Memory, Collective Memory), *Zmanim* 57 (1994): 4–13.

6. See a discussion of this state of affairs in my book on the literature of the second generation: Iris Milner, *Kiray Avar: Bographia, Zehut Vezikaron Besiporet Hador Hasheni* (*Past Present: Biography, Identity and Memory in Second Generation Literature*) (Tel Aviv: Am Oved, 2003), 36–43. Similar tendencies, stemming from different dynamics, may be identified in American Jewish responses to the Holocaust. See a discussion of it in Alan Mintz, "From Silence to Salience," in *Popular Culture and the Shaping of Holocaust Memory in America* (Seattle: University of Washington Press, 2001).

7. Cathy Caruth, "The Wound and the Voice," in *Unclaimed Experience: Trauma, Narrative and History* (Baltimore and London: Johns Hopkins University Press, 1996), 1–9.

8. Saul Friedlander, "Roundtable discussion," in *Writing and the Holocaust*, ed. Berel Lang (New York and London: Holmes and Meier, 1988), 287–89.

9. Anne Karpf, *The War After: Living With the Holocaust* (London: Minerva, 1997).

10. It is important to note that many of the veterans that comprised Israeli society at that time were themselves newcomers. They had arrived in Palestine a short while before World War II, in one of the waves of Jewish immigration, the last of which (before the war) took place during the 1930s. Though they positioned themselves at some distance from the Holocaust refugees (possibly as a psychological defense strategy), these veterans were very often personally affected by the Holocaust, as the families they left behind in Europe and their original communities were annihilated.

11. Hanoch Bartov, *Shesh Knafayim Le'echad* (*They Each Had Six Wings*) (1954; Tel Aviv: Am Oved, 1973).

12. Ibid., 11. Translation from Hebrew of the quotations from this novel are mine.

13. Ibid., 13.

14. Ibid., 14.

15. Ibid., 26.

16. On this concept, see Anita Shapira's essay "The Myth of the New Jew," in *Yehudim Chadashim, Yehudim Yeshanim* (*New Jews Old Jews*) (Tel Aviv: Am Oved, 1997), 155–74.

17. Bartov, *Shesh Knafayim Le'echad*, 26.

18. Ibid., 98.

19. Sigmund Freud defined these effects as "traumatic neurosis." His writings on the subject began in 1915 with "Thoughts for the Times of War and Death" (*The Standard Edition of the Complete Psychological Works of Sigmund Freud* [London: Hogarth, 1953] XIV: 289–300). They continued in his "Introduction to Psycho-analysis and the War Neuroses," published in 1919 (*Standard Edition* XVII: 205–15) and culminated in "Beyond the Pleasure Principle," published in 1920 (*Standard Edition* XVIII: 7–64).

20. Caruth bases her discussion of ineffability both on experimental research of traumatic states and on Freudian conceptualizations. Using the Freudian concept of *"Nachträglichkeit"* (belatedness, afterwardness), though somewhat altering its original meaning, she emphasizes the temporal characteristic of trauma—namely the fact that the symptoms of post-trauma appear only after a period of incubation, and with connection to a later event. See in Cathy Caruth, "The Wound and the Voice." See also Shoshana Felman, "Education and Crisis, or the Vicissitudes of Teaching," in *Trauma: Explorations in Memory*, ed. Cathy Caruth (Baltimore: The Johns Hopkins University Press, 1995), 13–60.

21. Primo Levi, *The Reawakening*, trans. Stuart Woolf (New York: Simon & Schuster, 1965).

22. Ibid., 207.

23. Ibid., 207–208.

24. Cathy Caruth, "Traumatic Awakenings (Freud, Lacan, and the Ethics of Memory)," in *Unclaimed Experience*, 91–112. Quotation is from p. 100.

25. A narrative of a happy ending is, of course, not a unique Israeli phenomenon. It also characterizes, for example, the American Holocaust narrative. The architecture of the Holocaust museums both in Jerusalem and in Washington, D.C. provides an interesting demonstration of this phenomenon. While the Yad Vashem Holocaust History Museum in Jerusalem is an underground building, shaped like a tunnel, that opens up to the lightened scenery of the Jerusalem mountains—thus narrating the story of redemption in the Israeli homeland—the tour of the United States Holocaust Memorial Museum in Washington, D.C. leads to a room devoted to American democracy. Obviously, in the latter, the redemptive closure is represented by the victory over Nazism of a democratic and humanistic America.

26. Yehudit Hendel, *Hachatser Shel Momo Hagdola* (Tel Aviv: Am Oved, 1969). The novel was republished in 1993 under the title *Hachamsin Ha'acharon* (*The Last Heatwave*) (Tel Aviv: Hakibbutz Hameuchad, 1993). References hereafter are to this retitled version.

27. Ibid., 7.

28. Ibid., 153.

29. Ibid.

30. Aharon Appelfeld, "*Aviv Meuchar*" (A Late Springtime), in *Ashan* (*Smoke*) (Jerusalem: Achshav Publishing, 1962), 49–58.

31. I refer particularly to Appelfeld's short stories, published during the first decade of his writing career in the 1960s, in the following collections: Aharon Appelfeld, *Ashan* (*Smoke*); *Bekomat Hakarka* (*Ground Floor*) (Tel Aviv: Daga Publishing, 1968); and *Adnei Hanahar* (*The River's Banks*) (Tel Aviv: Hakibbutz Hameuchad, 1968).

32. Yigal Schwartz discusses the presence of two opposing "poles" in these stories—the "closed space pole" as opposed to the "open space pole"—in his monographic study of Appelfeld's literature. See Yigal Schwartz, *Kinat Hayachid Venetzach Hashevet, Aharon Appelfeld: Tmunat Olam* (*Individual Lament and Tribal Eternity—Aharon Appelfeld: The Picture of his World*) (Jerusalem: Keter Publishing, 1996), 53–125.

33. Ibid., 104–109.

34. Aharon Appelfeld, "Brundeh," in *Adnei Hanahar*, 9–16.

35. Yoram Kaniuk, *Adam Ben Kelev* (*Adam Resurrected*) (1969; Tel Aviv: Sifriat Poalim, 1981).

36. The term "carnivalesque," coined by Russian formalist Mikhail Bakhtin, refers to a literary mode that subverts and liberates the assumptions of the dominant style or atmosphere through humor and chaos.

37. Second generation novels and short stories that are relevant to this discussion are (among others): Nava Semel, "*Mizvadot*" (Suitcases) and "*Raav*" (Hunger), in *Kovah Zechuchit* (*A Hat of Glass*) (Tel Aviv: Sifriat Poalim, 1986); Lily Perry-Amitai, *Golem Bama'agal* (*Golem in the Circle*) (Jerusalem: Keter Publishing, 1986); David Grossman, "Momik," in *See Under: Love*, trans. Betsy Rosenberg (New York: Farrar, Straus and Giroux, 1989), 3–88; Itamar Levi, *Agadat Ha'agamim Ha'atsuvim* (*The Legend of the Sad Lakes*) (Jerusalem: Keter Publishing, 1989); Benny Barabash, *My First Sony* (Tel Aviv: Hakibbutz Hameuchad, 1994); Michal Govrin, *Hashem* (*The Name*) (Tel Aviv: Hakibbutz Hameuchad, 1995); Lizzie Doron, *Lamah Lo Bat Lifnei Hamilchama* (*Why Didn't You Come Before the War*) (Tel Aviv: Halonot, 1998); Lizzie Doron, *Hayitah Po Pa'am Mishpacha* (*Once There Was a Family Here*) (Jerusalem: Keter Publishing, 2002); Lizzie Doron, *Yamim shel Sheket* (*Days of Tranquility*) (Jerusalem: Keter Publishing, 2003).

BIBLIOGRAPHY

Appelfeld, Aharon. "*Aviv Meuchar*" (A Late Springtime). In *Ashan* (*Smoke*). Jerusalem: Achshav Publishing, 1962, 49–58. [Hebrew]

———. *Ashan* (*Smoke*). Jerusalem: Achshav Publishing, 1962. [Hebrew]

———. *Bekomat Hakarka* (*Ground Floor*). Tel Aviv: Daga Publishing, 1968. [Hebrew]

———. "Brundeh." In *Adnei Hanahar* (*The River's Banks*). Tel Aviv: Hakibbutz Hameuchad, 1968, 9–16. [Hebrew]

———. *Adnei Hanahar* (*The River's Banks*). Tel Aviv: Hakibbutz Hameuchad, 1968. [Hebrew]

Barabash, Benny. *My First Sony*. Tel Aviv: Hakibbutz Hameuchad, 1994. [Hebrew]
Bartov, Hanoch. *Shesh Knafayim Le'echad* (*They Each Had Six Wings*). Tel Aviv: Am Oved, 1973. First published in 1954. [Hebrew]
Caruth, Cathy. "The Wound and the Voice." In *Unclaimed Experience: Trauma, Narrative and History*, 1–9. Baltimore: Johns Hopkins University Press, 1996.
———. "Traumatic Awakenings (Freud, Lacan, and the Ethics of Memory)." In *Unclaimed Experience: Trauma, Narrative and History*, 91–112. Baltimore: Johns Hopkins University Press, 1996.
Doron, Lizzie. *Lamah Lo Bat Lifnei Hamilchama* (*Why Didn't You Come Before the War*). Tel Aviv: Halonot, 1998. [Hebrew]
———. *Hayitah Po Pa'am Mishpacha* (*There Was Once a Family Here*). Jerusalem: Keter Publishing, 2002. [Hebrew]
———. *Yamim Shel Sheket* (*Days of Tranquility*). Jerusalem: Keter Publishing, 2003. [Hebrew]
Feldman, Yael. *Glory and Agony: Isaac's Sacrifice and National Narrative*. Stanford, CA: Stanford University Press, 2010.
Felman, Shoshana. "Education and Crisis, or the Vicissitudes of Teaching." In *Trauma: Explorations in Memory*, edited by Cathy Caruth, 13–60. Baltimore: Johns Hopkins University Press, 1995.
Freud, Sigmund. "Thoughts for the Times of War and Death." In *The Standard Edition of the Complete Psychological Works of Sigmund Freud*. London: Hogarth, 1953, XIV: 289–300.
———. "Introduction to Psycho-analysis and the War Neuroses." In *The Standard Edition of the Complete Psychological Works of Sigmund Freud*. London: Hogarth, 1955, XVII: 205–15.
———. "Beyond the Pleasure Principle." In *The Standard Edition of the Complete Psychological Works of Sigmund Freud*. London: Hogarth, 1955, XVIII: 7–64.
Friedlander, Saul. "Roundtable discussion." In *Writing and the Holocaust*, edited by Berel Lang, 287–89. New York and London: Holmes and Meier, 1988.
Gluzman, Michael. *Haguf Hatsioni: Leumiut, Migdar Uminiyut Basifrut Haivrit Hahadasha* (*The Zionist Body: Nationalism, Gender and Sexuality in Modern Hebrew Literature*). Tel Aviv: Hakibbutz Hameuchad, 2007. [Hebrew].
Govrin, Michal. *Hashem* (*The Name*). Tel Aviv: Hakibbutz Hameuchad, 1995. [Hebrew]
Grossman, David. "Momik." In *See Under: Love*, translated by Betsy Rosenberg, 3–88. New York: Farrar, Straus and Giroux, 1989.
Hendel, Yehudit. *Hachamsin Haacharon* (*The Last Heatwave*). Tel Aviv: Hakibbutz Hameuchad, 1993. First published as *Hachatar Shel Momo Hagdola* (*Big Momo's Courtyard*) in 1969. [Hebrew]
Kaniuk, Yoram. *Adam Ben Kelev* (*Adam Resurrected*). Tel Aviv: Sifriat Poalim, 1981. [Hebrew]
Karpf, Anne. *The War After: Living with the Holocaust*. London: Minerva, 1997.
Levi, Itamar. *Agadat Ha'agamim Haatsuvim* (*The Legend of the Sad Lakes*). Jerusalem: Keter Publishing, 1989. [Hebrew]

Levi, Primo. *The Reawakening*. Translated by Stuart Wolf. New York: Simon & Schuster, 1965.

Michman, Dan. *Holocaust Historiography: A Jewish Perspective*. Portland, OR: Vallentine-Mitchell & Company, 2003.

Milner, Iris. *Kiray Avar: Biographia, Zehut Vezikaron Besiporet Hador Hasheni (Past Present: Biography, Identity and Memory in Second Generation Literature)*. Tel Aviv: Am Oved, 2003. [Hebrew]

Mintz, Alan. "From Silence to Salience." In *Popular Culture and the Shaping of Holocaust Memory in America*. Seattle: University of Washington Press, 2001.

Perry-Amitai, Lily. *Golem Bama'agal (Golem in the Circle)*. Jerusalem: Keter Publishing, 1986. [Hebrew]

Shapira, Anita. "*Hashoah: Zikaron Prati, Zikaron Tsiburi*" (The Holocaust: Private Memory, Collective Memory). *Zmanim* 57 (1994): 4–13. [Hebrew]

———. "The Myth of the New Jew." In *Yehudim Chadashim Yehudim Yehsanim (New Jews Old Jews)*. Tel Aviv: Am Oved, 1997, 155–74. [Hebrew]

Schwartz, Yigal. *Kinat Hayachid Venetzach Hashevet, Aharon Appelfeld: Tmunat Olam (Individual Lament and Tribal Eternity—Aharon Appelfeld: The Picture of His World)*. Jerusalem: Keter Publishing, 1996. [Hebrew]

Semel, Nava. "*Mizvadot*" (Suitcases); "*Raav*" (Hunger). In *Kovaz Zekhukhit (A Hat of Glass)*. Tel Aviv: Sifriat Poalim, 1998, 83–104; 117–43. [Hebrew]

Zuckermann, Moshe. *Shoah Bacheder Haatum (Holocaust in the Sealed Room)*. Tel Aviv: M. Tsukerman Publication, 1993. [Hebrew]

Index

acting out: in *Gebürtig*, 16–19; melancholia reflected by, 16
Adam Ben Kelev (Kaniuk), 184
Adorno, Theodor, 50–51; on poetry, 27
affect, 129, 139n2
Alberich, 28
America: cinema, 6, 155; escape myth, 6, 152; film noir, 155; identity in, 130, 139n3; as land of opportunity, 6, 147; as melting pot, 6; perspective on Holocaust, 144; Roth on, 157n8; Spielberg and, 139n3; trauma theory and, 147
American Pastoral (Roth), 157n8
anti-Semitism: French, 34; Italian, 169; in *Life is Beautiful*, 169, 171; in Lithuania, 60; Milosz on, 86, 87; Poland, 85–87, 99; Vienna, 19
anti-Zionism, 110
Appelfeld, Aharon, 183
"The Arcadian Myth" (Milosz), 89
Armenian Genocide, 68
Arnds, Peter, 22n12
art, 45n18
Auschwitz, 15, 18, 31, 38; Carmelite convent on site, 85; children at, 119; crosses erected, 8586; design of, 119; gassing, 40; as muse,

153–54; name change proposed, 99; *sonderkommandos*, 40, 41; survivors, 119; victims and executioners, 146
"Auschwitz and the Professors" (Schoenberg), 157n6
Austria: national myth, 5; as no-mans land, 14; notions of normalcy, 4–5; Wendejahr, 13
Avisar, Ilan, 140n8
Aviv Meuchar (Appelfeld), 183–84

Bakhtin, Mikhail, 188n36
Baranczak, Stanislaw, 87, 94
Bartov, Hanoch, 178–79
Bartov, Omer, 25
Becker, Jurek, 6–7, 162–65, 172
Beckermann, Ruth, 14, 17
Befangenheit, 22n12
Benigni, Roberto, 6, 161, 167–72; fame of, 168, 171
Bernard-Donals, Michael, 140n7
Blake, William, 91
Blonski, Jan, 84–85
blood and soil, 92; pastoral and, 87–88
Bock, Gisela, 150
Bomba, Abraham, 40
Booth, W. James, 20
Braschi, Nicoletta, 168
Bresson, Robert, 55

191

About the Contributors

Ferzina Banaji is presently Senior Project Manager for BBC Media Action, the BBC's charity arm that uses media and communication to bring about social change. She was a post-doctoral research fellow at the University of Cambridge (2006–2009), affiliated with the Department of French, where she also completed an MPhil (2001–2002) and a PhD (2002–2006). She taught extensively while at Cambridge as well as at the University of Nottingham where she was a Visiting Lecturer in the French Department (2006–2007). She was awarded a Charles H. Revson Visiting Fellowship at the Center for Advanced Holocaust Studies at the United States Holocaust Memorial Museum in Washington, DC (2008) to complete primary research for her book *France, Film and the Holocaust: From Genocide to Shoah* (Palgrave-Macmillan, Studies in European Culture and History Series, 2012). She is the author of a number of articles on twentieth- and twenty-first-century French literature, philosophy and visual culture. She presently lives in New Delhi, India.

Donna Coffey is associate professor of English at Reinhardt University in Georgia. She holds an MA from the University of North Carolina at Chapel Hill, a PhD from the University of Virginia, and an MFA in Creative Writing from the Solstice Program at Pine Manor College. Her academic articles have appeared in *Women's Studies: An Interdisciplinary Journal*, *Science and Culture*, *Modern Fiction Studies*, and *Contemporary Women's Writing*. Her poems are forthcoming in the journals *Calyx* and *quarrtsiluni*.

Christina Guenther holds a PhD from the University of Wisconsin-Madison and is associate professor of German at Bowling Green State University, Ohio. Her teaching and research focus is on contemporary German and Austrian studies with an emphasis on Jewish identity, the Holocaust and Turkish-

German culture. Most recently, she has published articles on the work of Ruth Beckermann, Anna Mitgutsch, Barbara Honigmann, and Doron Rabinovici. She coedited the volume *Trajectories of Memory: Intergenerational Representations of History and the Arts* (Cambridge Scholars Press, 2008).

Sarah Hagelin is assistant professor of English at New Mexico State University where she teaches courses in film, gender theory, and American literature. She is the author of *Reel Vulnerability: Power, Pain, and Gender in Contemporary American Film and Television* (Rutgers University Press, 2013). She received her PhD in English in 2007 from the University of Virginia.

Phyllis Lassner is professor at the Crown Family Center for Jewish and Israel Studies, and in the Gender Studies and Writing Programs at Northwestern University. She is the author of two books on Elizabeth Bowen, as well as *British Women Writers of World War II: Battlegrounds of Their Own* (St. Martin's Press, 1998), *Colonial Strangers: Women Writing the End of the British Empire* (Rutgers University Press, 2004), numerous articles on Holocaust representation and on interwar and wartime women writers, and most recently, *Anglo-Jewish Women Writing the Holocaust* (Palgrave Macmillan, 2008). She created and edits the Northwestern University Press book series "Cultural Expressions of World War II and the Holocaust: Preludes, Responses, Memory."

Zofia Lesinska was born and raised in Warsaw Poland, where she earned her Master's degree in American literature at the University of Warsaw. She was later awarded the PhD in British and American Literature by the University of Iowa in Iowa City, where she also pursued the Master's degree in Library and Information Science. Since 2002, she has worked as a librarian at the University of Southern California in Los Angeles where she is currently Director of Public Services at the Doheny Memorial Library. Her book, *Perspectives of Four Women Writers on the Second World War: Gertrude Stein, Janet Flanner, Kay Boyle and Rebecca West*, was published by Peter Lang in 2002.

Iris Milner is senior lecturer in Tel Aviv University's Literature Department. She is also the head of the university's interdisciplinary undergraduate honors program in the Humanities and the Arts. Dr. Milner's main research areas are Holocaust literature and the literary representation of trauma. Her publications on these subjects include two books, *Past Present: Biography, Identity and Memory in Second Generation Literature* (Am Oved, 2003), and *Narratives of Holocaust Literature* (Ari Libsker, 2008), as well as essays on the literature of authors K. Tsetnik, Aharon Appelfeld, Ida Fink, Yehudit Hendel, Yoel Hoffman, and others.